REVOLUTION IN THE COUNTRYSIDE

REVOLUTION

JIM HANDY

IN THE COUNTRYSIDE

RURAL CONFLICT &

AGRARIAN REFORM

IN GUATEMALA,

1944–1954

THE UNIVERSITY OF NORTH CAROLINA PRESS • CHAPEL HILL & LONDON

Library of Congress Cataloging-in-Publication Data

Handy, Jim, 1952–

Revolution in the countryside : rural conflict and agrarian reform

in Guatemala, 1944–1954 / by Jim Handy.

p.   cm.

Includes bibliographical references and index.

ISBN 0-8078-2127-6 (alk. paper). — ISBN 0-8078-4438-1 (pbk.: alk. paper)

1. Guatemala — Politics and government — 1945–1985.   2. Social conflict —

Guatemala — History.   3. Peasantry — Guatemala — History.

4. Government, Resistance to — Guatemala — History.   5. Land reform —

Guatemala — History.   6. Guatemala — Rural conditions.   I. Title.

F1466.5.H29   1994

972.8105'2 — dc20   93-36112

CIP

Jim Handy, professor of history at the University of Saskatchewan,

is author of *Gift of the Devil: A History of Guatemala.*

The paper in this book meets the guidelines for

permanence and durability of the Committee on Production Guidelines

for Book Longevity of the Council on Library Resources.

98   97   96   95   94   5   4   3   2   1

CONTENTS

TABLES AND MAPS

PREFACE

Historians are taught to express certainty. We are trained to avoid "maybe" and "perhaps" as our stories unfold, no matter how perilous the leaps from "fact" to "fact" we employ in constructing our tales. I have followed that custom in this study.

This seems an opportune place, however, to admit to uncertainty. This study is the result of years of research. I have attempted to draw a picture of the revolution in specific Guatemalan villages and in that fashion piece together a broader image of the revolution in the countryside. I believe some insights have resulted, but huge gaps remain. I will never truly understand what the revolution meant to any single community. I will never know exactly how social relations changed, how political change affected perceptions of power and authority, or why some Guatemalans chose to use revolutionary institutions to better their economic circumstances and others did not.

Perhaps the area in which my research and the sources have failed me most is in trying to understand how the revolution affected women and gender relations. The sources do provide glimpses: in the few women who won positions in municipal governments, in the antigovernment protests led by market women in Guatemala City and Antigua, in the cases brought by female teachers against school supervisors for sexual harassment, in the active involvement of women teachers in peasant organizations, and in the attempts by the Alianza Femenina to create a credit fund for campesinas. But these glimpses are so rare and scattered that, for the most part, the questions they suggest have not been addressed. They await a different kind of study.

In addressing the questions this study does attempt to answer, I relied on the help and advice of many people. The book started out as a doctoral dissertation at the University of Toronto. My adviser, Dawn Raby, deserves my thanks for her gentle and unobtrusive encouragement at a time when she had every right to be wrapped up in her own concerns. The staff at a number of research facilities have been very helpful and patient over the years, including the U.S. National Archives, the Public Archives of Canada, the Manuscript Division of the Library of Congress, the Hemerotecas of the Archivo General de Centro América and the Guatemalan National

Library, and the Instituto Indigenista Nacional. I especially want to thank the staff at the Archivos Generales of the Instituto Nacional de Transformación Agraria, who shared their limited workspace, their lunches, their insights, and their friendship. The cheerful staff at the Centro de Investigaciones Regionales de Mesoamérica in Antigua were very helpful in preparing the final manuscript. I owe particular thanks to Steve Elliott and Guisela Asensio Lueg. The editorial staff at the University of North Carolina have been patient, helpful, and careful. I especially thank David Perry for his enthusiasm and support.

Over the last decade I have enjoyed an ongoing dialogue, primarily through panels at learned conferences, with some excellent scholars. I am sure they do not realize how much these discussions have helped deepen my understanding of Guatemala. Among those who have been most influential are Rick Adams, George Lovell, David McCreery, Carol Smith, John Watanabe, Robert Williams, and Lee Woodward. They, of course, share no blame for any shortcomings in this study.

Kris Inwood will always have my appreciation for his friendship and unfailing interest in this work, despite a busy research schedule of his own. Most importantly, I want to thank Annette, without whom this book would probably have been finished sooner, but without whom neither finishing this work nor anything else in my life would mean as much.

ABBREVIATIONS

AGA — Asociación General de Agricultores (General Association of Agriculturalists)

CAD — Comité Agrario Departamental (Departmental Agrarian Committee)

CAL — Comité Agrario Local (Local Agrarian Committee)

CAN — Consejo Agrario Nacional (National Agrarian Council)

CGTG — Confederación General de Trabajadores de Guatemala (General Confederation of Workers of Guatemala)

CNCG — Confederación Nacional Campesina de Guatemala (National Peasant Confederation of Guatemala)

CTAL — Confederación de Trabajadores de América Latina (Confederation of Workers of Latin America)

CTG — Confederación de Trabajadores Guatemaltecos (Confederation of Guatemalan Workers)

DAN — Departamento Agrario Nacional (National Agrarian Department)

DGAA — Dirección General de Asuntos Agrarios (General Office of Agrarian Issues)

FPL — Frente Popular Libertador (Popular Liberation Front)

FSG — Federación Sindical de Guatemala (Workers' Federation of Guatemala)

IGSS — Instituto Guatemalteco de Seguridad Social (Guatemalan Institute for Social Security)

INFOP — Instituto de Fomento de Producción (Institute for Encouraging Production)

IRCA — International Railways of Central America

PAR — Partido de Acción Revolucionaria (Revolutionary Action Party)

PGT — Partido Guatemalteco de Trabajadores (Guatemalan Workers' Party)

PIN	Partido de Integridad Nacional (National Integrity Party)
PRG	Partido de la Revolución Guatemalteca (Party of the Guatemalan Revolution)
PROG	Partido Revolucionario Obrero de Guatemala (Revolutionary Workers' Party of Guatemala)
PTRD	Partido de Trabajadores Regional Democrático (Regional Democratic Workers' Party)
Q	quetzal (the equivalent of one U.S. dollar)
RN	Renovación Nacional (National Renovation)
SAMF	Sindicato de Acción y Mejoramiento de Ferrocarriles (Union for Action and Improvement of Railroads)
STEG	Sindicato de Trabajadores de Educación Guatemaltecos (Union of Guatemalan Educational Workers)
UFCo	United Fruit Company

REVOLUTION IN THE COUNTRYSIDE

MAP 1. GENERAL POLITICAL DIVISIONS

INTRODUCTION

1

They are an introverted people,
consumed by internal fires which they
cannot or dare not express, eternally
chafing under the yoke of conquest, and
never for a moment forgetting that
they are a conquered people.

—Oliver LaFarge, *Santa Eulalia:*
The Religion of a Cuchumatán Indian Town

Shortly after eight o'clock on the evening of Sunday, 27 June 1954, President Jacobo Arbenz Guzmán informed the Guatemalan people that he was resigning from office and turning the government over to the head of the armed forces, Colonel Carlos Enrique Díaz. Despite continued support for the reforms his administration had fostered, Arbenz was giving up his office because, as he told his audience, "the sacrifice that I have asked for does not include the blood of Guatemalans."[1] Following Arbenz's resignation, the decade-long Guatemalan "revolution" quickly came to an end.

The overthrow of Jacobo Arbenz Guzmán is one of the most studied events in Central American history. But most of the works that have discussed his overthrow, and the history of Guatemala's ten years of reform between 1944 and 1954, have concentrated on national and international politics. As important as these studies have been, they leave much of the revolution unexamined. Guatemala was in the 1950s, as it is today, a predominantly rural country with an economy heavily dependent on agriculture. To understand the Guatemalan revolution, we need to examine the course of reform and reaction in the countryside.

From 1944 to 1954 the Guatemalan revolution embarked on a series of economic and social reforms. While for the first six years, under the presidency of Juan José Arévalo Bermejo, these reforms only superficially affected rural areas, from 1951 to 1954 the fortunes of the revolution were directly linked to the process of change in the countryside. It was in the countryside that the revolution prompted the most vehement opposition, and it was primarily because of the administration's activities in the countryside that relations between it and the military became strained. It was this opposition that was most important in forcing Arbenz's resignation.

This study is an attempt to provide a history of the revolution in the countryside and to link the changes that swept through Guatemalan *municipios* from 1944 to 1954 with the policies and politics of the "national" revolution. The reforms passed by the two administrations of the revolution (Juan José Arévalo Bermejo, 1945–51, and Jacobo Arbenz Guzmán, 1951–54) fostered a bewildering series of conflicts in rural Guatemala. These struggles took shape around a complex mix of class tensions and ethnic, geographic, and religious loyalties. These battles, in turn, forced alterations in national policies and programs as national politicians faced rural reality. To explain these conflicts and the role they played in shaping Guatemalan history, this study will proceed in four stages. First, it will provide a brief survey of rural history and a short theoretical discussion of

applyfied already
existing conflict

the role peasant communities played in Guatemala's national political and economic life. The second stage will present the major economic, social, and political currents of the revolution, with an emphasis on the sources of political instability. The third stage, which constitutes the major part of the study, will examine the activities of the national political organizations in rural Guatemala, the reaction of various elements of rural society to these activities, and the conflict that developed around them. A major focus of this section will be a discussion of the Agrarian Reform Law of 1952 and its application. Fourth, the role rural conflict played in hastening the end of the Arbenz administration will be analyzed. The study will conclude with a brief examination of the dismantling of the revolution in the countryside and an assessment of the legacy of this decade.

Community Formation in Guatemala

Guatemala, a relatively small country of slightly over 42,000 square miles, offers incredible diversity in climate and terrain primarily due to a back-bone of mountain ridges that passes through the country from the north-west to the southeast. These mountain ridges define the various geographic and climatic regions of Guatemala: the Pacific coastal plain and piedmont, the western and eastern highlands, the Cobán plain, the Atlantic coastal plain, and the vast Petén rain forest that stretches off to the northeast. The highlands and the extension of the western highlands into the Cobán region constitute approximately one-third of the total area of the country and contain the majority of the population. The mountain ridges and volcanoes create a mysteriously beautiful landscape of isolated valleys and high pla-teaus. It is in these western highlands and the Cobán that the bulk of the country's Indian population lives, most located in small towns and villages linked by paths trodden deep into the sides of the surrounding hills. The eastern highlands (often referred to as the Oriente), with poorer soils and inadequate rainfall, are less densely populated and have a higher percent-age of non-Indian residents. The melancholy beauty of the western high-lands is missing, but the sense of isolation is as apparent.

It is in the villages and towns of these three regions that most of the story of the revolution in the countryside takes place. Through centuries of history, these towns became strong but often conflictive communities, with a political and social structure deeply attached to local tradition. The Span-ish conquest, begun in the Guatemalan highlands in the 1520s, initiated a

MAP 2. GEOGRAPHIC REGIONS

terrible period of death and despair. The greatest toll was taken by European diseases that attacked even before the first meeting of Spaniard and
Indian and, through the course of a century and a half of sporadic epi-
demics, killed between 75 and 90 percent of the preconquest Indian population. This loss of life tore the social fabric of native society apart and
increased the burden of tribute and labor borne by those who survived.

However, Mayan communities in the highlands emerged from this destruction with a new culture — a conquest, peasant culture that integrated
Spanish and Indian influences. The Indian community was a product of
conquest, its subordinate and subjugated status constantly reinforced. The
core of the new culture was the community. "Community" in colonial
Guatemala was to some extent determined by the church and the crown

through the *reducciones* (forced settlement of natives in "congregations") carried out in the sixteenth century. These reducciones in turn established the basis for the over 300 municipios that existed during the revolution. But these communities also reflected preconquest settlement and customs. The community was organized around a religious/political hierarchy that was outwardly Catholic but essentially native. The primary focus of the community was land, and, while numerous types of landownership were recognized, most land was community controlled.

Various types of tensions were apparent in these communities. Colonial policy tended to condense social distinctions in native society, removing the higher levels of nobility from their exalted positions and freeing natives from enslavement, at least by other Indians. Nonetheless, social distinctions, often based on enduring noble status, continued to exist well into the nineteenth century. In addition, the reducciones had, in some cases, forced distinct Indian communities to merge. These prereducción entities maintained separate identities and competed for community resources.[2]

In the years between the formation of these communities and the revolution, a variety of influences emerged. Some fostered the disintegration of the community, some assisted social and economic differentiation within it, and some helped integrate rural communities into national politics and the economy. But other influences reinforced identification with the community, inhibited differentiation within it, and kept alive the memory of the conquest. In addition, a new element was added to rural society: Ladinos. Ladinos came in a variety of shades. The term was usually applied to those who were the product of Indian and Spanish miscegenation, but it was also used to identify Indians who no longer fit into "Indian" society. As such it was an arbitrary means for identifying those who had passed a very flexible line in the process of cultural borrowing. In the western highlands, where Indian population levels had remained higher than elsewhere in the country and where labor demands had been more moderate during much of the colonial period, Ladinos generally comprised a tiny minority of often impoverished rural petit bourgeoisie. In the eastern highlands, where Indian population levels were lower and labor demands had prompted many Indians to abandon their communities, Ladinos were often the majority; they were peasants and rural workers as well as shopkeepers and professionals.[3]

Even before the colonial period ended, the Bourbon monarchy had begun to attack many of the bases of these distinct peasant communities. With independence, the Liberal governments continued these policies even more forcefully in their desire for economic growth, national integration, and cultural assimilation. Communal landownership was discouraged, and the religious/political hierarchy that had developed around the church was attacked. Liberal administrations also began to tax Ladino peasants, both individually and collectively through charges against village funds. The Liberals' desire to shape Guatemala in the image of Europe was temporarily thwarted by a successful, combined Indian/Ladino peasant revolt led by Rafael Carrera in the 1830s. Carrera dominated Guatemalan politics for most of the next three decades, and during this time peasant landholding and village political and religious structures were under less pressure than they had been previously. This policy of benevolent neglect was assisted by the political dominance of Guatemala City merchants who depended on peasant producers for their major export crop, cochineal, and thus felt little incentive to alter landholding patterns.[4]

This respite came to an end in the 1870s when a new generation of Liberals swept to power on the coattails of a new, infinitely more profitable, export crop: coffee. In 1871, Liberal politicians in the capital and landowners in the western highlands, anxious for incentives to expand coffee cultivation, led a successful revolt that forced Carrera's successor from power. In the ensuing decades, a series of Liberal dictators passed laws that increasingly favored coffee planters in their struggle to attain sufficient land and labor.

Using an increasingly "professional" military with officers trained at a newly created military academy, the Escuela Politécnica, and a tightly controlled rural militia, the Liberal governments strengthened national control over rural areas. Political power in rural areas was often wielded through local caudillos with direct links to the president. But the economic dominance of Guatemala City, the importance of export agriculture, and the restricted development of internal, secondary market centers insured that few local caudillos were able to develop broad connections and thus challenge the power of the president. Consequently, Guatemala experienced a succession of strong presidents who developed stable and enduring regimes that, with the exception of a brief period of experimentation, moderate reform, and instability in the 1920s, continued until the coming of the revolution with the overthrow of General Jorge Ubico Castañeda in 1944.[5]

In the process of promoting the cultivation of coffee and other export crops, the Liberal regimes facilitated the development of two foreign enclaves in Guatemala. The most important of these was a group of German coffee planters who by 1913 owned 170 *fincas* (farms or plantations), 80 of them in the Cobán region, and marketed the bulk of Guatemalan coffee. The other significant enclave was the U.S.-owned United Fruit Company (UFCo) and its appendages: the International Railways of Central America (IRCA) and the UFCo Steamship Lines. Through its control of vast areas of land, rail and steamship transportation, and Guatemala's major port, Puerto Barrios, the UFCo (or the octopus, "el pulpo," as it became known in Guatemala) dominated much of the Guatemalan economy and wielded significant political clout.[6]

Coffee enjoyed great success in Guatemala. By the 1880s, Guatemala was the world's fourth largest coffee producer, and between 1870 and 1900 the volume of Guatemala's international trade multiplied twenty times. The Guatemalan elite had found the *produit moteur* that had been sought since the early days of the colony. Government policy was naturally directed toward assisting, in whatever ways necessary, that production.

One German resident of Guatemala called the Liberal victory in the 1870s a "triumph of the Ladino element of the population, over the Indian."[7] In many ways this assessment was correct. Positivist thought mingled with liberal economic philosophy to insure that little real protection was given to village land, the structure of peasant villages, or Indian culture. The increasingly racist attitudes of the Guatemalan elite served to justify the coercive means used to satisfy their major obsession — recruiting sufficient labor to work the rapidly expanding coffee harvest — and sought to foster increasing differentiation between Indians and Ladinos to assist in controlling the former. Liberal politicians and the coffee elite continually denounced the laziness of the Indians. As one German planter commented in 1886, the problem of obtaining sufficient labor was a "matter of life and death for the planters." He further observed, "It is a notorious fact that should the government cease to help the agriculturalists in securing laborers the cultivation of coffee would become an impossibility, because as everyone knows, the Indians despise working on the fincas."[8] Force was both needed and morally justifiable according to the *jefe político* of Chimaltenango in 1872, as it was "necessary to accustom [the Indians] to submission, for which it is indispensable to use some rigor because such is the deplorable condition of the race."[9]

While the *mandamiento* — similar to the colonial *repartimiento*, which required that each village supply a specified amount of labor every year — was applied with increasing vigor through the 1880s and 1890s, it eventually gave way to a no less coercive means of recruiting labor: debt bondage. All rural workers were required to carry with them the hated *libreto*, containing their work and debt records, and the labor contractor or *habilitador*, who advanced money to Indian peasants in return for labor contracts, became common in the western highlands. The habilitador often used alcohol to smooth the way to a contract, and for the price of a couple of drinks, many Indians were burdened with debts they could never pay. As one archaeologist reported upon seeing the operations of habilitadores in Nebaj in 1912, "The rum business and the coffee business work together in this country automatically. . . . Work leads to rum and rum leads to work."[10] As the British economic attaché described the situation in the early twentieth century, "From a creditor's point of view, the system is perfectly simple, and nothing but an inconvenient possession of a conscience can stand in the way of a quite indefinite furthering of his own interests. He has only to charge the cost of the unfortunate peon's living at a price that will prevent the man from ever getting out of debt."[11] Debt bondage was remarkably effective in forcing Indians in the highlands to seek wage labor on coffee fincas. Anthropologists working in the highlands in the 1920s and 1930s suggested that the majority of the male population of most villages was saddled with substantial debts to a finca or a labor contractor.[12]

Although Ubico abolished debt bondage in 1934, he replaced it with a vagrancy law that was almost equally coercive. Ubico's policies were inspired by the desire to centralize control over labor and challenge the political power of the coffee elite; they were not designed to allow those who did not wish to participate in the harvest to abstain from it. While the demand for labor declined due to reduced harvests during the 1930s and peasants benefited to some extent from government policies supporting increasing production of domestic-use agriculture, the basic coercive structures of Guatemala's rural economy were maintained.

Wages that were artificially depressed through the use of forced labor contributed to declining rural living standards for the bulk of the rural population despite the prosperity brought to the country by coffee production. David McCreery and R. L. Woodward, Jr., have estimated that daily agricultural wages expressed in terms of the cost of corn in the 1920s were only one-third to one-half what they had been in the period from 1853 to 1866. Depressed rural wages and low-cost labor increased the profits available to an elite of coffee planters. As one planter remarked, "Not the soil but rather the low wages of our laborers are the wealth of the Cobán."[13]

Liberal governments also initiated policies that affected Indian control over land. It has been argued that these administrations led a "massive assault on Indian land" designed primarily to force Indians to labor on the fincas. Recent research has suggested that Liberal land measures did not lead to immediate and widespread expropriation of Indian land, at least not to the extent previously believed in those areas where coffee was not profitably cultivated. Nonetheless, Liberal governments did pass laws that discouraged communal ownership and made it easier for individuals to gain access to land formerly controlled by Indian communities.[14]

Liberal labor and land measures decapitalized highland communities. David McCreery has argued that forced labor represented a "massive transfer of surplus to the export economy," while Robert Carmack estimated the forced, unpaid or marginally paid, labor provided by the municipality of Momostenango for plantation labor and public works to be approximately 336,000 man days per year.[15] But the demands of the Liberal governments and the negative aspects of coffee production had varying effects on different communities and on different sectors within the communities.

Most analysts suggest that Liberal policies helped lead to wealth and class differentiation within the community. Members of the village elite were occasionally able to avoid the demands of debt bondage and took advantage of the plight of their neighbors to accumulate land. In at least one community, village caciques became labor contractors, accumulated land through foreclosures on debts, and "were very ruthless with the lower caste or poorer Indians."[16] But the spread of coffee cultivation also inhibited differentiation in highland communities. Cash income from outside the community, small as it might be, allowed village inhabitants to maintain possession of plots of land too small for subsistence. Wages from plantation labor also allowed poorer community members to participate in the religious fiesta system. In addition, the finca provided a societal safety valve through which disruptive members of the community could be enticed to leave the village. Perhaps most importantly, the perceived rapacity of the Liberal attack on Indian labor and, to a lesser extent, land prompted the community to become more defensive and insular.[17]

Perhaps the most pervasive change in highland communities during the Liberal period was the loss of control by Indians over the municipal government. Throughout the late nineteenth and early twentieth centuries, the Liberal administrations issued a number of decrees that were designed to place Ladinos in positions of power in predominantly Indian communities. Finally, in 1927, the government officially decreed: "To promote the progress of these towns it is necessary and right that the Ladino minority should have representation in the governmental body, so that they might intervene in local administration and promote and control works of progress."

The decree went on to formalize a system of alternating posts for Indians and Ladinos, with the first *alcalde* (mayor or chief justice) always a Ladino and "preferring the election of those who speak Castillian, use the dress of the Ladino class, and know how to read and write."[18] Although government decrees did not necessarily reflect reality in rural Guatemala, this arrangement had in fact been in practice in many highland municipalities for decades. During the years following the Liberal victory in 1871, Indians steadily lost influence in municipal politics. This practice combined with other Liberal measures to increase dramatically racial tension throughout rural Guatemala.

Liberal measures also heightened tension over land in rural Guatemala. Land tenure in Guatemala was complicated, with municipios, *cantones* (districts of a municipio), *aldeas* (outlying hamlets), *cofradías* (brotherhoods honoring a specific saint), and individuals all having different rights to land. Conflict over land was endemic. It increased as many communities began to experience land shortages during the eighteenth and nineteenth centuries because of growing population, immigration of Ladinos into predominantly Indian areas, and the expansion of export agriculture. There were violent struggles over land among municipios in virtually every region of Guatemala, struggles that often lasted centuries, with simmering resentment lying dormant for decades before it would erupt again in violence. But not all disputes were between municipios. Often conflict occurred among cantones or aldeas within a municipio or between the outlying aldeas and the municipal capital or *cabacera*, reflecting lingering memories of prereducción social organizations. By the late nineteenth and early twentieth centuries, one common source of tension was the encroachment of Ladinos into the community and their dominance of municipally controlled land.[19]

Liberal labor, land, and political measures were so disruptive and rapacious that one scholar has called them a "second conquest."[20] The results of this conquest are apparent in studies of rural communities conducted in the 1940s by anthropologists and through a comparison of the 1893, 1921, and 1950 censuses. The surveys of fifty-six municipalities in the 1940s and 1950s done by the Instituto Indigenista Nacional indicate substantial variation among municipalities in almost all aspects of their political, social, and economic organization. Some villages had substantial community-controlled land, while others had little or none. In some municipalities, there appeared to be little ethnic conflict, but in others, such conflict was pervasive. Significant antagonism between wealthy and poor Indians existed in some communities; in others, little was apparent.[21]

Some similarities are evident, however. Almost all communities fought relatively constant battles over land. These battles were often simply conflicts among individuals over access to specific plots. But more often there was a corporate nature to these conflicts; they were fought between finqueros and the village, among various cantones within the municipality, between the municipal capital and the aldeas, or between neighboring municipalities. Disputes came to the surface in the form of a land invasion, a court case, or a minor battle.

There was a steady decline in the percentage of the population living in the highland departments between 1893 and 1950, as the population of departments hosting plantation agriculture grew. The two departments with the highest Indian populations in the core of the highlands, Totonicapán and Sololá, actually decreased in population between 1923 and 1950. While the percentage of the population considered to be Indian remained relatively constant between 1893 and 1923, between 1923 and 1950 the Indian population nationwide declined from 65 to 53.6 percent. This made little difference in the six departments in the western highlands, where the percentage of Indians changed little between 1893 and 1950 and remained close to 90 percent in 1950. In these areas, Ladinos continued to be a tiny minority, perhaps best described by Ruth Bunzel as "a group of under-privileged, debt-ridden shopkeepers, depending for their existence on patronage from above. They squeeze where they can. The Indians pay their tribute as the price of peace."[22]

The extent to which Ladinos had used their positions of dominance to accumulate land is apparent from the 1950 agricultural census. Ladinos operated 123,847 farms encompassing 4,321,907 *manzanas* (one manzana is approximately 1.7 acres), an average of almost 35 manzanas per farm. Indians operated 224,840 farms encompassing 993,568 manzanas (an average of 4.4 manzanas per farm). In the six departments in the western highlands, Ladinos made up 12 percent of the farm operators and controlled 66 percent of the land. There were significant variations from department to department, however. Bunzel's description of highland Ladinos is most appropriate in the two core Indian departments of Totonicapán and Sololá, where only 265 and 591 Ladinos, respectively, were involved in agricultural production.[23]

TABLE 1. POPULATION BY DEPARTMENT, 1950

Department	Population	% Maya
Totonicapán	99,354	96.8
Sololá	82,921	93.8
Alta Verapaz	189,812	93.4
El Quiché	174,911	84.1
Chimaltenango	121,480	77.6
Huehuetenango	200,101	73.3
San Marcos	232,591	72.5
Suchitepéquez	124,403	67.7
Quezaltenango	184,213	67.6
Chiquimula	112,841	61.9
Baja Verapaz	66,313	58.5
Retalhuleu	66,861	51.9
Sacatepéquez	60,124	51.6
Jalapa	75,190	50.5
El Petén	15,880	27.9
Jutiapa	138,925	19.6
Zacapa	69,536	19.2
Guatemala	438,913	18.1
Izabal	55,032	17.2
Escuintla	123,759	15.9
El Progreso	47,872	9.4
Santa Rosa	109,836	9.4
Total	2,790,868	53.6

Source: *Sexto censo de población, 1950* (1957), xxxii.

Liberal policies in the latter part of the nineteenth and first half of the twentieth centuries determined in many ways the social and economic structure of modern Guatemala. Liberal land, labor, and political reforms accentuated the dominance of a landowning elite. Peasant, particularly native, communities were decapitalized and, in some areas, depopulated. They became closed, suspicious places, viewing with entirely warranted apprehension any encroachment from outside. As Manning Nash has argued, the "twin goads of resource alienation . . . and social policies designed to ignore or crush evidence of Indian cultures . . . produced an indigestible, culturally hostile core of corporate Indian communities."[24] However, these communities were marked by a significant degree of social and economic differentiation and were pitted against each other in an increasingly violent competition for land.

Liberal policies also effectively stunted the growth of the state. While the Liberal state of the late nineteenth and early twentieth centuries was infinitely more powerful than its predecessors, this power was almost totally the result of the growing strength of the coercive apparatus of the state: the military, the Guardia Civil, and rural militias, all firmly in the hands of Ladinos. The racist/positivist attitudes of the coffee elite, their determination to force cheap labor from Indian villages, and their dominance of the instruments of the state insured that there were few attempts to inculcate nationalism and allegiance to state institutions among the majority of rural Guatemalans. Given the elite's determination to foster the elimination of Indian culture, it is doubtful that even if they had attempted to construct "hegemony" as opposed to employing the "armour of coercion," as Antonio Gramsci has described it, they would have met with much success. Especially in rural areas, the bulk of Guatemala's population were tied to the state with chains forged by coercion and violence.[25]

Modes of Production and the Village

Despite Liberal policies, in the 1940s village life, Indian culture, and peasant production were important features of Guatemalan society and contributed substantially to Guatemala's economy. It is necessary to recognize the continued importance of these elements, in the face of decades of pressure, before the revolution can be understood.

Peasants have been viewed primarily as remnants of precapitalist modes of production and thus doomed to disappear under the "steamroller of agrarian capitalism," as Mitchell Seligson has described it.[26] Marx predicted that the peasantry would continue to exist alongside capitalism in "gradual decay" with the spread of capitalist relations of production to the countryside. This gradual decay was seen primarily as the process of proletarianization or the differentiation of peasant communities into distinct classes: wealthy peasants (essentially capitalist landlords) and poor peasants (essentially wage earners).[27]

This perception has been widely accepted in studies of Latin American peasants. The extension of agrarian capitalism that accompanied the growth of export agriculture in much of Latin America in the mid-nineteenth century placed increasing pressure on peasant agriculture and on social cohesion in peasant communities and was thought to foster class differentiation.[28] But the continued existence and vitality of peasant production in some regions (including much of Guatemala) long after the expansion of export agriculture prompted some revisions to this argument.

Rosa Luxemburg argued that capitalism relied on noncapitalist forms of production for capital generation. One of the essential contradictions of capitalism, however, was that these latter would eventually be subsumed by capitalist relations of production.[29] The articulation of capitalist and noncapitalist modes of production as suggested by Luxemburg was elaborated upon by the French school of economic anthropologists, who drew their lessons from Africa. Claude Meillassoux argued that the value of the rural peasant community lay in its ability "to feed the temporarily unproductive workers of the capitalist system." He went on to suggest that "the agricultural communities, maintained as reserves of cheap labor, are being undermined and perpetuated at the same time, undergoing a prolonged crisis and not a smooth transition to capitalism."[30] Pierre-Phillipe Rey expanded on this discussion, suggesting three stages in this "prolonged crisis" based on the appropriation of surplus from the noncapitalist by the capitalist mode of production. Rey suggested that this appropriation of surplus was frequently accompanied by violence. Of particular interest, he argued that the final stage, the destruction of peasant production through economic competition caused by the investment of capital in traditional agricultural areas, is an unusual occurrence in the periphery.[31]

Others, of course, have argued against the idea of a "peasant" or "simple commodity" mode of production. Alain de Janvry has argued forcefully that "peasants are to be seen as a class or fraction of a class within different modes of production—a class that is essential in modes like feudalism and transitory (and hence only a fraction of a class) in others, like capitalism." Thus as capitalism slowly but inexorably replaces the precapitalist modes of production in Latin America, the existence of a peasant class in undermined. The peasantry is siphoned off to form either a rural bourgeoisie or a rural proletariat.[32]

Despite de Janvry's strong objection to the idea of a peasant mode of production, there is common ground between the two arguments. Both accept the continued existence and vitality of peasant production in the face of the expansion of capitalist agriculture, at least for extended periods of time. The survival of peasant production is not threatened by disadvantageous market relations or coercive labor recruitment; it is only threatened when extensive capital begins to penetrate peasant agricultural areas, Rey's third and final stage of articulation. The difference lies essentially in whether we believe peasant production carries with it an accompanying set of social relations distinct from capitalism, an argument that can logically be made.

Numerous case studies of peasant communities in Latin America have detailed the continued vitality of peasant or simple commodity production. The articulation of this mode of production with the dominant capitalist mode is accomplished through the market and through periodic or seasonal labor migration. Both help prevent differentiation in peasant communities. The inequitable terms of exchange in the market and the domination of the "critical nodes or means of exchange" by nonpeasants help drain the peasant community of surplus, restricting the amount available for investment in agriculture.[33] Seasonal labor, combined with peasant production on uneconomically small plots of land, impedes the mobility of factors of production and lessens differentiation. Perhaps most importantly, the violent fashion in which labor and to a lesser extent peasant products are induced from peasant communities heightens the defensive posture of these communities.

This defensive posture is exaggerated or more easily maintained when the community can also identify itself as ethnically distinct from the main components of the encroaching capitalist mode or when that ethnic distinction is purposely heightened by society outside of the community. The idea of internal colonialism has been used to argue that Indian peasant communities form distinct "refuge regions" within capitalist economies. Within these regions, class differentiation does not occur or develops in a weakened fashion partly because the community has erected obstacles to the intrusion of non-Indian influences that inhibit the extension of class relations and maintain "the caste-like social relations of Spanish colonialism." Surplus is extracted from these regions through market relations controlled by non-Indians, and even the customs and fiestas that surround village tradition are opportunities for the purveyors of "tawdry pageantry" to squeeze a profit out of the community. Both the place of the community and the shape of social relations within it are determined to some extent by these manners of articulation.[34]

Eric Wolf's discussion of closed corporate communities helps explain the way this articulation has helped shape peasant communities in Latin America. Wolf has suggested that during the colonial period, in response to pressures on peasant-controlled land and to the perceived rapaciousness of colonial society, many communities became increasingly closed and corporate. There have been legitimate criticisms leveled against this concept over the years. The perception of a dichotomy between open noncorporate and closed corporate communities has been questioned. There is a certain vagueness concerning the way in which these communities interacted with the outside economy. Also, there are questions concerning the timing of and reasons for the formation of the "closed" community. Especially in the case of Guatemala, it is clear that the pressures on the community did not become extremely onerous until the spread of coffee cultivation, and it was not pressure on land as much as pressure on labor that prompted the increasingly closed nature of the community.[35]

Still, Wolf's discussion is of importance in that he emphasized that the closed and corporate nature of these communities affected social relations within the community. According to Wolf, the corporate community "emphasizes resistance to influences from without which might threaten its integrity." In addition, "The corporate structure acts to impede the mobilization of capital and wealth within the community. . . . It thus blunts the impact of the main opening wedge calculated to set up new tensions within the community and thus hasten its disintegration." The corporate nature of the community not only leads to "a weak and distorted form of capitalism" but also helps maintain a certain measure of harmony within the community in the face of the extension of agrarian capitalism and the beginning of wealth differentiation within the community.[36]

Wolf's concept, with some revisions, seems to fit the case of Guatemalan municipios well and has been used extensively in discussions of them. A note of caution should be added here, however, concerning the "corporate" community. The closed and corporate nature of the community should not be seen as immutable. Nor should change always be expected in linear fashion, from closed to less closed. The Guatemalan experience demonstrates clearly not only that communities can become less closed and corporate in response to changes in their relations with the encircling economy and society, but also that they can retrench when outside pressures begin to foster concern for community integrity and resources once again. The closed and corporate nature of these communities thus should not be seen as a line of defense that, once breached, cannot be repaired; instead, corporate institutions act as a valve that can let in more or less outside influences depending on the perceived sympathy or rapacity of the agents of the national society and the economy.[37] It should also be noted that the challenges to the closed and corporate nature of peasant, Indian communities are not always inspired by economic considerations. As the state becomes increasingly interested in establishing "the hegemony of the ruling classes" by expanding the apparatus of civil society, the institutions of the community can be attacked, not because they represent a defense against economic penetration of the community, but precisely because they are the first line of defense against the cultural penetration that can accompany the economic expansion of the state. Indeed, the few studies that detail the development of corporate institutions in Guatemalan native communities during the colonial period stress that they acted primarily "to turn aside weak cultural and religious intrusion while giving in to economic exactions and trying to prepare for them."[38]

The history of native communities in the Guatemalan highlands — and to a lesser extent peasant communities in other regions of the country — should be seen in the light of these explanations for the continued vitality of peasant production and community identification. The surplus from peasant production was extracted through forced labor and market arrangements. Primarily because little capital was invested in areas of traditional agriculture, peasant production continued to exist and capitalist relations of production in the community were restricted. The prevailing ethnic distinction helped to further delineate the different modes of production. These forces helped shape a community that may not have been as closed as Wolf has suggested but that, nonetheless, developed a variety of mechanisms to strengthen community identification and reduce both class differentiation and the perception of class distinctions. The incomplete transition to capitalism that this entailed meant that there were conflicting processes at work in peasant communities. Wealth differentiation occurred; individual control over land increased; and some people were deprived of access to the means of production and formed a rural proletariat. On the other hand, community members were still defined by corporate badges of identity, primarily evident in distinct community dress; there was still a strong corporate nature to landownership; and the community maintained a powerful hold.[39] Conflict over land and other issues among peasant households was endemic, but it was often quickly subordinated to community issues. This helped protect community resources but also broadened individual complaints, transforming personal conflicts into community conflicts. Struggles between neighboring communities or among distinct entities of the municipio were the most common result. These conflicting pressures helped determine the manner in which economic, social, and political reforms were felt in rural communities during the revolution.

The revolution gave rise to widespread changes in social organization, to religious and political conflict, and to attempts to alter long-standing inequities in the access to political favor, credit, and, most importantly, land. Government policies were designed to assist in this process of transformation, but the policies had some unexpected results as they filtered down to the village level and as they percolated through institutions and conflicts that were centuries old. There was an ambiguous quality to the revolution in the countryside. It sought to champion the rural poor and lead them in struggle against the *terratenientes* or large landowners of "feudal" Guatemala, which in practice often meant supporting the interests of Indians against those of Ladinos. But the revolution also sought to diminish the prevalent racial distinctions and was a vigorous proponent of acculturation in its attempt to foster the spread of national culture. It sought to benefit peasants, and, indeed, in some ways the Arbenz administration dedicated itself to this task. Yet it also championed the extension of capitalist relations of production in the countryside. The revolution was intended to strengthen community, end the dominance of municipal government by a local Ladino elite, and halt the attacks on its resources by finqueros. Yet it also challenged many of the institutions of the community as reformers sought to expand the reach of the state and, at least in some municipalities, fostered an attack on community resources that was in some ways equal to that initiated by the Liberal administrations a half century before.

THE OCTOBER REVOLUTION

2

A new sun shines,

the young go forward

their ideas, a beacon

the young are a dawn

the young are a hymn

the young rise up

like the sun in the morning

illuminating the darkness

and adorning the mountains.

—Romelia Alarcón de Folgar,

"Romance del 20 de octubre"

The last of the Liberal dictators of Guatemala, General Jorge Ubico Castañeda, was forced from power in June 1944. The street demonstrations and protests that prompted his resignation were urban and middle class in composition and exuberant in character. There was a widely held expectation that the departure of Ubico would usher in a new era for Guatemala, an era symbolized by the young students, professionals, and officers who participated in the "October Revolution" and celebrated in song and poem.

The first administration following the revolution, that of Juan José Arévalo Bermejo, clearly reflected the middle-class and idealistic nature of the October Revolution. Espousing a confused political philosophy that concentrated on the intellectual and moral rejuvenation of the country, Arévalo tread carefully in the economic arena. Politicians scrambled after the perquisites of holding office as they formed and abandoned political parties at a dizzying rate. As the first blush of the new era faded, the political complexion of the revolution changed. Political opinion polarized. Less radical and less determined reformers were shunted aside as the goals of the revolution became more concrete.

Partly as a consequence, the Arévalo administration faced violent opposition from many sources. The church, businesspeople, landowners, and politicians who felt restricted by the opportunities offered by Arévalo's brand of political pluralism increasingly opposed much of the revolutionary legislation passed by congress during his term in office. The most serious opposition came from a divided military and U.S. business interests. Caught in a quagmire of conspiracy as opposition stiffened, Arévalo actively discouraged peasant and rural labor organization and did little to begin the social transformation of the country he heralded. He also bequeathed to his successor, Jacobo Arbenz Guzmán, a nation seething with conflict.

Arbenz concentrated on fostering economic development and independence. Central to that process was the Agrarian Reform Law of 1952. Despite attempts to forge a workable revolutionary coalition of political parties to help implement that law, he faced even greater political fragmentation than Arévalo had encountered. Increasingly, he sought support from competent and dedicated individuals, people many believed to be communists. Their involvement in the agrarian reform process and peasant organization spawned increasing opposition to the Arbenz government, culminating in his overthrow in June 1954.

The First Government of the Revolution and Spiritual Socialism

Ubico resigned from office on 29 June 1944, after ruling Guatemala for almost fourteen years. In his final years in office he had faced increasing opposition from a growing middle class, organized primarily around student groups who were clamoring for new economic policies and democratic opportunities. The substantial support Ubico enjoyed in the first few years of his regime had all but disappeared, and by 1944 he had clearly overstayed his welcome. In the face of growing unrest, after 311 prominent professionals and businesspeople submitted a petition calling for his departure, Ubico resigned, leaving power in the hands of a military triumvirate composed of Generals Federico Ponce Vaides, Buenaventura Piñeda, and Eduardo Villagrán Ariza. The country's leading newspaper expressed popular opinion when it commented that Ubico's government "fell like an overripe fruit."[1]

Immediately following Ubico's resignation, students and young professionals organized into political parties and searched for candidates for the promised presidential elections. The majority of them coalesced into two nascent organizations, the Popular Liberation Front (Frente Popular Libertador [FPL]) and the National Renovation (Renovación Nacional [RN]), and soon settled on Juan José Arévalo Bermejo, a professor living in exile in Argentina, as their presidential candidate. It was not long, however, before Ponce, who quickly dominated the junta, declared his candidacy for the presidency and unleashed a wave of repression designed to insure his success in the promised elections.[2]

On 20 October members of the Guardia de Honor military battalion and the company of cadets from the Escuela Politécnica led a revolt. Quickly joined by civilians, the "October Revolution" succeeded in forcing Ponce, the "tentacle of *ubiquismo*," to capitulate after a bitter battle. These rebels, in turn, established a junta composed of the commander of the Guardia de Honor, Major Francisco Arana; a former commander of the company of cadets, Captain Jacobo Arbenz Guzmán; and a prominent civilian, Jorge Toriello.[3]

A few days after the October coup, Arévalo, now the front-running candidate in the elections set for December, described the importance of the event in a radio address: "What has occurred in Guatemala is not a *golpe de estado*; it is something more profound and more beneficial: it is a revolution. . . . It is a revolution that will go to the roots of the political system. . . . In a word: it is a revolution called to wash, to purify our political life, to quiet everyone and to honor Guatemala."[4] The first steps in this purification and the junta's major tasks were to oversee the election of a new president and to begin the process of drafting a new constitution. It performed both carefully and legally.

Framing a new constitution provided the neophyte politicians in the constitutional assembly with a quick lesson in the problems of legislating. Debate on many points was long and acrimonious. But the most bitter debate was reserved for provisions concerning the abolition of the vagrancy law and the granting of voting rights to illiterates. During the discussion of the vagrancy law, the assembly resounded with age-old arguments concerning Indians' unwillingness to work and the necessity of a strictly enforced vagrancy law. One delegate declared that these points were widely known in Guatemala and that history showed that earlier governments were overwhelmed by the "enormous difficulties they found with rural workers, especially the Indian." Others responded that the law made it appear as if peasants did not work, which was both factually and morally incorrect, for "if anyone works in Guatemala, it is peasants." Finally, the president of the assembly, Jorge García Granados, was able to push through a much less coercive vagrancy law. The difficulties of presenting moderate legislation in a society still dominated by the landed oligarchy were remarked upon by a sympathetic member of the U.S. embassy, who commented, "His (García Granados's) sponsorship of this measure, moreover, is a typical example of the sort of ordinary progressive action which is sufficient in Guatemala to label a public official as 'communist' " (a comment that would prove to be somewhat ironic given the later views of U.S. officials).[5]

The discussion of voting rights for illiterates was no less heated. Some of the assembly's members defended a restricted franchise by pointing out that Liberal dictators had "driven thousands and thousands of illiterates carrying a portrait of the candidate to deposit docilely their vote." But others disagreed vehemently. Representatives of the newly formed Workers' National Party (Partido Nacional de Trabajadores) argued, "To be illiterate is not synonymous with a lack of conscience or with imbecility. To be illiterate is a consequence not a cause." After almost a month of debate, literate women were allowed to vote and illiterate men were permitted a public oral vote.[6]

Other articles of the constitution caused less bitter but still intense debate. Nevertheless, the assembly finally emerged with a new constitution that was a peculiar blend of traditional liberal thought interspersed with some minor socialist measures. It left many problems unresolved, however.

Arévalo easily won the elections held in December 1944, and the junta handed over power to him on 1 March 1945. His political philosophy was a curious mix of somewhat confused social and economic concerns, ardent antifascism, nationalism, and corporatism. The core of his intellectual ideals lay in his concept of "spiritual socialism." According to Arévalo: "Spiritual socialism, like liberalism, will begin to restore to the moral and civil personality all of its grandeur; but it will go farther than liberalism and remove the insularity of man, obliging him to embrace the atmosphere of social values, necessities, and ends, understood simultaneously as an economic and social entity." Spiritual socialism was not essentially materialist. Arévalo did not believe that "man was primarily stomach." Rather, he stressed the importance of dignity. Spiritual socialism did not aim for the "ingenious redistribution of material goods, based on the foolish economic comparison of economically different men. Our socialism is going to liberate men psychologically." For Arévalo, "to socialize a republic is not simply to exploit industries in cooperation with workers, but before this to make each worker a man in the absolute fullness of his psychological and moral being."[7]

Although these concepts were vague, Arévalo left no doubt on his inauguration as to where the sympathies of his government would lie. He vowed: "There has been a fundamental lack of sympathy for the worker, and the slightest clamor for justice was avoided and punished as if one were trying to squash an outbreak of a terrifying epidemic. We are going to install a period of sympathy for the man who works in the fields, in the workshops, in the barracks, in commerce. . . . We are going to join justice and happiness to order, because order based on injustice and humiliation serves no one."[8]

The first government of the revolution passed a cornucopia of social and economic legislation, much of it inspired by Arévalo's philosophy. The economic and social policies of the Arévalo administration reflected a somewhat contradictory faith in the benefits of capitalism coupled with a determination to structure policies to benefit the less well-off. An editorial in the official *Revista de economía* in 1950 entitled "Principles of the State's Economic Policy" detailed this view clearly. It argued, "There is no reason to hope for prosperity in an economy in which one class benefits exclusively from the work of another. The orderly expansion of the economy with benefits equally divided gives to workers the purchasing power to acquire the necessities and the commodities of modern life, from which comes opportunities for profitable investment of capital in plants, equipment, and houses." However, the government's rhetoric was more impressive than the economic changes it fostered.[9]

Much of the government's economic policy in rural areas was directed toward expanding agricultural production, both agricultural exports and domestic-use agriculture. The most important legislation promoting the latter was designed to stimulate corn cultivation by providing rural workers with land. In 1946, after bad climatic conditions resulted in a severe decline in corn production, the government passed the Agricultural Emergency Law. This law and two subsequent Laws of Forced Rental, which allowed peasants to demand that they be allowed to rent unused land at set percentages of the harvest, were seen as harbingers of more drastic agrarian legislation.[10]

The government attempted to provide increased credit at reasonable rates to small farmers. In 1948, the Institute for Encouraging Production (Instituto de Fomento de Producción [INFOP]) was formed, its mandate to concentrate on increasing the production of basic foodstuffs through expanding credit. Augusto Charnaud MacDonald, the minister of economy, explained that the government had acted on the assumption that "in a country where 99 percent of the inhabitants had been dispossessed of their land" commercial credit was not sufficient. In its first full year of operation, the INFOP gave out Q4,500,000 in loans to over 4,000 people. By 1950, this figure had reached Q7 million per year.[11] Arévalo also promoted agricultural cooperatives "to defend the small peasant from the vicious exploitation of usury." The economic gains were not the only benefits to be gained from the cooperative program; the director of the program felt the process of organizing was a "magnificent school of popular education" that served to unite the peasantry in their struggle for economic liberation.[12]

These policies appear to have had only a limited impact on the mix of agricultural production in Guatemala. While the value of agricultural exports (especially bananas) fluctuated during the Arévalo administration because of climatic and political disruption, the production of agricultural goods for domestic consumption increased steadily from 1944 to 1950. This increase, however, was matched or surpassed by Costa Rica and El Salvador with less radical political change.[13]

In the social sphere, Arévalo's two major initiatives were expanding the education system and constructing an extensive social security network. As expected of a former teacher, Arévalo placed great stress on the need for public education, particularly in rural areas. Facilities for literacy training were greatly expanded with special emphasis on making the teaching methods applicable to Indians.[14] In addition, the Guatemalan Institute for Social Security (Instituto Guatemalteco de Seguridad Social [IGSS]) was formed in October 1946. The bill originally provided for benefits only to workers who suffered debilitating accidents on the job, but by mid-1949 coverage was extended to include all accidents, whether or not they occurred on the job. By 1951, 181,286 workers were affiliated with the IGSS throughout Guatemala. Maternity benefits and child care provisions were included in the scheme in 1953. The IGSS was a broad stroke on the revolutionary canvas; its benefits reached many poor citizens and were concrete reflections of the government's changing priorities.[15]

In general, the economic policies of the Arévalo administration proved to be a modest success. The economy benefited most from an increase in the international price for coffee beginning in 1946, for which the administration, of course, could take no credit. Guatemala's gross domestic product increased at a respectable rate throughout the period. There were, however, a number of problems. The most important were a high inflation rate and a growing government deficit. The government's attempts to reduce the deficit and make the tax system more equitable by taxing imports, increasing export taxes on agricultural goods, and introducing a restricted income tax spurred vehement opposition. Indeed, the income tax law first proposed in 1950 was never passed.[16]

Labor and the Revolution

Another area of significant legislative endeavor during the Arévalo administration was in the field of labor relations. The growth of unions and their influence on the government became one of the major sources of conflict. While labor unions took a relatively moderate stance toward Guatemalan-owned businesses, they made increasing demands on foreign-owned companies. Their perceived influence on the government and strengthening connections to the communist-linked Confederation of Workers of Latin America (Confederación de Trabajadores de América Latina [CTAL]) were important reasons for heightened opposition to Arévalo on the part of other sectors of society by the end of his term in office.

The railway workers' union, Union for Action and Improvement of

Railroads (Sindicato de Acción y Mejoramiento de Ferrocarriles [SAMF]), with approximately 4,500 members, was the best-organized and largest workers' union in the country. It quickly dominated the labor movement and the Confederation of Guatemalan Workers (Confederación de Trabajadores Guatemaltecos [CTG]), formed in October 1944. The SAMF adopted an extremely belligerent attitude toward the U.S.-owned railway, the IRCA. It struck in 1944, 1945, 1946, 1947, 1949, and 1950. Many of these strikes were linked to the union's aggressive nationalist stance, expressed in 1949 when it declared it would support "any national firm that competes with or establishes national services similar to those foreign companies have at the present time in a monopolistic form."[17]

Other U.S. firms operating in Guatemala were also subject to frequent work stoppages. Perhaps the most frequent and bitter strikes occurred at the various UFCo plantations. From March 1945 throughout the Arévalo administration, almost constant labor unrest engulfed one plantation after another. Most of the disputes concerned wages, but as in the SAMF strikes, nationalist rhetoric was often employed. In appealing for government support for its strike in 1946, one union leader declared, "We believe our government must embrace the cause of the workers, despoiled, scoffed at, and humiliated in their own fatherland by the haughtiness and despotism of foreigners accustomed to the practices of many years of dictatorship."[18]

The only union able to challenge the dominance of the SAMF and the UFCo unions in the labor movement was the teachers' union, the Union of Guatemalan Educational Workers (Sindicato de Trabajadores de Educación Guatemaltecos [STEG]). STEG officials argued that "teaching professionals are the nerves, the antennae, and the spirit of the working class and the people" and believed that the continued survival of the revolution depended on the vigilance of the union. Teachers were especially important in the formation of rural unions since many of them had been working in rural posts for years. They were often the only people in the community or the finca outside of the military with national connections.[19]

A general labor congress, the CTG, was formed in October 1944, primarily by the SAMF, members of the printers' union, and some returned exiles. But the congress was soon split between unions representing the best-paid, best-organized industrial workers (railway, cement factory, and brewery workers and skilled employees such as printers and bus drivers) and less well organized laborers and rural workers' unions, to a large extent led by teachers. Friction was apparent in three broad, linked areas: the extent of union involvement in politics, international affiliation for the

CTG, and "communist" influence. Protesting communist influence, the best-organized unions broke from the CTG in 1945 and were later joined by the SAMF, forming their own Workers' Federation of Guatemala (Federación Sindical de Guatemala [FSG]) in 1946. The two union federations opposed each other for much of the Arévalo administration. However, in December 1946, they did form a committee for labor unity to coordinate activities. It was not until the first year of the Arbenz administration that the two organizations reintegrated with the formation of the General Confederation of Workers of Guatemala (Confederación General de Trabajadores de Guatemala [CGTG]), headed by a former teacher, Víctor Manuel Gutiérrez.[20]

Arévalo welcomed union organization and supported the unions with a new Labor Code in 1947 and substantial revisions of the code in 1948. The Code was a fairly generous recognition of labor rights. It established an eight-hour day and a six-day week. It set minimum wages, encouraged union organization, and established a series of labor tribunals to arbitrate disputes. However, union organization on farms was restricted to those employing more than 500 people. The 1948 revisions eased the restrictions but still limited the right to strike and organize in the countryside.[21]

The Labor Code and its revisions provoked bitter opposition. The General Association of Agriculturalists (Asociación General de Agricultores [AGA]), representing large landowners, steadfastly opposed both. But the most bitter denunciations came from the UFCo. The company viewed the provisions for union organization only in large agricultural enterprises as discrimination, arguing (erroneously) that it was the only such firm in the country. Its efforts to persuade the U.S. embassy to act in its defense prompted much debate within the embassy and the State Department. The labor officer for the Office of Regional American Affairs, John W. Fishburn, believed the law was reasonable and fit with international practice. He warned that embassy action on behalf of the UFCo could only lead to disastrous results, strengthen radical labor segments, undermine the Guatemalan government, and "threaten our entire Good Neighbor Policy." Fishburn's thoughts on the code were echoed by the Office of International Trade Policy, but the Office of Middle American Affairs dismissed Fishburn as being "way off the beam" and the State Department acted as a vigorous negotiator for the company on the issue.[22]

The Arévalo administration usually enjoyed the support of organized labor, but this support was not unequivocal. Wages increased dramatically, but the booming inflation rate ate up most of the real gains in income. Labor leaders repeatedly complained about their inability to win substantial pay increases because of the restrictions on strikes in the Labor Code. In addition, the government often acted vigorously against even legal strikes. The military, particularly before the chief of the armed forces, Colonel Francisco Arana, was killed in 1949, often reacted violently to work stoppages in the countryside. While Arévalo and most members of his government theoretically defended the rights of labor, they were concerned enough about the effects labor organization and work stoppages might have on production and in promoting opposition to the revolution that they were frequently prepared to deny those rights in practice.[23]

"Democracy Is Not a Dog Fight"

With growing cooperation between the CTG and the FSG, labor was a more unified and, thus, more effective political force by the end of Arévalo's term in office. This cohesiveness stood in sharp contrast to the increasingly splintered state of the political parties supporting the government in congress. The rather decentralized fashion in which Arévalo viewed government meant that he needed to rely heavily on both cabinet ministers and supporters in congress. Throughout his presidency, he depended on a shifting alliance of revolutionary parties. These parties easily dominated congress, but they were continually torn apart by personal rivalries and battles over party advantage. Conflicts among revolutionary politicians weakened the Arévalo administration tremendously.

Guatemala had a population in 1950 of close to 3 million. Of this number, only a very small percentage were involved in the political battles in Guatemala City. Most of the politicians active during the revolution had attended the University of San Carlos or had gone through the Escuela Politécnica together. Personal connections, either friendships or longstanding feuds, dominated politics. As Arévalo once expressed it, "We are a small town and here we know each other too well."[24]

The newspapers followed the various personal battles with barely concealed delight. Interspersed with calls for "everyone to cooperate in the work of salvation and collective well-being," *El Imparcial* gave full play to feuds between politicians. These stories helped deepen the discord.[25]

Not all battles were personal in nature, however. One constant among the revolutionary parties was a conflict between "moderate" and "radical" wings of the movement. Following Arévalo's victory in 1944, with the government facing a strengthened opposition in municipal elections, the two "government" parties, the RN and the FPL, merged to form the Revolutionary Action Party (Partido de Acción Revolucionaria [PAR]) in order to "maintain the revolution." But in July 1946 the RN split from the new party, promising it would "always be in solidarity with them through a common denominator: the revolution of 20 October and the grand patriotic aspirations of arevalismo." Even the remaining members of the PAR were divided, and later that year, when the PAR executive agreed to cooperate with the labor federation in selecting some deputies for election to the assembly, some members began to complain about "extremism" in the party executive. Unable to unseat the executive, a majority of the members split to re-form the FPL. Like the RN dissidents, these members reaffirmed their commitment to the revolution and the "leftist line." They made it clear, however, that they could not work with the more radical members of the PAR, which continued as a party despite these desertions. They described the difference between the PAR and the FPL as that between "anarchy" and a "rational, historic approach to the consummation of the revolution."[26]

These conflicts caused serious realignments in politics and prompted the government to take action against the most radical of the PAR members, even though they supported the Arévalo administration. Many of the FPL and RN members approached change in rural Guatemala cautiously. Following a wave of labor agitation in the countryside in 1945, the FPL leaders and the military forced the president to assign the most radical labor organizers to foreign diplomatic posts. These postings reflected the very tentative approach to change in the countryside that was followed during the early years of Arévalo's term in office. Even the usually conservative *El Imparcial* called these new postings "repression with a silk glove." It went on to argue that in Guatemala at that time this proved that "toward the right one can be as extremist or reactionary as one wishes, but if one is inclined to the left, no matter how little, one is lost."[27]

Although the PAR and the RN were able to cooperate in elections and in congress, the FPL was increasingly leery of the strength of organized labor and communist influence in the PAR. The parties were unable to agree on an electoral coalition for the municipal and congressional elections in 1948, leading to some gains for the opposition and intense conflict in rural areas.

The parties splintered from within as well. There was constant conflict in the PAR between José Manuel Fortuny and Augusto Charnaud Mac-

Donald, both important figures on the PAR executive, conflict that ended only when Fortuny left the party in 1950. Also, the RN convention in 1948 tore the party apart and ended in violence when the old executive refused to give way to the newly elected one. These internal conflicts became even more apparent during the presidential elections in 1950. The FPL separated into two factions, both running candidates. The RN was weakened by defections, and the PAR lost a number of its most active members, who later formed a communist party. Shortly after the elections, Charnaud and many others left the PAR to form the Socialist Party.[28]

This instability influenced Arévalo's relationship with the parties and congress and affected his ability to get legislation passed. Arguing that "democracy is not a dog-fight," he vowed that his government would function only with honorable men who "exhibit a minimum of cleanliness in their life." But he was quickly disillusioned with the constant squabbles and bemoaned "the cells, the unhealthy longings, the suicidal propaganda the revolutionary groups make against each other."[29]

Caught in this atmosphere of intrigue, where political and personal battles intermingled and were fought in party conventions, congress, and the press, Arévalo walked gingerly along a thin line between nonpartisanship among the revolutionary parties and fighting for support in congress. He constantly had to balance his cabinet to smooth the ruffled feathers of one or another party.[30] But the most "radical" of the government supporters were, by and large, the most dedicated and hardest working deputies and cabinet ministers. Although such members were not exclusively supporters of the PAR, they did constitute a larger proportion of members of that party. The PAR also most ardently supported the president in congress. Consequently, while the more moderate FPL continued to be the largest party until the end of the Arévalo administration, the PAR was soon obviously the most vigorous and in some ways the most favored.

Reactionaries and Revolutionaries

The instability of the revolutionary parties was a major concern as the Arévalo administration was confronted with serious opposition, much of it violent. Beginning with the refusal of his major opponent, Adrian Recinos, to accept the results of the presidential election in 1944 and continuing almost to the very day of turning the government over to Jacobo Arbenz Guzmán, Arévalo was attacked relentlessly. He withstood close to thirty attempted coups, many with significant involvement of military officers.

Much of this opposition was directed at the government's economic policies. The landowners' association, the AGA, was probably the most vehement critic. It was initially disturbed by the abolition of the coercive vagrancy law used by Ubico to insure labor for the harvest. It also soon began to protest what its members perceived to be heightened unrest in the countryside after 1944. The AGA, along with the Chamber of Commerce, also complained about the government's limited attempt to implement a "planned economy," arguing, "The truth is that there does not exist a human brain capable of substituting for this natural law [supply and demand] without causing the most deplorable economic disturbances to the people they try to favor with artificial systems." By 1948, the AGA was complaining that government intervention and the actions of unscrupulous political leaders were causing a severe shortage of workers. In order to win the votes of the workers, these leaders, the AGA argued, had created artificial problems between labor and capital, "exalting or exaggerating the rights of labor, without mentioning their responsibilities, kindling the most ruinous passions." In this way they had "destroyed social harmony, so necessary in order that the factors of production fulfill with success their noble goals of creating and increasing the national wealth."[31]

However, the numerous attempted coups Arévalo endured were primarily the result of intrigues by conservative political parties that failed to do well at the polls. There was much discussion concerning the failure of opposition parties to abide by the rules of the political game. Arévalo blamed the political unrest on the inability of these parties to understand that "after a civic defeat they have to resign themselves to wait for new elections to demonstrate that they have improved their position before the public conscience." Even *El Imparcial*, often critical of the government, denounced the opposition parties, stating, "Reasonable opposition, dignified, elevated, without egoism, without violence, is as indispensable in a democracy as the air we breathe. . . . Why do we not have parties of this type in Guatemala?"[32] The opposition parties blamed their failure at the polls on government interference and fraud. While isolated instances of electoral fraud did occur during the various contests that took place in the first few years of the revolution, for the most part elections were a fair reflection of the popular will.[33]

But if the opposition deserved censure for refusing to abide by elections, the government parties were also somewhat to blame since they contributed to the unrest. Revolutionary politicians were often too quick to paint all those who disagreed, often only mildly, with government policy as "reactionaries." As *El Imparcial* editorialized, "The government and its supporters were interested in confusing . . . acceptance of the regime, which is transitory, with the ideal of liberty and democracy, which is permanent and immovable." The broad brush with which government supporters painted all opponents contributed to political unrest and strengthened the violent opposition.[34]

The most inflammatory issue around which political opposition gathered was the existence of communists in Guatemala. The 1945 constitution declared that no political organization with international links would be allowed to operate in Guatemala. This provision quickly became the rallying point for opposition to the government's acceptance of radical labor leaders. At times the labels were absurd; Arévalo himself was often called a communist or communist sympathizer despite the fact that he had repeatedly called communism one of the greatest dangers to democracy, had insisted that Guatemalan peasants would never accept Marxism, and on occasion had acted against "communists" operating in Guatemala by expelling foreign activists, closing the Escuela Claridad (a Marxist study school), and denouncing rural unrest. Throughout his presidency, no openly communist party existed in the country. Probably the most absurd episode of this red scare came when Kenneth De Courcy, a British journalist, wrote a story carried by the United Press in Guatemala that claimed the Soviets were planning to establish a base for submarines in Guatemalan waters and that underwater supply centers already existed to service them. The Guatemalan government immediately invited him to Guatemala to "help us discover" the bases.[35]

The concern over communism was understandable, however. Many of Guatemala's young reform politicians were ardent students of political theory and used Marxist rhetoric and a history of class conflict to describe their ideals. The CTG and the PAR, particularly, were considered to be dominated by communists. The head of the CTG, Víctor Manuel Gutiérrez, was openly communist by the midpoint of Arévalo's term in office and later joined the Guatemalan Communist Party created by José Manuel Fortuny in 1951. Gutiérrez's domination of the CTG, along with the labor agitation fostered by such people as Carlos Manuel Pellecer, who had contacts with communists outside of Guatemala, insured that opposition to the labor federation reached a fever pitch. To many in Guatemala, the PAR was tarnished with the same communist stain, again, an understandable conclusion given the temper of the times. After the FPL split from the coalition that created the PAR, the young radicals remaining in the PAR saw themselves as both the most trustworthy defenders of the revolution and the surest allies of workers and peasants. Given this orientation, those in the party who demonstrated the most zeal in the cause were esteemed. Party debates over specific issues often became discussions of political theory; those who could quote Marx and Lenin most fully, however imperfectly, won the most points.[36]

The national debate over communism affected Guatemalan relations with the United States and became intertwined with Guatemala's treatment of U.S. business interests. Arévalo shuffled cabinet ministers, abandoned legislation, and restricted labor to placate U.S. concerns. Even so, increasing U.S. opposition to the Arévalo administration encouraged violent opposition to the government.[37] *resistance starting building of Arbenz but,*

The mounting concern over communist influence in the government *yes* reached a crescendo in 1949 and 1950 with the killing of the chief of *b/c of* the armed forces, Colonel Francisco Arana, the emergence of a nascent *Communism* Communist Party, and the election campaign to succeed Arévalo. Colonel Arana, the most powerful officer in the country, had become increasingly linked to conservative opposition to the government. His killing in 1949 prompted the most serious military revolt Arévalo faced and divided the military almost in half. The revolt was only defeated after Colonel Jacobo Arbenz Guzmán, the defense minister, armed politicians and workers. Following the revolt, tension remained high as the military demanded the return of weapons given out to workers. The unions delayed for weeks, finally agreeing to place their trust in what was now "a true army of the revolution."[38]

In June 1950, ten of the most radical leaders of the PAR resigned from the party. This group began publishing a newspaper with a clearly Marxist perspective, *Octubre*, in the same month and opened a new Marxist study school named Jacobo Sanchéz. The school, the newspaper, and the expectation that these ten would form a communist party dominated political discussion for months. There was much debate over whether they were in violation of the constitution forbidding international political organizations until finally the minister of *gobernación*, Colonel Elfego Monzón, closed both the newspaper and the school. Although Monzón was forced to resign from his post because of the protests in congress over his action, the school and the newspaper remained closed until after the presidential elections.[39]

There was even more concern over the role of the political committees of the labor federations during the election. Following the death of Arana, Arbenz began to test gingerly the political waters in preparation for a plunge into the presidential campaign. Although he was first nominated by a new, moderate, regional party from his hometown of Quezaltenango, the National Integrity Party (Partido de Integridad Nacional [PIN]), it was the vocal support of the political committees of the labor unions that caused him to be chosen by the PAR and the RN as their candidate. The prominent position of labor in the campaign, another military revolt led by Colonel Carlos Castillo Armas, street battles prompted by protests over the killing of Arana, and continual charges of electoral fraud in the works increased the tension and apprehension as the elections approached. Nonetheless, the worst fears were not realized. The elections proceeded relatively smoothly with little violence. Arbenz emerged as the clear winner in a ten-candidate race and, surprisingly, began to be seen as something of a conciliatory candidate who it was hoped would dampen the political fires that raged.[40]

The Second Government of the Revolution

Colonel Jacobo Arbenz Guzmán was inaugurated as president on 15 March 1951. Many saw Arbenz as the personification of the aspirations of workers and peasants. Even more than Arévalo, he was portrayed as a man of the people. Some suspected that he had little control over his government and that the labor federations or communist advisers actually determined policy. Yet Arbenz's economic and political philosophies were decidedly pragmatic and capitalist in temper. Government policy sought to stimulate industry, foster economic independence, and encourage production.

The second government of the revolution was much more secure than the first. The Arbenz administration was spared the onslaught of coup attempts that had plagued Arévalo. Yet under Arbenz, opposition to government reforms became more widespread and more determined. Increasingly, the issue of communist control over the government overshadowed all others, despite the capitalist temper of Arbenz's reforms. In the end, the question became increasingly intermingled with the agrarian reform and the expansion of labor and peasant organizations in the countryside.

In many ways, Arbenz had been a surprising choice as the presidential candidate of the majority of the revolutionary politicians in 1950. There was concern about the nomination of an officer, as many distrusted the military establishment and the political ambitions of soldiers. In addition, while Arbenz received his most important support, at least initially, from the labor federations, he had cultivated a convenient political ambiguity while serving as minister of defense. But his support for nationalist measures and his prominent role in the overthrow of Ponce and in defeating the revolt following Arana's death insured that he was increasingly seen as the "soldier of the people" and the staunchest defender of the revolution in the military.[41]

Arbenz approached the elections with solid support. The PAR and the RN, two of the three most powerful parties in the country, supported him. The third, the FPL, was split and ran two candidates. One of these, Manuel Galich, withdrew his name shortly before the vote and called on his supporters to cast their ballots for Arbenz. There were serious challenges, however. Jorge García Granados, a respected politician and former president of the assembly, ran in opposition to Arbenz, and it was feared that he would divide the revolutionary vote. The most important opposition came from General Miguel Ydígoras Fuentes. While Ydígoras gained support from many sectors fearful of government economic and political reforms, his campaign focused exclusively on the communist threat. In one of his first campaign speeches, he assured his supporters, "I know that you have joined me so that, by our united efforts, we can rescue Guatemala from the sharp claws of Marxism, which under the guise of 'spiritual socialism,' is beginning to loom dangerously over it."[42]

The presidential elections were held in a period of intense unrest. Anticommunist demonstrations abounded, street battles erupted between these demonstrators and revolutionary supporters, a military coup was attempted, and government supporters feared more unrest. Many believed Ydígoras and his followers were linked to the coup attempts, and although there was little evidence of his involvement, a warrant was issued for his arrest. He fought much of the election in hiding, while his full-page advertisements in the country's major newspaper continued. There was also concern for Arbenz's safety. He dropped out of sight for long periods; there were persistent rumors he had left the country; and his home and headquarters were described as a fortress, with armed guards at all entrances.[43] Nevertheless, Arbenz easily won the elections. While there were irregularities in the election, his margin of victory — 266,778 votes to Ydígoras's 71,180 — accurately reflected the relative sizes of their constituencies.[44]

Out of the debris of civic unrest, coup attempts, and charges of fraud, a movement toward national reconciliation grew. Arbenz, despite his connections to labor, was seen by many to represent a step toward political and economic moderation after the idealism of Arévalo. Despite disturbing calls for agrarian reform in his election campaign, many of his speeches were considered to be less inflammatory than Arévalo's had been. All sectors of Guatemala's elite attended Arbenz's inauguration ball, and the U.S. embassy staff commented favorably on the "national honeymoon spirit." Indeed, the commentator believed that the "new administration comes into power in an atmosphere of greater general confidence than has existed in [the] country since [the] early days of the Arévalo regime."[45]

For the most part, Arbenz lived up to these expectations in the first year of his administration. In his inaugural address, he presented his plans in the practical, pragmatic, and somewhat conciliatory tones he was to use for most of his term in office. He announced that his government was going to encourage the economic development of the country with the following three goals: "to convert our country from a dependent nation with a semi-colonial economy into an economically independent one; to convert Guatemala from a backward country with a predominantly feudal economy into a modern capitalist country, and to carry out this transformation in a way that will bring with it the greatest increase possible in the standard of living of the greatest mass of the people." He went on to affirm that in order to achieve this transformation, "it is absolutely clear that our political economy must be based on private initiative, the development of Guatemalan capital, in whose hands we must find the fundamental activities of the national economy." He also extended an invitation to foreign capitalists as long as their investment "adjusts to local conditions, is always subordinate to Guatemalan laws, cooperates in the economic development of the country, and abstains strictly from involvement in the political and social life of the nation."

In the course of his short address, he also stressed the need for the abolition of latifundia, industrialization, the construction of an improved transportation network, and more accessible means of credit for small farmers. He vowed "to conserve at whatever cost the democratic regime, in which citizens maintain the right to think and believe as they wish, to organize and dedicate themselves to whatever legal activities they elect." The U.S. embassy saw this address, "with its call to national unity and absence of class appeal," as a major step in reducing the bitterness provoked by the elections.[46]

A few months after his inaugural address, Arbenz expanded on the economic development he envisaged. He emphasized the importance of economic independence and agrarian reform. He stressed that economic autonomy was so important that "even if prosperity and independence were incompatible, . . . I am sure the great majority of Guatemalans would prefer to continue being a poor but free nation." Luckily, he argued, independence was not only compatible with prosperity but indispensable for it. To obtain this independence, he suggested, Guatemala needed to expand its agricultural production, diversify, and process more agricultural products. Consequently, industrialization could not occur without an agrarian reform. For Arbenz, agrarian reform meant primarily that Guatemalan agriculture, suffering still from a "feudal" attitude on the part of large landowners, needed to be turned into a capitalist venture. Unused land and fincas not run in a "capitalist" manner would be subject to expropriation. He also reasserted that the final goal of government action must be to increase the income of the majority of the population. "How wrong it would be," he suggested, "if we confused the means with the ends, erecting financial stability or economic prosperity into supreme political objectives and sacrificing to them the possibility of encouraging the immediate well-being of the great majority."[47]

Much of the economic program of the Arbenz administration was based on the recommendations made in an International Bank for Reconstruction and Development survey headed by George Britnell, an economist at the University of Saskatchewan in Canada. Britnell stressed the need for increased agricultural production and diversification, the integration of the highland peasantry into the national economy, and the necessity of raising the peasantry's disposable income. He was especially critical of large landowners on the Pacific slopes who kept idle some of the best agricultural land in the Americas. The report, completed in late 1950, had been submitted to a meeting of the National Economic Council in 1951 and had been approved virtually intact.[48]

An important goal of Arbenz's economic program was to challenge the monopoly on transport and shipping held by the IRCA and the allied UFCo. The most important project in this regard was the construction of a highway to the Atlantic to rival the railway. The road was hailed as a "Symbol of Liberation" by the official newspaper, and Arbenz continually pointed to it as one of the most important government projects. By 1952, Arbenz announced that this highway was to be joined by the construction of a new port, Santo Tomás, on the Caribbean to challenge the UFCo-controlled Puerto Barrios.[49]

The most important and most controversial aspect of Arbenz's program was the Agrarian Reform Law. Many in the Arbenz administration believed the government had a moral obligation to alter landholding patterns and that none of the goals of the administration's economic program could be achieved without an effective agrarian reform. There was little consensus about what shape that reform would take, however. The actual Agrarian Reform Law proposed by Arbenz in May 1952 had diverse roots and had been the result of years of debate among revolutionary organizations. It, and the peasant and rural worker organization that it helped spawn, prompted immense opposition.

As part of his attempt to win support for his program among diverse sectors, Arbenz sought landlord input on and acceptance of his projects. At first he was reasonably successful. Immediately after his inauguration, the AGA welcomed Arbenz's policies, promising, "In this field, and faithful to its rigid apolitical tradition, the association is ready to contribute patriotically with constructive cooperation to promote the desired development of agriculture."[50] But the amicable relations were destroyed with the Agrarian Reform Law.

The most dramatic demonstration of Arbenz's determination to reduce tensions in the country was his handling of labor. Although Arbenz was accused of being controlled by organized labor, almost immediately after he assumed office his actions revealed that this perception was erroneous. The two labor federations had become increasingly restless during the latter part of the Arévalo administration, largely because they believed their political strength had not been matched by economic gains. Following the presidential elections, they attempted to remedy this with a series of bitter strikes. Railway workers, customs workers, teachers, and employees of the government-owned national fincas went on strike. Truckers, postal employees, and telegraph operators threatened to join them. Arbenz at first seemed reluctant to respond, which, according to the Canadian trade commissioner, prompted the nickname "Sleeping Beauty" among his critics. But Arbenz soon took action to end the strikes. He personally mediated the disputes, ending the strikes by the SAMF, teachers, and finca workers and preventing the truckers' strike.[51]

Perhaps the clearest indication of Arbenz's ability and determination to persuade the labor federations to temper their demands and cooperate with his economic program was his veto of proposed revisions to the Labor Code in 1952 after congress had overwhelmingly passed the changes. Following a series of meetings with the revolutionary parties, he even won their support for the veto. *El Imparcial* was particularly full of praise for this action, suggesting that it demonstrated the government possessed "sufficient character to continue on its own plan . . . and to attend to the just demands of reasonable organizations presented in defense of the economic, political, and social well-being of the country."[52]

Politicians and Peasants

While Arévalo believed in the virtue of competing institutions as a means for insuring against dictatorship, Arbenz was clearly more interested in centralizing power in the presidency to facilitate the implementation of his economic program. Partly as a consequence, more of his administration took place behind closed doors. The president's office became especially important as individuals sought to affect legislation, to receive personal favors, or to win political advantage through the personal intervention of the president or his associates. In direct contrast to the confused and fluid political smorgasbord served up during the Arévalo administration, national political power increasingly centered on a dozen or so men and women, who acted, according to the Canadian trade commissioner, as "an iron wall keeping [Arbenz] out of touch with events and people." In the process, the political parties that had been the major support, unsteady as they might have been, for Arévalo, disintegrated into a myriad of competing factions.[53]

The PAR emerged from the presidential elections in 1950 as the major political force in the country and retained that distinction throughout Arbenz's presidency. Its dominance was assisted by the decline of the other two revolutionary parties. The RN never developed grass roots organizations and more and more functioned like a wing of the PAR. It was also so divided that at the party convention in March 1954, one delegate pulled a gun, killing one policeman and seriously wounding two delegates.[54] The FPL was torn apart by the presidential elections and was never again a powerful political force. The PAR's strength was the result of its relative organizational solidarity, its willing acceptance of Arbenz early in the election campaign, its connections to increasingly powerful organized labor, and its readiness to work more or less diligently to implement legislation passed by congress.

But the PAR also suffered from internal conflict. In the midst of the presidential election campaign in 1950, José Manuel Fortuny and nine other "radicals" split from the party and later formed the Communist Party of Guatemala. In December 1952, its name was changed to the Guatemalan Workers' Party (Partido Guatemalteco de Trabajadores [PGT]). Their withdrawal from the PAR was probably the result of a struggle between Fortuny and Augusto Charnaud MacDonald and an attempt by Charnaud's followers to reduce the influence of the more radical wing. At the 1949 party convention, many of the "radicals" had been defeated in their bid to continue in executive posts, and many of them left with Fortuny. The split in some ways strengthened the PAR as it allowed Arbenz to rely more heavily on the party, to some extent free from the taint of communist collaboration.[55]

Charnaud soon faced opposition from within the party as well as from the "radicals" who had resigned. Part of this opposition was generated because of the founding of a peasant league, the National Peasant Confederation of Guatemala (Confederación Nacional Campesina de Guatemala [CNCG]). Efforts to organize peasants (as distinct from rural workers) had been carried on with some success during 1949 and 1950. In May 1950, peasants formed a national confederation and in February 1951 held their first national congress with 275 delegates attending. The formation of the CNCG was an important event and a major step forward in extending the revolution to the countryside, but it was viewed with apprehension by many people. The most powerful figure in the organization was Leonardo Castillo Flores, a teacher and PAR deputy in congress. The labor federations, newly united in the CGTG, complained bitterly that a separate formation of peasants would divide peasants from workers and weaken the revolution. Charnaud and Castillo Flores were close political allies, and many people believed the CNCG would be used by Charnaud to develop a mass following that would insure his national political dominance and his election as the next president. They saw it as one more example of the "caudillismo of Charnaud MacDonald" and warned that his attempt to "place the peasant movement under the control of the bourgeoisie" would be dangerous for the revolution.[56]

Partly because of this growing criticism, Charnaud was defeated in his bid to retain the position of secretary-general at the party convention in 1951. He resigned from the party in May of that year, citing "undemocratic" conduct in the convention and apparently concerned that the new party officials would wean the CNCG from him. The leaders of the CNCG also resigned from the party, saying, "We must keep faith with those who trust us." They swore they would only join another political organization "if it genuinely represents the aspirations of the farmer and working classes."[57]

Charnaud soon announced the formation of a new party, the Socialist

Party, which seriously challenged PAR dominance. With Charnaud and a few other refugees from the PAR as a political base and the burgeoning CNCG as an allied grass roots organization, it looked to be a powerful political organization. The party soon attracted a number of politicians from other parties. But the most important influence on the party's political commission was exerted by leaders of the peasant federation, including Castillo Flores and Amor Velasco, secretary-general and secretary of organization of the CNCG, respectively. Immediately after the formation of the party, numerous PAR affiliates in villages throughout the country abandoned the PAR for the Socialists. However, the squabbles also threatened to tear the CNCG apart as many of the *uniones campesinas*, the peasant organizations that were locals of the CNCG, refused to follow the executive's lead and announced they were staying with the PAR.[58]

Partly because of the PAR's fear of the strength of the Socialists, it soon launched movements to effect some sort of conciliation between the two. This attempt at cooperation is best seen in the context of the periodic "unity" appeals floating back and forth among the six parties that now occasionally cooperated on government policy: PAR, RN, FPL, PIN, the Communists, and the Socialists. This already complex situation was further confused by the existence of such nonparty but politically important revolutionary organizations as the CGTG, the *octubrist* group (linked to the communist newspaper), the CNCG, and, until 1952, Víctor Manuel Gutiérrez's Revolutionary Workers' Party of Guatemala (Partido Revolucionario Obrero de Guatemala [PROG]). Most often attempts to form an effective coalition floundered on the shoals of anticommunist feeling on the part of the PIN, the FPL, and sometimes the RN and the Socialists. These parties steadfastly refused to join a coalition that included the Communist Party, no matter how small a component it was. The PIN especially vowed to "fight to prevent exotic theories that come to perturb our tranquility and attack the democratic principles apparent since 1944 from infiltrating the country."[59]

Finally, in 1952, with Arbenz's urging and a battle over the proposed agrarian reform looming, the PAR and the Socialists announced they had formed a "vigorous alliance" to protect the revolution. They agreed on shared priorities, including such disparate elements as a battle against inflation, correct application of the Law of Forced Rental, the realization of agrarian reform, the improvement of the living conditions of intellectuals, full incorporation of women into society, protection for infants, international peace, and "a fight to promote the best development of Indian nationalities." Both parties promised they would put an end to "personal feuds that must be subordinated to the high goals of the revolution and progress." A little over a month later, the RN and the FPL agreed to join the alliance.[60]

The passage of the Agrarian Reform Law in June 1952 inspired a new onslaught of attacks on the government. In the face of this opposition, the alliance became more ambitious; the PAR and the Socialists began to discuss a true amalgamation of the two parties. They reached a tentative agreement that same month and enticed the RN, the FPL, and the PIN to join in the agreement. On 2 July all the component parties dissolved to form the Party of the Guatemalan Revolution (Partido de la Revolución Guatemalteca [PRG]).[61]

The creation of the new party was a grand stroke promising a solid front of revolutionary politicians to buttress Arbenz's attempts at economic reform. But there were too many differences among the various parties for it to be effective. Many politicians continued to view Charnaud with suspicion and to suspect the PRG of being a tool to further his career. Partly because of his influence, many PAR members considered the PRG executive to have "APRISTA tendencies" — by which they meant the PRG was composed of conservative nationalists — and to be in bed with the reactionaries. On the other hand, many of the politicians in the other parties were concerned by the radical nature of the PAR politicians and their connections to communists.[62]

This "mysterious united conglomeration," as it was called by the PAR executive, quickly fell apart. Much of the trouble began in the local affiliates of the parties. In many communities, the merging of the various parties threw together people representing the two extremes of local political expression, whatever their parties might represent in the national arena. When it was time to pick candidates for the assembly and municipal elections in 1952, the PRG locals split into warring sides with local representatives of the PAR most often complaining that the PRG was supporting reactionaries for positions. Finally, in late July, PAR and RN members left the new party and applied for official inscription of their original parties. The PRG continued, with a Socialist Party core and dominated by Charnaud but retaining many politicians from the other parties, including the PAR.[63]

Immediately after the coalition dissolved, Castillo Flores announced that the peasant league would no longer be affiliated with any party. From that point, he attempted to maintain an apolitical, but progovernment, stance in the CNCG. Nonetheless, when he and most of the CNCG leaders left the PRG and rejoined the PAR, the latter regained much of its lost strength in rural areas. In 1954, the PAR realistically estimated that 60 to 70 percent of the peasants in the CNCG were allied with the party. Nonetheless, the PRG remained powerful, especially in the "Oriente," where its local affiliates were more organized. For most of the Arbenz administration, these two parties (the PAR and the PRG) were the major actors in the government coalition and dominated the assembly. But both parties also continued to suffer from internal dissent, and by March 1954 the independents — six refugees from the PRG and five ex-PAR members — were the second largest political group in the assembly, after the PAR, though they never formed an organization and had no local bases.[64]

The game of musical chairs that went on with increasing bitterness among the various government parties had an effect on the functioning of government. Congress, particularly, turned into a kind of circus. Kalman Silvert, a U.S. political scientist who spent some time observing the operations of government in the early 1950s, commented on the often exuberant and heated debates in congress. Silvert suggested, "The result was often noisy, but clearly indicative that Congress is one of the most sensitive organs of the government." It was a boisterous expression of democracy. But as the Arbenz administration continued, it became increasingly difficult to pass legislation. A quorum was almost impossible to obtain, party leaders were frequently drunk, spectators were uncontrollable, and deputies at times were frightened for their lives.[65]

Some of this disintegration can be traced to the fact that deputies were still, by and large, young, impatient men with little stomach for the tedious business of a democratic assembly. In 1953, two-thirds of the deputies were under thirty-five. But a good deal of the unrest can be traced to a growing sense among deputies that the real decisions of government were not made in congress. Arbenz's penchant for surrounding himself with close confidants and ruling through them helped trivialize the role of congress.[66]

Communism and Anticommunism

As these various revolutionary parties shattered into a myriad of competing factions, tenuously glued themselves back together, and then split apart once again, Arbenz sought competent administrative personnel to help implement government policy. To some extent he succeeded by appointing technicians who kept aloof from party politics: cabinet ministers like Roberto Fanjul and Guillermo Toriello. He also relied heavily on the military, appointing officers to administrative posts in a variety of government departments. Still, as government initiatives penetrated the depths of rural Guatemala, he needed reliable administrators with influence in rural areas. To a great extent, he was forced to dig into the CGTG and the CNCG for such people. His reliance on members of organized labor and peasants added fuel to the anticommunist movements.

While the PGT never had much official power — at its height the party had only five deputies in congress and no cabinet ministers — its influence was not easily dismissed. The closed nature of Arbenz's administration heightened the power of a few close advisers. Important among them were Fortuny of the PGT and members of other parties who were thought to be communists. María Cristina de Villanova, Arbenz's wife, was considered to be both a communist and an important influence on the president. In addition, the CGTG was steadily growing more powerful, and dedicated individuals in both the CGTG and the PGT, such as Víctor Manuel Gutiérrez and Carlos Manuel Pellecer, were gaining widespread personal followings.[67] Without a doubt, however, it was the increasing importance of peasant and rural worker organization, the unrest that accompanied that organization, and the powerful position of supposed communists in that organization that prompted the most opposition and engulfed Guatemala in unrest in the final years of the Arbenz administration.

"A SEA OF INDIANS": RURAL ORGANIZATION AND ETHNIC CONFLICT

The Indian is an inexhaustible layer of
exploitation, and his best song
is his taciturnity. . . . Guatemala is
sad; a desperate, horrid, fearful
sadness. Its people are sad, they live
introspectively, without sensation or
passions. Mute, withdrawn, hushed. . . .
We are a sad people . . . living with
a totally alien world within us.

—Ernesto Juan Fonfrías,
"Guatemala: un pueblo triste"

The populist ex-president of Mexico, Lázaro Cárdenas, remarked that Guatemala had made an urban revolution in a rural country.[1] Cárdenas pointed out the basic dilemma of the revolution. Most of the young politicians involved in the two administrations between 1944 and 1954 had little understanding of rural Guatemala and the conflicts buried there. They were intense nationalists with an eager desire for national integration. Their vision of a new Guatemala had little space for an Indian culture or an Indian worldview if it differed fundamentally from their own.

It was in the countryside that the most virulent opposition to reform emanated. Landowners and the rural Ladino middle class had an entrenched interest in the maintenance of the prevailing systems of land tenure, labor recruitment, and market and credit arrangements. But opposition to reform in the countryside was not exclusively a reflection of the economic interests of a dominant Ladino elite. An almost paranoid fear of Indian uprising had been deeply ingrained in the psyche of rural Ladinos, a fear that had been purposely fostered during the Liberal decades. Surrounded by a sea of Indians, many viewed any organization among Indians or the rural poor with apprehension. They feared any awakening of that "totally alien world" described by Fonfrías. For these reasons, reforms in the countryside before the Agrarian Reform Law of 1952 were tentative.

The various political parties and revolutionary institutions that sometimes collaborated and occasionally quarreled with each other in national affairs fought bitterly in the countryside. The result was unsettling and contradictory. Cárdenas's statement describes perfectly a movement that needed to extend the revolution to the countryside in order to survive yet had no program for doing so and was constantly frightened by the changes it did foment. In the end, this schizophrenic approach to rural Guatemala helped hasten the revolution's end.

National Views of Rural Reform

The October Revolution sprang from the frustrated dreams of an urban middle class. Their concerns in the first few years of the revolution rarely strayed far from that comfortable urban environment and the understandable, if tempestuous, arena of national politics. For many urban Guatemalans, the preponderance of Indian blood among rural inhabitants made the countryside a place of impenetrable superstition, irrational and incomprehensible. Even the most reformist of the Guatemalan elite and those most concerned with conditions in rural Guatemala before the revolution espoused ideas little changed from the "positivist" philosophy that pervaded Liberal thinking at the turn of the century.

The inspiration for much of the social and economic thought of the revolutionaries during the early years of the revolution came from the ideas propounded by the "Generation of the 1920s," the graduates of the University of San Carlos who had come of age around the earthquake of 1917 and the overthrow of Manuel Estrada Cabrera in 1920. The leading lights of that generation, men like Jorge García Granados and Miguel Angel Asturias, were important figures in the revolution as well. Yet if we can judge from their writings in the 1920s, their approach to Indian cultures, while perhaps sympathetic, stressed cultural and political assimilation. Asturias's *El Problema social del indio*, in particular, was an important contribution to indigenista ideas following 1923 when it first saw light as a thesis at the University of San Carlos.

El Problema was an impassioned plea for action to better the living conditions of Guatemala's Indians, but it was action designed to turn Guatemala from a largely "Indian" nation into one more closely resembling European countries. The Indian was seen as "a child that from the night to morning was turned into an adult." Asturias identified two levels on which action could be taken to effect more completely this transformation from child to adult: the first involved improved education, better nutrition, and relief from long periods of exhausting work; but the second was the most important and most necessary. Indians could be improved only if they were incorporated into non-Indian society, which could only be done biologically. Miscegenation was "a wide door to pass from their primitive social state to the social state that European civilization left in these soils." But the intermingling of European and Indian threatened to clog the "vigorous blood" necessary for progress. The only means of preventing the inevitable debasement of the Ladino was infusions of new blood through immigration into Guatemala from such pure stocks as those found in Switzerland, Belgium, Holland, and Germany.[2]

This approach was evident in writings on the Indian throughout the "ten years of spring." During the revolution the "Indian" novel flowered as a literary genre. While occasionally addressing real economic and social problems of Indian peasants, the novels depicted Indians' lives as straight out of fantastical legends. These novels and the earlier writings of the 1920s did little to provide an understanding of the Indian cultures that surrounded the urban reformers. They certainly provided nothing on which to base a positive plan for social and economic action.[3]

Some attention was paid to Indian and peasant problems in the early days of the revolution, however. *El Imparcial* ran frequent editorials on the need for an enlightened policy in rural areas. The place of Indian cultures in national society was debated at length during the constitutional assembly, where a suggestion of separate laws for Indians prompted an attack from some of the most determined reformers, who argued that separate laws would "give strength to the reactionaries." The more conservative David Vela countered forcefully, suggesting that "if we want to arrive at true equality before the law, it cannot be along the simple path of classical liberalism, but through . . . respecting the resources of the current civilization and, at the same time, bringing the ideas of universal cultures to these classes. . . . In this way . . . the racial discrimination that exists will cease to do so." Prompted largely by Vela's defense, the constitution called for the state to implement "an integral policy for the economic, social, and cultural advances of indigenous groups. Toward this end, laws, regulations, and special dispositions may be adopted for indigenous groups, taking into account their needs, conditions, practices, usages, and customs." A later section of the constitution also empowered the president "to create and maintain institutions or dependencies that may concentrate their attention on Indian problems, and may guarantee the effective employment of the services of the government toward the resolution of their problems."[4]

One of the first applications of these ideas was the government's decision to agree to the provisions of the Instituto Indigenista Interamericano created at the Pátzcuaro conference in Mexico in 1940. Accepting the accords of the convention committed Guatemala to the implementation of a wide range of measures to ameliorate the problems of the Indian majority in the country. One of the most important of those provisions called for governments to "conserve and fortify the social discipline existing in the Indian community and coordinate the common aspirations of the group with the national aspirations of each country." The conference also encouraged governments to "take measures to protect the small individual and collective property of the Indians, considering it inalienable."[5] These provisions, which in effect called for the preservation of Indian subcultures, conflicted with the generally assimilationist views of Guatemalan reformers, provoking quite sharp debates within the most radical of the revolutionary organizations.

Out of the decision to agree to the Pátzcuaro provisions came the creation of the Instituto Indigenista Nacional. Headed by Antonio Goubaud Carrera, an anthropologist trained at the University of Chicago, the institute was charged with carrying out a broad investigation into the living conditions and needs of the Indians in Guatemala. One of its first tasks was to devise a formula for determining who was and who was not an Indian. The somewhat surprising conclusion of the investigation was that there was no general agreement on what constituted an Indian and that the few criteria that did exist changed from department to department.[6]

The institute also embarked on an investigation of conditions in a number of rural communities. These investigations, carried out based on a guide devised by a North American anthropologist, looked into both the political and social organization of these communities and the basis of the local economies. They were the first of a long series of economic and social studies that helped pave the way for the Agrarian Reform Law in 1952. Despite the rhetoric of the institute, however, it was imbued with the same kind of contradictory attitudes toward Indian cultures evident within the revolution itself. Goubaud, reflecting the traditional Guatemalan assumption about the virtue of assimilation, suggested in the first bulletin of the institute that "indigenismo is the manifestation, the symptom, of a certain social ill-health."[7]

This contradiction can best be seen in the institute's policies to assist in Indian education. In June 1945, it sponsored a conference of Indian teachers in Cobán designed to incorporate the observations of these teachers in the development of rural schools. Besides recommending that the school serve such social functions as providing showers and sanitary facilities for the community, it proposed that education be in the native language up to the third grade and that the school should be used to protect the Indian way of life.[8] Nevertheless, the education system was designed primarily to act as an agent for cultural assimilation. Arévalo saw the school as a means for "bringing the doctrine of the revolution" to rural areas. The assimilationist role of education was probably best represented in the Misiones Ambulantes de Cultura, a concept borrowed from the Mexican Misiones Culturales. The missions were roving bands of cultural emissaries trundled off to rural areas and given broad responsibilities. Stress was placed on their mandate "to disperse to the farthest corners of the republic the cult of patriotic symbols and historic values of the nation" and the "moral origin and social sentiment" of the revolution. The changes proposed to the education system were the clearest attempt by the Arévalo administration to begin to construct a modern state in Guatemala that tied its citizens to the institutions of the state.[9]

The ability of the government to impose a "national" culture on rural areas was limited, however. This was particularly the case as most politicians active in the constitutional assembly and in the Arévalo administration had an abiding attachment as well to local autonomy, partly in reaction to Ubico's centralizing tendencies. This attachment was best reflected in the Municipal Law, decree 226, passed in April 1946. The law reaffirmed the municipality's legal status and described the general duties of the various local government officials. It envisioned local government as an active force in the day-to-day functioning of the municipio, intervening constantly in the social, economic, and cultural affairs of the community. Municipal governments were required to establish commissions for financial and municipal resources, public health, public works, culture, education, and agriculture. They were to have responsibility for, among other things, stimulating agricultural production in the municipio, protecting land from erosion, enforcing the forestry law, assisting in the organization of cooperatives, building municipal silos to protect harvests, and insuring the proper observance of the Labor Code. They were also called upon to carry out a long list of cultural and educational duties. The municipal alcaldes were granted substantial powers.[10]

"Like Patzicía"

Perhaps the most controversial legislation concerning rural areas in the early years of the revolution involved labor regulations controlling the rural population. The constitution took a moderate, measured approach to labor regulations. Nevertheless, the hated libreto, a document listing the number of days worked on public works and fincas that most Indians in the highlands had been required to carry under the vagrancy law of 1934, was abolished despite protests by conservative politicians. The constitution declared labor to be a "right of the individual and a social obligation" and made vagrancy punishable, but it gave no guidelines as to the minimal amount of labor demanded of an individual or provisions for punishment. Debt contracting was made more difficult, and the maximum amount of debt was fixed at a level easily paid back by the laborer. The constitution also guaranteed the right of free organization for "socioeconomic purposes," set specific guidelines concerning hours and conditions of work, and called for the establishment of minimum wages to be set by committees in various regions of the country.[11]

The coffee economy of Guatemala depended on the availability of a large supply of agricultural laborers, both permanent and seasonal; the U.S. embassy estimated the number in the 1940s at 425,000, with close to 150,000 of these being seasonal migrant workers (for 11,200 coffee fincas).[12] Since the 1870s, the major preoccupation of coffee finqueros and the government was insuring an adequate supply of this labor. Consequently, government attempts to amend the vagrancy law were met with plentiful opposition. This opposition became even more intense when the worst fears of coffee finqueros seemed to be realized as the number of migrant laborers fell dramatically after the abolition of the law. The danger this posed to the interests of the coffee finqueros was heightened with the spread of labor organizations in rural areas and agitation for better working conditions and increased salaries.[13]

Throughout the revolution, these concerns were continually expressed in the denunciations of the revolution by landowners and the rural Ladino elite. Unrestricted organization among rural laborers, the landowners' association shrilly protested, not only would lead to a disastrous collapse of Guatemala's rural economy but also would provoke Indians to rebellion. Fear of Indian revolt was such a prominent part of rural Ladinos' psyche that they viewed any relaxation of the constant scrutiny and tight control employed by Ubico in rural areas as an invitation to bloody Indian uprising.

Ethnic conflict, of course, had been a prevailing source of tension in Guatemala since the conquest. Widespread Indian revolt was rare in Guatemala, being most notable in the period from the beginning of the nineteenth century to the overthrow of the Liberals by Rafael Carrera in the 1830s. The Liberal regimes of the late nineteenth and early twentieth centuries strengthened the military and gained control of many village governments. Liberal measures prompted Indian villages to turn inward more determinedly and pitted village against village as they gave land to some and took land from others. As a result, the few revolts that broke out in the late nineteenth and early twentieth centuries were kept isolated and were easily put down.

Nonetheless, local revolts occurred. In the 1870s, there was a serious uprising in Momostenango. In 1884, the Indian government of the municipality of Cantel steadfastly resisted the expansion of a textile factory onto community land; the government members were all killed by federal troops. During the 1890s, there were periodic revolts in the region around Cobán. In 1898, Indians in San Juan Ixcoy killed most of the Ladinos in the town, and in the 1930s Indians in Nebaj rose in protest against attempts to collect debts prompted by the impending abolition of debt bondage.[14]

Despite the absence of wide-scale revolt, these incidents served to make more palpable the resentment Indians felt toward the local Ladino elite. While one anthropologist writing in the 1930s talked about "culture contact without conflict," most stressed the serious nature of that conflict. In the large Indian town of Chichicastenango, the local priest warned one anthropologist, "If armed and a bit educated the Indians might some night massacre all of the Ladinos."[15] The Ladino population in many areas of the country felt surrounded by a sea of potentially hostile Indians whose apparent docility and servility only made them appear more threatening.

This fear was fanned in October 1944 by events at Patzicía. General Ponce had attempted to use the government's control over Indian communities to subdue the growing urban opposition to his presidential ambitions. Armed peasants were brought into the city and paraded through the streets on Liberal Party marches. In rural areas, he tried to win support for these tactics by promising land to Indian peasants. With Ponce's overthrow, many Indians were frustrated because now these promises would not be fulfilled. In the town of Patzicía, Chimaltenango, not far from Guatemala City, this resentment was spurred on by the local military commander in a futile attempt to support Ponce. On the night of 22 October 1944 a couple of dozen Indians, mostly from two extended families, gathered on the outskirts of the town. Shouting "Viva el Partido Liberal," the Indians began what *El Imparcial* described as a "horrifying massacre and pillage." Demanding promised land, they reportedly killed fourteen Ladinos living in the center of town. As one eyewitness recounted, "The scenes were those of horror: the Indians . . . entered the homes and killed all those they encountered."[16]

The violence was not simply a response to the exhortations of a commandant loyal to Ponce, as the Guatemala City newspapers tried to portray it. The wealthier Ladinos of the town center had monopolized land and credit in a community in which 75 percent of the 7,000 inhabitants were Indian but in which 313 Ladino families owned more land than all the Indians. This wealthy Ladino elite dominated local government as well as marketing and credit arrangements and controlled the municipally owned land. Partly as a consequence, the municipality was marked by intense racial animosity, which often took the shape of battles between the Indian-controlled aldeas and the Ladino-dominated cabacera. Simmering resentment against this Ladino elite finally bubbled to the surface that night.[17]

Nonetheless, Guatemala City newspapers presented the incident as an Indian revolt against all authority, another example of the smoldering racial hatred that threatened to erupt in rural Guatemala with any relaxation of scrutiny. The image of an Indian chopping off a nine-year-old boy's head with a machete that was drawn so graphically by *El Imparcial* continued to trouble rural Guatemala long after thirty-four Indians in the community were sentenced to death or long periods of imprisonment.[18] As in the more famous *matanza* in El Salvador in 1932, few people seemed concerned by the "uncountable bodies of Indians" that resulted from Ladino reprisals for the attack.[19]

This fear of rural, primarily Indian, unrest was stoked by stories in Guatemala City's major newspapers and other publications. One that effectively combined the two greatest horrors of many Guatemalans — Indian revolt and communism — must have been particularly effective. In a book entitled *Communist Revolution: Guatemala in Danger* published in 1946, Jorge Schlesinger provided a graphic account of *la matanza* in El Salvador in the 1930s, replete with gory pictures. Although most modern accounts focus on the rather brutal response of General Maximiliano Hernández Martínez and the Salvadoran military to the uprising, there was little mention of that aspect of the incident in Schlesinger's book. Instead, the Indian peasant uprising fostered by land dispossession, the effects of the depression, and agitation by communist organizers stressed the horror of the Indian attack. The book was not subtle in pointing out the lessons Guatemalans needed to draw from *la matanza*; the introduction ended with, "The communist revolution of El Salvador teaches us to what lengths a people oppressed by hunger and stimulated by promises of immediate social vindication can go: and history repeats itself."[20]

With Patzicía and *la matanza* as convenient reminders, much of the peasant and labor agitation in the countryside was greeted with shrill warnings of imminent Indian revolt. One of the first such combinations of Indian organization and vehement response occurred in Rabinal, Baja Verapaz. The town of Rabinal itself had 2,743 inhabitants, mostly Ladino, while the outlying municipio contained slightly over 9,000 Pokoman Indians. Four hundred and forty Ladino families owned slightly over half the land in the municipio and dominated business in the cabacera.[21]

El Imparcial reported that a leader of the Indian *comunidad campesina* (a peasant organization) in Rabinal organized a large demonstration for May Day in 1945. At the public gathering he declared that it was time for the Indians to adopt Ladino tools of exploitation and robbery to wrest control of their lands from the Ladinos. The Ladinos who opposed them when they took back their lands would be run out of town. The next day the women in the comunidad went to the market proclaiming they would take sticks to merchants and burn their stores. Consequently, the next evening when groups of Indians congregated in various locations around the community, the Ladino residents of the town center called for the governor to send troops. *El Imparcial*'s informants claimed the troops arrived barely in time to prevent an attack, and one eyewitness, in a peculiarly mixed metaphor, described the Indians from the outlying aldeas as being "rounded up like cattle in dense groups and distributed in diverse sites of the town, waiting to pounce." *El Imparcial* ran the story with a big front-page headline declaring that Rabinal was on the verge of a bloody uprising "like Patzicía."[22]

The labor federation, the CTG, provided a different view of the situation. Its spokesperson argued that there was no reason for apprehension. The Indians had simply been gathering for a May Day parade, and the Ladino alcalde became inordinately alarmed at seeing a large congregation of Indians. Nonetheless, a month later reports from the district continued to stress the simmering unrest. Ladino residents reported that families were leaving the town. One resident warned that 2,000 Indians in the aldeas were constantly on the verge of attack. "It isn't true," he said, "as you have been informed that the agitation among the campesinos has ended. Lately they have accentuated their hostile attitude toward the Ladino population, to such an extreme that we are in danger of perishing, massacred by the crowd excited by the demagogic campaign that has been made among them."[23]

Similar reports of Indian unrest flooded the offices of *El Imparcial* and of the minister of gobernación in the early years of the revolution; to judge by the accounts in the newspaper, massacres always seemed to threaten but for some reason never occurred. Newspapers published reports that the town center of Camotán, Chiquimula, had been attacked by Indians from the outlying districts and that several Ladinos had been killed. The CTG refuted this claim, saying the Indians had been assembling for a torchlight parade to commemorate turning over the municipal government to its new officers when they were fired on by soldiers. They retaliated, attacking the soldiers and taking over the municipal building. The report of a somewhat similar incident in Villa Canales only about twenty miles from Guatemala

City was particularly alarming. Indians reportedly killed the local military commander in San Andrés Itzapa in 1944 and battled with the Guardia Civil in Olopa, Chiquimula, in September 1945. Alarmed Ladinos complained of armed Indians in the aldea of Montúfar, San Juan Sacatepéquez, in 1947 and sent urgent requests for protection after large numbers of Indians arrived in the region waiting for the government to partition a finca it had purchased several weeks earlier. Throughout rural Guatemala, the fear of Indian revolt spread from municipio to municipio, fanned by small incidents of unrest and a few isolated cases of violent conflict.[24]

Political Parties and Municipal Elections

Conflict in rural areas, both ethnic and class based, was often expressed through elections for municipal posts. Because of the extensive autonomy granted local government and the significant powers allowed alcaldes, national political parties felt it necessary to grasp control of municipal politics to consolidate their political position and to insure that reform legislation was enacted. Without the cooperation of local governments, most of the reforms of the revolution could not have been implemented in rural areas. It was primarily for this reason that the peasant league, after its formation in 1951, also pushed its members to get involved in local politics, warning that "if we don't win elections and gain the *alcaldía* [local government] . . . it will be extremely difficult to resolve the problems of [the peasants]." Very quickly after the October Revolution, political parties began to present slates of candidates for election to municipal office. As a result, throughout the revolution, local elections in many of Guatemala's 314 municipios occasioned intense conflict.[25]

Municipal government in Guatemala was incredibly complex and varied from region to region, from municipio to municipio, and even from cantón to cantón within the same municipality. The definition of "community" varied from place to place. In some locales, the municipal government truly reflected a cohesive entity, and the system of a dual hierarchy of religious and secular offices controlled by a board of governors embodied in the *principales* was energetic and responsive. In others, the term "community" more closely corresponded to an aldea some distance from the municipio capital or a separate cantón within but distinct from the capital itself.

In many municipalities, the government was controlled by wealthier

Ladinos who used their positions to maintain their domination over the surrounding Indian population. In other municipalities, the Indian hierarchy was not challenged by local Ladinos, yet in their own right they represented a local elite, wealthy by community standards, and used their positions of influence within the community to insure preferential access to community-controlled resources. Despite this diversity, some generalities held true: the town center was the site of economic and political power and was most often dominated by Ladinos, and where substantial ethnic separation existed, it tended to override other sources of tension.

In most areas, municipal elections were intensely fought contests during the revolution. National political parties shaped themselves around a variety of local confrontations to win adherents. While class conflict found expression in many local political contests, the municipal elections also reflected ethnic divisions, powerful attachments to the aldea or cantón, and personal feuds.

In particular, the 1948 municipal elections prompted violent encounters in rural areas. In the year prior to these elections, the Revolutionary Action Party and the workers' federation organized poorer sectors of local society into affiliates. During the elections, these sectors challenged the local Ladino elite or the traditional hierarchy, often for the first time in recent history. Partly as a result of this, there was an increasing rift between the PAR/RN and the FPL at the national level. The PAR and the RN had been able to agree on combined slates in congressional elections and in many municipal contests. Although approached by the PAR, the FPL refused to cooperate, suggesting that it would face a revolt from its local organizations if it attempted to align itself with the more radical PAR adherents in local areas.[26]

One example of the kind of conflict this rift inspired occurred in the municipality of El Tumbador in the department of San Marcos. The municipality had almost doubled in size between 1893 and 1950 — 8,310 to 16,551 — but the increasing importance of the cabacera was demonstrated by the fact that it had almost quadrupled during the same time to a population of 661. It was situated in a region of dramatic land concentration and ethnic conflict. Only 1,408 families in the municipality controlled any land. Several thousand people earned their living as laborers on the surrounding coffee fincas. Most, although certainly not all, were Indians, who made up 60 percent of the population. Seven hundred and three Indian farm operators had access to an average of less than one manzana apiece, while 645 Ladinos averaged thirty-five manzanas each.[27]

In 1948, a meeting of PAR-affiliated workers at a local finca was broken up by members of the FPL, which dominated local politics. The PAR organizer, Ernesto Marroquín Wyss, hurried to town to complain but was stopped along the way by "opposition peasants" who threatened to lynch him. The FPL alcalde, learning of the incident, took Marroquín Wyss to the local jail, perhaps for his own protection, perhaps en route to prison. On hearing of his arrest, workers from the finca marched in protest to town but were prevented from entering by armed opponents. When the alcalde showed up at the confrontation, the workers stoned his entourage. While everyone else in the group was able to flee, the alcalde, who was sixty years old and "extremely corpulent," fell beneath the hail of stones and was hacked to death with machetes.[28]

The FPL executive in the community claimed that this was an elaborate ambush, and Marroquín Wyss, despite being in jail at the time, was charged with complicity in the murder and spent eighteen months in jail before being released, never standing trial. The town and the surrounding region were embroiled in intense conflict for months to come. The residents of the town blamed the PAR, claiming that Marroquín Wyss controlled "a mass of 3,000 peasants that maintain a perpetual menace toward the finqueros of the department." They claimed that the soldiers dispatched to El Tumbador following the killing of the alcalde arrived in the town just in time to prevent their slaughter at the hands of the campesinos. When a national delegation of the PAR arrived to investigate the incident, it was immediately driven from the town. Over 100 people were arrested, mostly Indian workers from the neighboring fincas, and there were reports that over 1,000 others fled into the hills to avoid attacks by the finqueros and their agents.[29]

The incident gained national prominence, with FPL alcaldes from all over the country urging that the full weight of the law be brought to bear on the killers "to prevent similar incidents from occurring in other places in the country," while the PAR, although somewhat hesitantly, defended its organizers. Not coincidentally, the town was one of the first to organize an anticommunist civic committee that was a vocal critic of the PAR's rural labor organization. It warned that the peasants could be turned into "an easy instrument in the hands of unscrupulous men, of demagogues that abound in the party they call revolutionary."[30]

The PAR was also accused of being responsible for the bloody events surrounding the municipal elections in Asunción Mita in the department of Jutiapa. Asunción Mita was an almost entirely Ladino municipality of

close to 16,000 people, mostly peasants in aldeas surrounding the municipal capital. There was heated conflict between the poorer peasantry in these
aldeas and the wealthier landowners and merchants in the town center. The
PAR leader and deputy for the department, Alvaro Hugo Salguero, was
accused of inspiring a multitude of armed assaults on FPL members by the
"illiterate masses" during the election campaign. In return, *El Imparcial*
reported that FPL members in the cabecera had used their influence with
the governor to prompt a vicious attack by the military against peasants in
the community, forcing 500 of them to flee into the mountains.[31]

Numerous other complaints surrounding the 1948 elections poured into
Guatemala City from around the country. The PAR complained that much
of the unrest was a ploy on the part of the FPL to prevent the PAR from
taking municipal seats it had won. The FPL had been so successful that in
"almost all the municipalities won legally by the PAR, there is danger that
the elections will be annulled and there are places that . . . could be
considered in a state of emergency." Despite the alleged tactics of the FPL
adherents, the PAR emerged from the 1948 elections in control of almost
one-third of the municipal governments in the country. Its strong second-
place finish to the dominant FPL illustrated its increasing power in rural
Guatemala and reflected some quite dramatic victories for the organized
peasantry and rural workers.[32]

The violence surrounding the elections led Arévalo to call José Manuel
Fortuny, the secretary-general of the PAR, and Ricardo Asturias Valenzuela, the secretary-general of the FPL, into his office to try to bring about
an accord. *El Imparcial* devoted much attention to the problem, most often
openly critical of PAR actions. The paper commented that unrest was so
prevalent that "blood runs almost to the point of becoming a river; . . . rare
are the communities in which the elections were conducted with tranquility
and where the people are satisfied with the events. . . . We are a month from
the elections and the waters . . . have not calmed."[33]

Subsequent elections were no calmer. In 1950 they were held in the
midst of the intense conflict in the capital surrounding the revolt following
the death of Arana, the confrontation between government supporters and
those protesting Arana's killing that occurred during the Arbenz election
campaign, and the attempted coup led by Carlos Castillo Armas. As a
result of these disturbances, the elections were delayed two months past
their scheduled dates. There were questions concerning the legality of any
municipal acts passed in the intervening period. Again there were numerous charges of fraud and continuing unrest for many months following

the elections. Not only small, isolated, rural towns suffered. In the town of Coatepeque in the department of Quezaltenango, with 6,272 people, an anticommunist civic committee supported by the FPL won the elections, reportedly using fraud and intimidation. The town was primarily a Ladino merchant center servicing the surrounding coffee-growing area. The victors were steadfastly opposed by peasants in the surrounding aldeas and workers in the coffee *beneficios* who were mostly organized by the PAR but who included numerous RN and PIN supporters as well. When the results of the election were announced, a strike of agricultural workers was called. The strike enjoyed wide support in the community. At one point, the strikers held a day-long demonstration in the town park. They were served lunch by a brigade of women led by the town's two beauty queens, the Belle de Quezaltenango and the Flor de Coatepeque. After the alcalde called in members of the Guardia Civil, the strikers broke into a spirited rendition of the national anthem and the commander refused to move against them. The strike lasted close to a month and only ended when new elections were called.[34]

As the example of Coatepeque illustrates, the growing strength of anticommunist civic groups added a new dimension to municipal elections and demonstrates the increasing importance of the issue of communism in Guatemalan politics in general. One of the most interesting ramifications of this new source of conflict occurred in Antigua following the 1950 municipal elections. Antigua, the old colonial capital, was a rich town in the middle of one of the best coffee-growing regions in the country. The conservative opposition in the town had been strong since the beginning of the revolution. Surrounded as it was by coffee fincas and readily accessible to the capital, it also had powerful workers' and peasants' organizations. In 1950, a PAR slate won the elections, but the newly elected alcalde soon resigned from his post. After consultation with the Departmental Electoral Board, another member of the alcaldía took over the duties of the alcalde until new elections could be held. However, during the interim, the municipal council passed a law imposing new taxes on the merchants in the local market. Those opposed to the PAR and hoping to overturn the elections used this as a spark to foster an increasing demand for immediate new elections. The merchants and supporters invaded a meeting of the council, forced its members to resign, and elected a new council from among themselves.

In response, the PAR deputy for the department and two teachers at the local boys' school (one of whom was secretary-general of the peasant league) entered the municipal chamber and forced the new council to disband. It was reported that the deputy punctuated his demands by opening fire in the street with a machine gun. The departmental governor and the deputy requested assistance from the national government, which dispatched police reinforcements to Antigua. Many of the protesters elected to the new council were arrested. The situation never completely returned to normal, and Antigua continued to be one of the most violent and polarized towns in the country for the rest of the revolution.[35]

Conflict, charges of fraud, and violence accompanied all subsequent municipal elections during the revolution. The FPL gradually lost its rural base following the presidential elections in 1950, removing one avenue through which conflict had been expressed. But the anticommunist civic committees provided a more than adequate replacement in many areas. In addition, the Party of the Guatemalan Revolution quickly developed a strong rural base and, particularly in the Oriente, challenged the PAR. While nationally the PAR and the PRG consistently forged electoral fronts in which they attempted to agree on common slates in most communities or at least not to oppose each other, these agreements rarely filtered down to the local level. PRG and PAR organizers competed bitterly in many communities, with the struggle often complicated by ties to the unión campesina or, alternately, the local workers' sindicato.[36]

Municipal elections during the revolution reflected a variety of different conflicts. As national political parties began to extend themselves into rural areas, they often shaped themselves around these long-standing disputes. The most prevalent conflict was between Indians and Ladinos or between rural workers and peasants and a local elite. More rarely, a traditional Indian hierarchy was challenged by a coalition of Ladino and Indian poor. Occasionally, various geographic entities (cantones or aldeas) within the municipality opposed each other or the municipal capital. Ethnic differences, local loyalties, and personal feuds all played parts in increasing tensions. The political parties, regardless of their national stances, often indiscriminately reflected these various differences. Even the most "revolutionary" political party found itself with local affiliates that attempted to impede the extension of the government reforms to the municipality and that were opposed by a large number of peasants and workers.

Although the U.S. State Department, in summing up the 1950 municipal elections, suggested that fraud perpetuated by those with national political connections insured their dominance, such a conclusion does not seem accurate. The biggest winner of both the 1948 and 1950 elections was the

FPL. Its success in the municipal elections reflected its dominant position as the party of the rural Ladino middle class, who were the quickest at organizing in rural areas. The PAR's position in second place in 1948 and 1950 reflected its expanding presence among rural workers and peasants. As rural sindicatos grew, the PAR's presence in rural areas strengthened, easily eclipsing the FPL shortly after 1950. With the creation of the peasant league and the strong organization of the PRG, the PAR was challenged and the PRG carried a respectable number of municipal governments. During the Arbenz administration, they were the only political parties that exerted the required effort to organize in the countryside, link local affiliates to the national party, and conscientiously address the concerns of their members. The Communist Party was able to win a few municipalities in Escuintla and around Guatemala City, but it was never a powerful force in municipal politics. As political opinion polarized with the extension of the agrarian reform, the more conservative civic committees were able to win a few scattered municipalities. But they had a very limited appeal, no national organization, and no consistent policies. Municipal elections throughout the revolution, by and large, accurately reflected the wishes of the majority of community members.[37]

"The Pernicious Action of Demagogic Agitators"

"Like cattle . . . waiting to pounce": this peculiar imagery used in describing Indian actions in the previously discussed incident in Rabinal in many ways summed up the attitude of many Ladinos toward the Indian population. There was a contradictory nature about the reaction to rural unrest in Guatemala in the early years of the revolution. While the Ladino elite believed that Indians were a dangerous element, easily prompted to violent revolt, they placed most of the blame for this unrest on non-Indian, non-peasant agitators. Those most often blamed were members of the CTG and the PAR.

Shortly after its formation, the CTG began an aggressive campaign in the countryside. Prominent among the CTG activists were Carlos Manuel Pellecer (who often served as grievance secretary for the CTG) in Escuintla and Marroquín Wyss in San Marcos. Their work was met with strident denunciations. A petition to the president from finqueros in Escuintla in June 1945 complaining of the "communist propaganda being carried on by a group of people headed by . . . Carlos Manuel Pellecer" illustrates the tone well. The petitioners warned that Pellecer counseled anarchy on the fincas and that he told workers that if they could not gain their demands any other way, they should "make justice with their own hands." As he would do for the rest of the decade, Pellecer refused to bow to pressure and readily admitted he had stirred the workers to make demands. If someone must be blamed, he responded, "I accept the guilt because I want slavery . . . to be abolished in Guatemala, but I deny categorically the accusation that I am provoking 'massacres.' " Pellecer, who came from a wealthy family, went on to issue a challenge to the landowners, saying, "Fortunately, I know almost all of my accusers. I know with certainty their systems of exploitation. I have lived with them and they cannot ignore that I know them and . . . the manner in which they have enriched themselves."[38]

In response to complaints against Pellecer, frequently expressed concerns about unrest in the countryside, and increasing military pressure to act to curtail the disturbances, Arévalo took prompt action. In 1945, the government rescinded some of the guarantees provided by the constitution and passed an emergency measure temporarily prohibiting the organization of agricultural laborers "to maintain harmony and order so necessary in the difficult moment through which the republic is passing."[39] The CTG gave the suspension hesitant support but warned that it could not control the rural unions, many of which threatened to separate from the federation if they were restricted by the central. A number of commissions representing political parties and the CTG toured the countryside explaining the new restrictions, while Arévalo agreed to meet with delegations of rural workers to reassure them that these restrictions did not signal a return to dictatorship.[40]

Despite these measures, the unrest continued. During the 1945/46 harvest, conflict was most apparent in the department of San Marcos. The manager of the Banco de Occidente estimated that 30 percent of the coffee crop in the region would be lost that year due to the shortage of labor since only 4,000 of the 40,000 contracted workers showed up for the harvest in a protest over wages. As the "strikes" continued in the San Marcos area, Colonel Arana took an even firmer stand than Arévalo and called in the troops to force the workers back to the fincas in time to save the harvest.[41]

In the aftermath of the strikes, the cabinet sent a commission to the department to investigate. It issued a report that blasted the CTG in general and one of its organizers, Amor Velasco, in particular. The report pointed to a "vast organization" centered in the town of Malacatán that "practically controls all the workers in the department of San Marcos." The organization, linked to the CTG, was charged with forcing workers to pay illegal dues and with promising to divide local fincas among them. The local organization was disbanded, but Velasco denied the accusations against him, saying he had only visited Malacatán twice in the last year and a half and had not received a penny from the workers in the organization.[42]

While the CTG bore the brunt of the charges from the AGA, the army, and some members of Arévalo's cabinet, it is clear they had little control over these rural federations. The CTG accepted the army intervention in the strikes in San Marcos and consistently attempted to control the most radical of the rural organizers. Activists like Pellecer espoused a confrontational approach and helped heighten tension in some departments, but in most areas the demands of local unions represented the collective and long-standing grievances of agricultural workers against the Ladino elite; little outside agitation was necessary. The CTG could not chastise local unions too severely or it would lose its position in the forefront of labor organization in the countryside.

Arévalo, after intense pressure from politicians and the military, forced the most radical of the CTG and PAR organizers (including Pellecer) out of the country on diplomatic posts. The army issued stern warnings against any unrest. In November an army spokesperson announced that the military would accept no disruption of the 1946/47 harvest. He warned: "Whenever the necessary resources for maintaining normal conditions are exhausted or when illegal strike movements are clearly concerned, the Army of Guatemala will intervene to maintain normal conditions in the country. . . . Among the functions of the Army is that of keeping all of the country within a margin of tranquility; consequently, whenever these national principles are menaced, the Army will take the measures which its duty towards the country may determine."[43]

Nonetheless, strikes soon erupted throughout the country. One of the largest began in December 1946 at the finca El Pilar in San Juan Sacatepéquez. The 200 strikers in the finca reported that they had been promised raises from the current salary of 5 cents to 15 cents a day (at a time when studies done for the CTG indicated that 50 cents a day was the bare minimum necessary for subsistence), but the owners had failed to comply with their promises. The strikers were ordered back to work by Colonel Arana after four days. When they refused, they were attacked by the military and 93 of the 200 were arrested. The rest still refused to work, however, and fled to the hills. Finally, after the finca owners petitioned the government, the arrested workers were released and most of the others returned to the harvest. Again, responsibility for the unrest was laid at the feet of "outside agitators," this time José Manuel Fortuny and Leonidas Acevedo of the PAR.[44]

Numerous other strikes occurred during the harvest that year. The military most often responded with violence. In January, when Indian workers at the finca Candelaría in Alotenango in the department of Sacatepéquez announced they were preparing to strike, demanding 30 cents a day, the military governor of the department suggested that "responsible" residents in the community be armed to *"prevent violence"* (emphasis added). In this instance, it was the finca owner who prevented further unrest by accepting most of the demands of the workers, including the removal of the administrator. Similarly, several months later when peasants on the national finca Cerro Redondo in the department of Santa Rosa took over part of the property as a protest over their treatment by the managers, Arana immediately called the army in and declared that it would "punish with all energy those responsible for this occurrence because of the danger that this class of rebellion brings to the tranquility of the country and the security of our institutions."[45]

The 1947 Labor Code maintained the restriction on the formation of rural unions by forbidding union organization in fincas employing less than 500 people. This provision, in practice, prevented organization of rural workers except on some of the national fincas operated by the government, the farms owned by the UFCo and its subsidiaries, and two other privately owned farms. Jorge García Granados, the ambassador to the United States at the time, explained to the State Department that the law was not meant to discriminate against the UFCo but to differentiate between large plantations where Ladinos were the bulk of laborers and smaller farms where Indians, "who were underdeveloped in respect to social or moral conscience and know nothing of trade union organization," were the majority.[46]

The administration's handling of rural labor prompted much opposition from both sides of the political spectrum. Arévalo was clearly under tremendous pressure from landowners and the military to restrict labor organization in the countryside. He probably shared some of their concerns about unfettered organization in rural areas, having come from a moderately wealthy rural Ladino background. Indeed, he once responded to a delegation of AGA members concerned over labor measures by saying he was "in a certain sense, a finquero." Thus, he assured them he would not institute laws that would hurt their interests or agriculture in general.[47] Most of his cabinet and many deputies in congress shared this view of rural

Guatemala. They, therefore, more often than not supported the restrictions on rural organization and the military's constant intervention. They had little choice, for they realized all too well that any attempt to prevent the military from imposing order in rural areas would heighten the army's fears about the administration and leave the government open to the next coup attempt.

This attitude was not shared by all in the government coalition, however. Many of the more radical PAR members had been very active in organizing rural labor and saw it as a necessary part of their local party organization. They bridled at the restrictions constantly placed on them by the government and the military.

By 1947 the conflict between the PAR activists and more cautious politicians linked to the FPL and the RN came to a head. In July, the minister of gobernación issued a circular warning against rural agitation and threatening to arrest those responsible for "social crimes." The warning met with an immediate critical response. José Manuel Fortuny led the PAR attack, arguing that the minister could not create laws and punishment at will and that the threat "signifies a regression to the methods of the past when it was left to the will of officials to dispose of the freedom and lives of the farm workers. This . . . indicates a Ubico-like mind" (the ultimate insult in revolutionary Guatemala). Even the relatively conservative, if erratic, Clemente Marroquín Rojas railed against the circular in his paper, *La Hora*. He called on the political parties "to state frankly and categorically whether they support the minister who has done this . . . or assume their position at the side of the workers who brought them to power. . . . Guatemala already knows how 'social crime' has been used — applied in a most elastic manner. . . . To appeal to a law that is the most odious, most terrible and most criminal that has ever been dictated in America by a despot is something that will forever shame the government of Doctor Arévalo."[48]

If this circular served as "one of the opening guns in the struggle between the FPL and the PAR" as the U.S. embassy suggested, the PAR clearly won the encounter. Slightly more than a month after issuing the warning, the minister was forced to "clarify" his statement and left the country on vacation.[49]

Although somewhat less violence was associated with rural labor organization after 1947, unrest continued. Finqueros and the AGA continually complained about the rural activists in a losing battle to prevent change in the countryside. After a finquero was hacked to death with machetes following his refusal to comply with labor court orders near Retalhuleu in late

1947, the AGA increased its demands for protection from rural workers and peasants. In 1948, when revisions to the Labor Code were being discussed, the AGA sent an extensive public denunciation to the government protesting conditions throughout much of the country. The AGA said that it was subjected to "the insistent clamor" of its members, who were "every day more alarmed" by the "hostile disposition" of the workers as a consequence of the "pernicious action of demagogic agitators." The AGA warned that this agitation was damaging "indispensable discipline" in the centers of production and complained especially about the labor inspectors who were in charge of arbitrating and ruling on labor disputes. Finqueros in Cuilapa claimed the inspectors were actually instigating labor unrest. Also, the AGA cited reports from its members in Rabinal that "it is now common in this zone for workers to do their work as they wish and when they wish, because if they are reprimanded, even with good cause, they abandon their work and plant complaints against the bosses, counting on the partiality of the labor authorities and occasioning great loss of time for the bosses."[50]

The reports of the various labor inspectors indicate that while they were clearly sympathetic to the problems of rural laborers, the inspectors performed their duties with an admirable degree of restraint. Most disputes were settled before strikes occurred. The report of one such inspector, José Domingo Seguro, for January 1953 seems to have been fairly typical. Of the twenty-two disputes he handled, eleven were settled through conciliation, four ended without any conciliation, seven were still in dispute but were being actively discussed, and none had gone to trial. In all the disputes, a total of Q174 was awarded workers. Some conflicts were not easily settled, however. In October 1952, Domingo investigated a complaint that the owner of a large finca in the department of Quezaltenango had continually insulted the Indians, addressing them as "indios brutos." When Domingo confronted the owner with the complaint, the owner remarked that the Indians were all fools and deserved such treatment. Domingo immediately brought action against him for violation of five articles of the Labor Code.[51]

Nevertheless, complaints about unrest and disobedience in the countryside continued. In 1950, the AGA denounced the "series of crimes that have been perpetrated against agriculturalists in different zones of the country." The newspapers of the capital, especially *El Imparcial*, gave rural unrest prominent coverage, both in news reports and in rather alarmist editorials. In October 1951, the newspaper printed an account of yet another attack on a finquero, suggesting some regions in Guatemala were

experiencing "days like those of the pioneers that opened the savage fron-
tiers of the far west of North America in the past century. The ranchers of
the region of Malacatán and Ayutla in San Marcos are enduring a prevalent
reign of terror, illegality and almost complete abandon on the part of the
authorities."[52]

The revisions to the Labor Code in 1948 lifted many of the restrictions
on labor organization in the countryside, although it was still illegal to
strike during the harvest. Many sectors of the Guatemalan labor movement
responded enthusiastically, especially the CTG. The CTG was invaluably
assisted in forming rural unions by members of the teachers' union, the
STEG. With 998 teachers in schools on private fincas and a good number
more in official schools on the national fincas, teachers were in a unique
position to influence rural workers. Partly because of their assistance and
because of the tireless work of such men as Gutiérrez, Pellecer, Velasco,
and Marroquín Wyss, the CTG was able to expand its rural base rapidly
after 1948. By 1951 there were close to 200 unions of rural workers in the
country, the majority of them affiliated with the CTG.[53]

The government controlled over 100 fincas — collectively called national fincas — that had been taken from Germans during World War II or
from generals and associates close to Ponce and Ubico. Although they had
been under government control since 1941, the national fincas were not
officially expropriated until 1951. Combined, the national fincas were the
largest economic enterprise in Central America, with 50,000 employees,
approximately 150,000 field workers, and over 30 percent of the best
coffee fincas in the country.[54] While potentially an important economic
asset, the fincas were poorly run by inefficient administrators. They also
became a political football, especially after Mariano Arévalo, the president's brother, became director. There were constant squabbles between
the PAR, which represented most of the field workers, and the FPL, which
included most of the administrators in its ranks.[55]

Labor organization in rural areas was not an easy task. Rural activists
were faced with opposition from finqueros as well as the fear and antipathy
of many workers. Many found labor organization most fruitful on national
fincas, but even there success did not always come easily. Workers often
blamed CTG organizers for creating unrest and sided with finca managers.
For example, on the national finca Cerro Redondo, workers told *El Imparcial* that the CTG was causing problems on the finca and warned that if the
director of the finca, who had been denounced by the CTG, was removed,
"blood would flow." The CTG representative, for his part, described the

divisions in the finca as between two groups, "one with the law and reason were organizing a sindicato as protection and the other with brute force, intrigue and violence . . . opposed that organization." Numerous other complaints indicate that in many fincas the CTG was finding it difficult to gain the support of the workers. One of the problems was simply that the monthly dues of 5 cents that the union demanded was a considerable amount of money. With little return immediately obvious from union organization, many national finca workers were unsympathetic or openly hostile to the union.[56]

Despite the CTG's modest expansion in rural areas between 1948 and 1951, it became apparent that it needed some substantial successes benefiting rural workers before it could become a powerful force in the countryside. This success came with its campaign for a minimum agricultural wage. Between 1949 and 1951, a series of illegal strikes during the harvest broke out on national fincas as workers clamored for a substantial increase in the daily wage, which ranged from 15 to 55 cents a day. The campaign was pushed aggressively by the communist newspaper, *Octubre*, after its founding in 1950, and by 1951 a minimum wage of 80 cents a day was the main rallying cry at the May Day parade. Partly in response, on 12 May 1951, Arbenz promised that an 80-cent wage would be the standard in all national fincas.[57]

Arbenz's announcement sparked intense opposition, with many people arguing that the national fincas could not afford to pay wages at that level. The conflict very clearly became a struggle between the CTG and the PAR on one side and the more cautious government parties on the other. A number of studies were commissioned to determine if the national fincas could afford the increase, and the CTG continued to pressure the government through periodic strikes. The most important was a walkout by the almost 2,000 workers in the national finca Concepción that began during the 1950/51 harvest.[58]

It appeared that the CTG had lost the struggle when the commission reporting on Concepción argued that the finca could not afford the higher wages. However, Arbenz intervened directly and convinced the commission's members that they had "erred" in their study. Soon commissions studying other national fincas also approved the minimum wage. By December, the minimum wage of 80 cents a day was established for all national fincas, and commissions had been set up to determine ways of reorganizing the fincas in order to provide better conditions for workers. In January 1952, the campaign shifted to the largest private fincas. Throughout 1952 and 1953, this agitation helped insure that 80 cents a day for field work was the national standard, although many fincas continued to pay less.[59]

The minimum wage campaign had been a major success for both rural workers and the CTG. After a number of years of only partial acceptance on fincas, the CTG had concrete benefits to demonstrate to potential members. The success of the campaign was both an indication of the CTG's growing importance in the countryside and influence within the government and a spark to augment further organization.

The distinction between peasants and rural workers in the Guatemalan context was somewhat artificial. Consequently, it was not long after the CTG began organizing rural workers in earnest that it turned its attention to the much more numerous rural peasantry. CTG rhetoric concerning peasant organization emphasized ending the "feudal" arrangement of sharecropping and *trabajo necesario*, in which, it claimed, peasants were often forced to work six times the amount of land for the owner as they received. The CTG called for the return of land taken from peasant communities illegally during the various Liberal regimes. It also proposed a number of ways to eliminate "the backwardness that affects Indians from the racial and cultural point of view, . . . to lift the Indian nationalities to the level of white inhabitants, [and] at the same time . . . respect their origins, their communal unity, their customs, and their language."[60]

Teachers were extremely important in assisting peasant organization. As Gutiérrez explained in one of his regular pep talks in the STEG bulletin: "Of all the workers' organizations that exist in the capital . . . there are few that . . . can count on affiliates in the various regions of the republic. . . . STEG has in front of it a national labor that can give it much prestige and the opportunity to guide the magnificent forces of workers and peasants that are dispersed throughout all the territory of our country."[61] Not all teachers shared Gutiérrez's desire for work among peasants, however, despite his often infectious enthusiasm. STEG executives complained of constant difficulties in convincing teachers to accept postings in rural areas, despite an "army of unemployed teachers" in the cities. Even when they were able to persuade teachers to accept these positions, problems occurred. The teachers were seldom Indian, rarely demonstrated respect for Indian culture, and even more rarely spoke a native language. Rural teachers often did not attend to their duties with diligence. There were constant complaints about teachers who seldom bothered to teach anything, or even show up for classes, and who demonstrated little interest in the community.

One village that had gone to the trouble of building a school when it was promised a teacher was particularly upset that the teacher spent all her time in the nearest large town and rarely made an appearance in the village. In another, the teacher sent Indian and poor Ladino children home, telling them to dress properly.[62]

Nevertheless, Gutiérrez's call was heeded. In many communities, teachers were instrumental in forming organizations affiliated with the CTG as well as in integrating peasants into local affiliates of national political parties. Indeed, in many towns the teacher was the secretary-general of the local sindicato, the leader of the local PAR, RN, or PRG affiliate, or even the alcalde.

Still, there was much criticism from within the CTG concerning its ineffectual efforts to organize peasants. José Luis Ramos, sometime secretary of peasant relations for the CTG, observed in 1950 that efforts to establish unions among rural agriculturalists had primarily involved shipping a flood of propaganda and information on government programs to rural areas. There was a decided lack of dedicated workers prepared to spend time in rural areas and win the trust of the peasants. In the headlong rush to bring about reform that characterized the efforts of the most dynamic of the young politicians involved in the revolution, there was little patience for the slow work of peasant organization. Therefore, Luis Ramos argued, "we must recognize that the revolution has not arrived in the field, that there has not been attention paid to the needs of peasants. . . . The peasants are harassed and fined by the same people who call themselves revolutionaries and friends of the working class and collect their votes to win municipal posts."[63]

Much of the problem the CTG encountered in its attempt to organize peasants was caused by its insistence on strict unity between peasants and agricultural workers. Peasants from neighboring communities often viewed workers on fincas with distrust, the product of decades of battling with the fincas for land. It was partly the CTG's and Gutiérrez's determination to link peasants and workers that fostered the growth of a new peasant organization, the CNCG, in 1949 and 1950.

Headed by Leonardo Castillo Flores and other teachers, PAR activists, and former CTG workers, the organization spread rapidly. Teachers were an even more important part of the CNCG than they were of the CTG. But Castillo Flores had an equally difficult task inspiring sufficient numbers of teachers to heed the revolutionary call. He continually needed to strengthen the revolutionary resolve of teachers working in isolated communities who were attempting to organize peasants, most of whom were scattered throughout the outlying aldeas, while they lived and taught in the town center surrounded by an antagonistic Ladino elite. To one such fellow threatened with dismissal, Castillo Flores advised, "Don't worry at all about what you refer to as your work — the best work a teacher can accomplish is to orient the peasantry to defend their interests."[64]

With the exception of the sporadic efforts of the CTG, it was primarily through the CNCG that the peasantry found a national institution prepared to serve as an important broker — and in many ways a protector — within the complex and competitive political arena in Guatemala City. In the process, because of its widespread support in the countryside, the CNCG became an important political voice and its leader, Castillo Flores, one of the most powerful men in the country.

Despite Castillo Flores's repeated assurances that the CNCG wished to develop the closest possible relations with the workers' union, the CNCG was seen as a challenge to the CTG. Both the CTG and *Octubre* assailed the peasant league and Castillo Flores throughout 1950, denouncing his "divisionist attitude" and the lack of true peasant leaders in the federation. On one occasion, *Octubre* devoted much of the front page to a long denunciation of the federation, arguing, "Nobody can deny — history demonstrates it with total clarity — that the revolutionary actions of the working class inevitably fail when they do not have peasants at their side and that the revolutionary actions of the peasants fail when they cannot count on the workers of the city on their side." The newspaper went on to say that this was why the labor federation had decided to unite peasants and workers in one grand federation with one leadership. Although the leaders of the CTG regretted the formation of the peasant league, they admitted that the two federations must now work together. They were encouraged by the assurances of the leaders of the CNCG but doubted that the peasant league could live up to the promises of cooperation. They reached this conclusion because "at the side of the undeniable activity of Castillo Flores in the field are Charnaud MacDonald and collaborators like Alejandro Silva Falla [and] Joaquin García Manzo . . . whose preoccupation is not to forge an alliance of the workers and peasants but to the contrary to create an organization of the masses under their control to use for their own political ends."[65]

Castillo Flores continued to make conciliatory gestures toward the CTG despite these and other rather harsh criticisms. Soon a national accord was worked out pledging cooperation between the two and guaranteeing that fields sown by one central would not be harvested by the other. There were still constant local skirmishes between the two, however, as they battled for national prominence, skirmishes that became more frequent and violent after the passage of the Agrarian Reform Law.[66]

The CNCG experienced numerous problems. It was difficult to find capable organizers. Many of those who did come forward had little patience with peasants and distrusted them, creating tension and conflict in the community. The peasant league was also constantly short of funds and could do little to increase its income, being reliant on an impoverished peasantry for its dues. The 10 cents a month membership fee was already too much to bear for many.

Nevertheless, peasant organizations sprang up around the country. By February 1950, there were five departmental federations of peasants (in Jalapa, Chiquimula, Guatemala, Zacapa, and Jutiapa) linked to the fledgling organization. Throughout the spring of 1950, numerous uniones campesinas were set up and granted official recognition by the government, mostly in the Oriente but also including many in the Indian highlands. Finally, in May 1950, the CNCG was inaugurated at a conference with 200 delegates from 36 unions attending. It was given official recognition in September of that year.[67]

At the first national conference of the federation in 1951, 275 delegates representing almost all departments in the country attended. By August 1952, the CNCG claimed to represent 215,000 people in 1,600 unions. By 1954, 7,500 delegates attended the national conference, and the *Tribuna popular* claimed they represented 2,500 unions. Although there has been much disagreement over the actual strength of the CNCG, there appears to be no reason to question the CNCG claims, even though some exaggeration undoubtedly did occur and many unions were obviously very small and/or inactive. Certainly by 1954, there was a functioning peasant union in all but the most isolated and the smallest communities.[68]

The CNCG's success had much to do with the nature of its resolutions in favor of the peasants and with the character of Castillo Flores. The peasant league concentrated its demands on acquiring land for peasants to cultivate. The first resolution of the national federation was to demand that the government clarify the Law of Forced Rental, decree 712, and its first major success was in helping to bring about the government's substantial revision of the law in 1951 in decree 853. It continually pressured municipal alcaldes and government officials to act more vigorously in applying the law, but its major objective from the beginning was the enactment of "democratic" agrarian reform.[69]

Castillo Flores was an important reason for the CNCG's success. He was somewhat imperious, determined to maintain his control over the CNCG, and reluctant to delegate authority. This led to conflict with others in the executive, and as a result, several of the most powerful founding members left the federation.[70] Nevertheless, Castillo Flores worked diligently in the service of the CNCG. He was particularly interested in helping communities develop their resources through their own initiatives, for example, working to get government money to fund an irrigation project, to build a community library, or to repair a bridge. In addition, Castillo Flores, like Gutiérrez and Pellecer of the CTG, patiently responded to individual requests for aid, the kind of wearying but indispensable organizational work that over the long run resulted in an increased CNCG presence in the countryside. He sought permission for a homeless family to use an abandoned government-owned house, arranged for medical attention for injured peasants, organized brigades to respond to crop infections, intervened with forestry inspectors to get licenses to chop wood for needed fuel, and on one occasion even arranged to have a football sent to a community so peasants waiting for land would be a little less restless. Perhaps his most important activity in this regard was intervening with the Guardia Civil and departmental governors to effect the release of people imprisoned through arbitrary measures. In the process, Castillo Flores became a powerful figure in Guatemala. Like Gutiérrez, Pellecer, and even María Arbenz, he was bombarded with requests from other powerful politicians to use his influence with the government for one cause or another. The fortunes of Castillo Flores and the CNCG increased dramatically with the passage of the Agrarian Reform Law in 1952.[71]

By 1952, the Guatemalan countryside was beginning to change in fundamental and radical ways. The growing strength of peasant and rural worker unions led to increased fears among the Ladino elite about the ability of the government to control the unreasoned passions and racial hatred that they believed dominated rural Guatemala. Many who had supported the urban and political reforms of the revolution began to look back with nostalgia on the order in the countryside during the days of Ubico. Some saw the choice as clearly one of despotism or continued unrest and made it plain which they preferred. As Carlos Titu stated in an editorial in *El Imparcial* entitled "From Life in the Towns: The Headache of the Alcaldes":

Before, the campesino . . . was fully dedicated to his agricultural labors. . . . Because of this, time was for him as precious as gold for the avaricious. After a hard day's labor under the burning sun . . . he did not think of anything but returning to the side of his children, to his home, to rest during the night without greater worries. Now, in contrast, though they say that liberty obtained by the revolution of '44 has brought guarantees to the man of the field . . . so many violent attacks occur among campesinos and humble people, many of which result in death, that a dark cloud of pain has been carried to the home that before lived in peace and harmony.[72]

AGRARIAN REFORM: "THE MOST PRECIOUS FRUIT OF THE REVOLUTION"

One day wine and another day bread;

A day of fire and scarlet,

A powerful day

foretold in the annals,

. . . .

a day, grand, eternal, unfathomable

the day man gets land.

—Otto Raúl González,

"El Encuentro del hombre con la tierra"

n his 1953 address to congress, Arbenz declared, "The Agrarian Reform Law begins the economic transformation of Guatemala; it is the most precious fruit of the revolution and the fundamental base of the destiny of the nation as a new country." He went on to affirm that the law formed "a part of the heavy debt the ruling class and governors contracted with the humble people, with the people of the field with cheap cotton shirts and palm-leaf sombreros who do not have shoes, or medicine, or money, or education, or land."[1]

In Guatemala, the issue of control over agricultural land was the preeminent political and social question. In 1950, over two-thirds of the population depended on agriculture for a living. Decades of land dispossession and government policy that had fostered economic disparity in the countryside bound the majority of the population in chains of poverty and helped create a deeply divided society. Even some of the young urban politicians who struggled to enact reforms during the revolution realized agrarian reform was the major issue in Guatemala; all other acts of the revolution paled in comparison.

However, agrarian reform faced significant opposition from many sectors. As envisioned by Arbenz and his closest advisers, agrarian reform required the active participation of the rural poor. Peasant activism accompanying the implementation of agrarian reform helped provoke a storm of protest against the Arbenz administration. Eventually, it was the agrarian reform, the most precious fruit and the most indispensable measure of the revolution, that led to the overthrow of the Arbenz administration and the collapse of the revolution.

"To Liberate the Oppressed"

Since the Bourbon reforms in the eighteenth century, governments in Guatemala had been preoccupied with the need to increase agricultural production. Each major change in government brought a spate of new laws affecting agriculture and landownership. The Liberals in the 1820s and 1830s tried to break down what they saw as an impediment to agricultural development by removing what protection existed for community-controlled land. After the peasant revolt that defeated the Liberals in 1838 and eventually brought Rafael Carrera to power, Carrera initiated measures to protect community lands. The Liberal regimes that held power from the 1870s to 1931 enacted legislation designed to alter village control over land and foster colonization of uncultivated, often uninhabited areas of the country. Even Jorge Ubico Castañeda, shortly after coming to power, offered free land to those people who would leave the crowded highlands and settle in the undeveloped lowlands, an offer promptly rescinded when landowners complained about the potential loss of workers.[2]

It is not surprising, then, that agrarian reform quickly became a topic of discussion following the resignation of Ubico and the overthrow of Ponce. Debate over agrarian reform and landownership dominated the constitutional assembly for days. The tiny but influential Vanguardia Nacional, an embryonic socialist party, was the most active champion in the assembly. In February 1945 the party declared that the first priority of the state should be to "regulate the national economy to benefit the collective" and urged the government to begin a concerted attack on latifundia and "feudal" property.

There were resounding cries that this resolution attacked the sacred right of private property and set the stage for the spread of communism in the country. The members of the party vehemently denied that this was their intention. Rather, they asserted that to argue for the total dominion of absolute private right over land was absurd; they were simply suggesting that land had a "social function" and that private ownership of land must "always be limited and subject to the general interest." Carlos Manuel Pellecer was a strong supporter of this measure in the assembly. But his explanation that "all we wish, all we are trying to do, is to liberate the oppressed, the weak, from the sabotage of the strong," while popular with the gallery, did not calm the fears of many of those opposed to change in the countryside.[3]

Nonetheless, through the strong urging of the Vanguardia and the efforts of the president of the constitutional assembly, Jorge García Granados, a number of important agrarian provisions were contained in the constitution. After article 90 made assurances that the state recognized private property and guaranteed it by law, article 91 prohibited latifundia and called for the return of that land to the national patrimony. Article 92 allowed for expropriation of private property with prior indemnification in the interests of public welfare. Article 93 declared that the dominion of the state over the national patrimony was inalienable but that the state had the right to extend usufruct (the right to use property, generally for life) of this property, preferably in cooperatives. Finally, article 96 protected the ejido (municipally owned land) and other community lands and declared them inalienable, neither subject to expropriation nor divisible.[4]

The land provisions of the constitution prompted much concern among various sectors in Guatemala. *El Imparcial* argued that the idea of expropriating property and parceling it out to small proprietors might be attractive in theory, but it was only "tortas y pan pintado" when the government faced the more "practical" problems of the economy. The paper predicted that agricultural colonies would be the "proving ground for future agrarian policy."[5] Arévalo appeared to agree. In an interview for a Mexican newspaper, he suggested that in Guatemala there was not "what you could appropriately call an agrarian problem." Rather, rural laborers and peasants "have lived in a psychological and political climate that has prevented the expression of the yearnings to work the land." Thus, what was required was to allow peasants to "work in a more effective manner."[6]

Arévalo's major initiative in agrarian reform was a project to create an agricultural colony at Poptún in the largely unpopulated Petén. While the Poptún scheme was devised primarily through collaboration with Argentinian colonization experts, it had a number of precedents in Guatemalan history, the most immediate being Jorge García Granados's suggestion in the 1920s that the government "ship Indians en masse to the wilds of the Petén."[7] Colonization of El Petén reflected a natural desire to foster the development of Guatemala's vast frontier region. It was also used to help stifle demands for the division of land in the more populated and fertile Pacific coast region, which was increasingly attractive for banana and cotton cultivation. But even this minor measure was angrily attacked by the AGA when there was a suggestion that teachers at finca schools encourage volunteers for the program. The AGA expressed concern about a shortage of workers for the harvest.[8] The Poptún colony, considered at its inception to be one of the government's major initiatives, was never a success. Thousands of dollars were spent on the colony with little result before the government unofficially abandoned it in 1952. Colonization proved to be too slow and too expensive a proposition.[9]

Other government measures to alter land tenure before 1952 were sporadic and indecisive. Some smaller colonization projects were attempted. A few fincas expropriated from associates of Ubico and Ponce were divided among peasants or turned into cooperatives. Congress was asked to provide Q50,000 to be used to buy land to augment municipal property, and provisions were passed regularizing the rental of municipal land. The government even bought land from some landowners to distribute to neighboring peasants. But these were isolated incidents responding to local conditions; they represented no coherent government program.[10]

The Law of Forced Rental, passed in 1949, was a major initiative. Despite its limited application and the problems the government encountered in getting alcaldes to enact faithfully the provisions of the law, it provided an effective way for peasants in some municipalities to obtain land to cultivate at affordable rates. In the village of Chinautla, for example, a number of peasants who traditionally traveled to the coast to work during the harvest used the law to rent land there. Although they continued to live in the highland village, they were able to harvest two corn crops a year on the coastal land. The land on the coast offered an opportunity for the peasants to improve their standard of living measurably while retaining their connection to the village. Reports to the CTG and the CNCG from other villages throughout the country indicated that, at least in some areas, the law provided valuable opportunities.[11]

However, a chorus calling for more substantial agrarian measures was mounting. Every major economic publication in the country not linked to the AGA argued that the agrarian structure needed to be altered. Particularly vocal was the influential *El Mes económico y financiero*. Throughout the Arévalo administration, all the government political parties joined the harmony supporting agrarian reform, and many of the most influential members of congress were proponents. As early as 1946, the PAR declared that the realization of a "democratic agrarian reform through the collectivization of nationally owned land, the suppression of the latifundia, an increase in the amount of land cultivated, and an increment in agricultural credit to small proprietors" was one of the bases of its political program.[12]

Perhaps the strongest push came from the labor federation, the CTG. At its national congress in 1946, the federation urged that land be expropriated from "feudal" property larger than 145 manzanas. The confiscated land was to be sold to the rural poor at a price set at the value of one year's crop and paid for in the space of ten to twenty years. The CTG continually pushed agrarian reform as one its major priorities and kept up a constant campaign denouncing "feudal" practices on fincas.[13]

The rural poor added their own voices to the chorus. Delegations from Indian communities traveled to the capital to petition Arévalo for land. Peasants and rural workers occupied land on both private fincas and municipal property. In addition, workers on the national fincas joined in a concerted campaign to force the government not to return the German properties to their former owners and to divide them among themselves. In a few instances, they were successful in fostering the formation of experimental cooperatives watched closely by agricultural economists.[14]

Guatemala suffered from a double-edged problem caused by its extremely inequitable structure of land tenure: large amounts of potentially productive land were left uncultivated on private estates while a land-hungry peasantry struggled for existence in the highlands. This problem became increasingly apparent during the revolution as a result of various studies carried out by the revolutionary governments. A preliminary analysis of landownership and land use was requested by Arévalo for the "triangulo" at Escuintla in 1945, a discussion among government representatives, employers, and workers. The report, prepared by Antonio Cerezo Ruiz, signified the beginning of serious inquiry into land tenure. The studies of communities conducted by the Instituto Indigenista Nacional provided further fodder for those clamoring for agrarian reform. Even more important were surveys done by the Ministry of Agriculture in 1947 indicating that of the 3,803,974 manzanas in private hands in the country, only 449,103 were cultivated; a further 773,084 were used as pasture.[15]

The same year congress formed an Agrarian Studies Commission under the chairmanship of Mario Monteforte Toledo. Members of the commission, the CTG, and the PAR visited or studied agrarian legislation in Mexico, Israel, Costa Rica, and many of the Eastern bloc countries. Their work was augmented in the early 1950s by George Britnell's report for the International Bank for Reconstruction and Development, in which he saved his strongest condemnation for large landowners in the Pacific piedmont who let some of the best farmland in the Americas lie uncultivated and argued most forcefully that peasant agriculture must be stimulated before any substantial economic progress could be made.[16]

The most important statistics on landownership came from the agricultural census carried out in 1950. Although the full results of the census were not available until 1954, many of its preliminary findings were reported in the monthly bulletin of the General Office of Statistics or in *El Mes económico y financiero* after 1950. The census indicated that 72 percent of the agricultural land in the country was controlled by slightly more than 2 percent of the farming units, while 88 percent of the farming units controlled only 14 percent of the land. This meant that in a country where close to 70 percent of the population depended on agriculture for a living, almost half of the farming units, representing 165,850 families, had less than two manzanas each, a figure suggested as the bare minimum needed for subsistence. On the other hand, twenty-two fincas controlled among them 13 percent of the agricultural land in the country.[17]

The agricultural census itself, commissioned in 1948, was the result of

TABLE 2. LANDOWNERSHIP, 1950

Size of property	Number of fincas	Total manzanas
Less than 1 manzana	74,269	40,822
1–2	91,581	135,077
2–5	99,779	302,987
5–10	42,444	282,730
10–32	29,615	444,164
32–64	6,125	271,308
1 caballería–10	6,488	1,161,803
10–20	569	506,100
20–50	358	707,869
50–100	104	468,070
100–200	32	280,476
More than 200 caballerías	22	714,069
Total	348,687	5,315,473

Source: *Censo agropecuario, 1950* (1954), 1:19.

an appeal by the Food and Agricultural Organization of the United Nations for a global study of food production and landownership. Supported by the United States, the organization's appeal proved to be an important incentive for discussion of agrarian reform throughout Latin America. By 1950/51 there was significant international pressure for reform. At the Inter-American Agricultural Conference held in Montevideo, Uruguay, in 1950, it was resolved that each country in America take such measures as were necessary to insure that "democratic norms prevail in the agricultural field." That year the United Nations established a special council to investigate agrarian reform, and the next year the U.S. under secretary of agriculture, in a submission to the council, declared that "economic progress and political stability are closely related to the systems of agricultural economics in force" and called for measures to reduce the causes of "agrarian agitation, political instability, and to foment an elevation in the living standards of agricultural workers." Information concerning these resolutions was distributed throughout Guatemala as a means of increasing support for agrarian reform within the country.[18]

These calls for reform prompted opposition. Again, most of it came from the AGA. After Max Ricardo Cuenca published a pamphlet under the auspices of the CTG calling for a "democratic agrarian reform" in 1947, the AGA and the CTG engaged in a public debate over the prospect. The AGA suggested that the accusation of the existence of "feudalism" in the countryside was "simply a product of sectarian fantasy." It warned that the projected reform "would be an error of the most unfortunate type for the country." Other conservative sectors of society also publicly opposed such measures. The church, through a regular article by "Juan sin Tierra" in the *Acción social cristiana*, called agrarianism the "worst plague" affecting Guatemala. It argued that all the talk of reform was imported from Mexico, where it had been "a rich vein continually exploited by unscrupulous politicians" and had led to falling production and "extreme misery" for peasants. It urged that a "grand campaign" be initiated to inoculate Guatemala against the spreading sickness.[19]

But opposition to agrarian reform came from some unexpected sources as well. The moderate Regional Democratic Workers' Party (Partido de Trabajadores Regional Democrático [PTRD]) and the FSG were leery of it. The PTRD suggested that, in a country like Guatemala where the attitudes of the majority of plantation owners toward their workers "if not perfect, are acceptable," the best means for economic development was to better conditions for agricultural laborers rather than dividing the land among peasants and "having them vegetate on it, . . . paralyzed by their ignorance and poor farming habits." The FSG argued that dividing land among peasants and agricultural workers was not "the step necessary to begin capitalist development" and suggested that the creation of a large class of small farmers would "aggravate" Guatemala's agrarian problems.[20]

Nonetheless, by the time of the 1950 election campaign, agrarian reform was one of the priorities of the revolutionary parties and revolutionary organizations. At the PAR and RN conventions, in which Arbenz was chosen as their presidential candidate, the importance of agrarian reform in their political platforms was clearly demonstrated. Both conventions were heavily attended by peasants, who pledged that the local affiliates would support the candidacy of "el soldado del pueblo" but clearly linked that support to the promise of agrarian reform. Víctor Manuel Gutiérrez's small party, the Revolutionary Workers' Party of Guatemala (Partido Revolucionario Obrero de Guatemala [PROG]), also strongly supported Arbenz and agrarian reform.[21]

It was therefore not surprising that agrarian reform was a major element in Arbenz's election campaign. By July 1950, Arbenz had made eleven campaign speeches and agrarian reform had been stressed in each of them. In his inaugural address, he affirmed, "In our program agrarian reform has capital importance in order to liquidate latifundia and make fundamental changes in primitive methods of work, that is to say, to effect a better distribution of uncultivated land or that land in which feudal customs continue."[22]

The most determined of the revolutionary forces kept up a supportive but constant pressure on Arbenz following his inauguration to insure that promises of agrarian reform were kept. The agrarian commission of congress was strengthened, and Gutiérrez was named chairman. His party, PROG, shortly before it dissolved, published a pamphlet on the various laws affecting agriculture in Guatemala's history to facilitate discussion, and Gutiérrez presented his own project for reform to congress in April 1951. *El Libertador*, the PAR newspaper, issued one of the most forthright demands for agrarian reform a few months later, declaring:

> The realization of agrarian reform through the abolition of latifundia and the distribution of land to the campesinos who work it . . . is the fundamental prerequisite for all economic, political and social reforms of the October Revolution. No democratic conquest will be stable or permanent without the previous achievement of agrarian reform. . . . Without the achievement of agrarian reform, the political democracy that we have built since 1944 ought to be considered as a structure that is erected on shaky ground. Without the realization of the agrarian reform, the sovereignty of the republic will always be threatened and the people will continue living in poverty.[23]

The Communist Party and *Octubre* contributed their share to this campaign. Following the passage of the second Law of Forced Rental in 1951, decree 853, the newspaper warned against complacency. Observing that the law was a positive step, it counseled, "It would be a grave error to consider that decree 853 signifies the solution to the essential problem of the peasants. On the contrary, the Communist Party has demanded and continues to demand with greater firmness, the promulgation of a law of agrarian reform." It also applied pressure by publishing a series of exposés of "feudal" fincas. One of the first such stories was a direct response to AGA claims that feudalism did not exist in Guatemala. It is worth quoting at length as it captures the baiting tone the newspaper used when dealing with the AGA. It observed:

> To find proof of the regimen of feudal exploitation in the countryside in Guatemala it is not necessary to organize expeditions, like those who decide to find a strange tribe in the heart of Africa. No sir! Here

not more than a half hour from the capital in the municipio of Ama-titlán, peasants of the aldea of Llana de Animas cultivate in small parcels of a manzana or two products of diverse types. In order to meet their necessities they need to rent land from some finqueros (Eugenio Mejicanos and Miguel Soto, not to cite names) who give them the land on the condition that they WORK THEIR COFFEE FREE AND ALSO! THEY MUST GIVE THEM PART OF THE FRIJOL AND OTHER PRODUCTS THAT THE EXPLOITED PEASANTS CULTIVATE. In such a manner these señores through typical feudal exploitation produce cof-fee without paying a single penny. Those who know the price of a *quintal* [100 pounds] of coffee . . . will realize how much these "poor victims of the communist government of doctor Arévalo" profit.[24]

The CNCG joined the chorus with a strong call for agrarian reform at its first national congress in 1951. The association of agricultural experts lent their voices in support. The national radio station presented a dialogue be-tween the agriculture minister, an agriculturalist, a member of the agrarian commission of congress, and Leonardo Castillo Flores. Otto Raúl Gon-zález even wrote a play entitled "El Tiempo del respeto está cercano o la Reforma Agraria en Guatemala," which played briefly in Guatemala City. Finally, at the May Day parade in 1952, CGTG and CNCG representatives, backed by thousands of peasants and workers, presented a petition to Arbenz that read in part, "For many years the agrarian reform has not been more than a promise and an inspiration. The workers and peasants demand the government quickly pass an agrarian reform." Perhaps this was the final prompting — if Arbenz needed one — for less than two weeks later, almost eight years after Ubico's resignation, Arbenz sent an Agrarian Re-form Law to congress.[25]

The Agrarian Reform Law

At 1:10 on the morning of 17 June 1952, congress gave its approval to the Agrarian Reform Law, decree 900. The bill had diverse origins. Between 1949 and 1952, no less than six serious projected agrarian reform laws were presented to congress or the president for consideration. The proposal most closely resembling the actual law was presented in congress in 1951 by Víctor Manuel Gutiérrez and Ignacio Humberto Ortiz, both members of the Agrarian Studies Commission. The law proposed to congress was very much the product of Arbenz and his closest advisers, particularly José Manuel Fortuny of the Communist Party and Víctor Manuel Gutiérrez. There were differences, however; Gutiérrez's original proposal had advocated the incorporation of expropriated land into cooperatives, a provision not mentioned in Arbenz's proposed law and allowed for, but not stressed, in the final draft passed by congress. This became an important distinction in the course of the application of the law.[26]

Despite numerous indications during the preceding few years that some sort of agrarian reform was imminent, Arbenz's proposal prompted a whirlwind of activity. The most obvious support came from the revolutionary forces. *Octubre* continued to denounce "feudal" fincas. The CNCG called a special assembly that attracted thousands of people, filled the National Theater to capacity, and allowed representatives from each of the revolutionary organizations to promise their support. Even the moderately conservative PIN, after some hesitation, came out in favor of the law. The pressure placed on Nicolás Brol, the minister of agriculture and leader of the PIN, over the issue is of interest. Although Brol was ultimately credited with prompting the PIN to support the law, during an initial period in which he was having difficulty gaining the support of party members, Carlos Manuel Pellecer provided some persuasion of his own by denouncing the labor practices Brol employed on his finca and threatening a strike. Brol energetically responded to Pellecer's criticisms, but it is probably not simply coincidence that the matter was dropped after the PIN agreed to support the law. Just before the law was sent to congress, even *El Imparcial* suggested it was time for such changes and expressed confidence that the government would not listen to special interests and would take into consideration the "interest of the collective, of all the Guatemalan people."[27]

The two organizations that had pushed most vigorously for the agrarian reform — the CGTG and the CNCG — took a moderate but supportive stance toward the law. The CNCG was pleased with the law, but before making elaborate statements, it took the proposed law to its members and awaited their response. In this way, it argued, not only the interests of the AGA and the politicians would be taken into account in the debate but also those of "the thousands and thousands of peasants, agricultural workers, and urban workers" who would be most affected. The Communist Party also supported the law, arguing that although the party's ultimate goal was to eliminate private property in Guatemala, it accepted the fact that "in no way . . . could anyone think that the conditions exist to apply the principle of 'land for those who work it.' . . . Conditions only exist to destroy the most backward forms of feudal production."[28]

It is not surprising that the most vehement opposition to the law came from the AGA and associated organizations. The AGA held a stormy meeting with Arbenz on 15 May, five days after the reform had been presented to congress, and four days later it submitted its own proposal for agrarian reform. The draft attacked a number of provisions in the proposed law. The most important of these were the arrangements made for the expropriation of land and the basis for indemnification. It was also concerned that some beneficiaries would get land in usufruct rather than outright ownership. The AGA, as it had in the past, especially criticized the government's determination to attack all property on which rent was paid in the form of labor (trabajo necesario) by declaring it to be latifundia and subject to expropriation.

Instead of attempting to answer the AGA objections, the government issued a strongly worded critique of the AGA proposal. The document revealed the theoretical perspective of the people ensconced in the president's office. The critique traced the history of attempted reforms by the two administrations of the revolution, pointing out that the AGA had sought to avoid or sabotage all serious proposals. It suggested that there was a fundamental difference between capitalist enterprises and feudal ones, because while capitalists extracted "surplus product," they at least reinvested some of that product to increase production, benefiting the national economy and workers in the long run. Under capitalism, workers received salaries that allowed them to accumulate savings and to advance. Latifundistas, on the other hand, simply collected the product of the workers without investment, and thus "the owner, without worries, without anxiety, without risks, lives in the city, goes now and again to visit the finca, travels through European countries and plays in Monte Carlo." To be a latifundista "does not require intellect, exceptional talent, superior ingenuity. All that is necessary is a heart as hard as a rock, to uproot the peasant without respite or compassion."

As a result of the latifundistas' power over previous governments, twenty-two owners controlled more land than 249,169 peasant families, the critique argued. The painful legacy of this inequality haunted the country:

Barefoot, threadbare, badly clothed, exposed to the bites of the vipers, always subject to the punishment of the weather, the campesino comes and goes like a phantom, a phantom of the latifundios. . . . He doesn't know how to read or write. He doesn't know how to count past one hundred. He doesn't know how to defend his elemental right to an hourly wage. He doesn't know anything. Advanced in years, his culture is lost at the level of a child at kindergarten. . . . With [feudalism] he will always live in the same inhuman condition that in the past his parents lived in, his grandparents, his great grandparents, his ancient ancestors.

If all the unpaid labor that peasants had been forced to perform in the past were now rewarded, the critique went on, they would become the legitimate lords of all the national property.

It was their knowledge of these facts, their realization that the latifundia would be destroyed by capitalism, that prompted the AGA's attacks on the agrarian reform, the president's office argued. This was why the landlords lent all their forces to support "reactionary dictators." "Unfortunately for the latifundistas," it predicted, "the reconquest of political power is difficult, better said, is impossible. The Revolution of October has converted the state into a revolutionary fortress . . . untakeable by force, by cunning, or by any other means. Eight years of continuous violent assault . . . have proved this irrefutably."[29]

The government's response to the AGA proposal revealed a willingness to challenge landowners in the process of implementing an agrarian reform. It was the angriest denunciation of the AGA yet offered by the president and marked the final divorce of the landowners' association from the Arbenz administration after two years of attempted conciliation. Despite continuing calls from the government for cooperation from "progressive" landowners (some of whom did cooperate), this exchange between it and the AGA clearly illustrated that the government foresaw the process as a battle between the bulk of the large landowners and the forces of the revolution, a battle that was to rage freely in the countryside for the next two years.

Despite the prominent position of such communists as José Manuel Fortuny and Víctor Manuel Gutiérrez in framing the Agrarian Reform Law, it was at heart capitalist. It focused on the prevailing preoccupation of the administration to attack "feudalism" in the countryside and to inspire both more productive and more equitable agricultural enterprises. The law abolished all forms of *servidumbre* (which the administration defined as near slavery in the countryside) and latifundia with the essential objectives of developing the "capitalist peasant economy and the capitalist agricultural economy in general"; giving land to peasants, *mozos colonos* or resident workers, and agricultural workers who possessed insufficient land; facilitating the investment of new capital in agriculture through the rental of national lands; introducing new methods of cultivation to peasants; and increasing agricultural credit to all peasants and capitalist agriculturalists.

Land was to be expropriated from a variety of types of agricultural enterprises and distributed to peasants and workers in one of three forms. The law provided for substantial protection for medium-sized and/or efficient farms. No finca less than two *caballerías* (one caballería equals approximately 110 acres) in size was to be affected by the law, whether cultivated or not. No finca larger than two caballerías and smaller than six caballerías on which at least two-thirds of the property was cultivated was to be affected, but if two-thirds of the property was not directly in use, uncultivated land or rented land could be expropriated. All property of the national fincas was subject to distribution under the law, as was any land in fincas larger than six caballerías that was not in use or was rented in return for personal service, in lieu of or "to complete unsatisfactory salaries," during the last three years. Municipal land denounced by *comunidades indígenas* or *comunidades campesinas* (local organizations given legal status under the Arévalo administration) could also be expropriated and distributed to members of the comunidad.

Private property expropriated under the law was to be paid for through agrarian bonds, with the price set at the declared value of the property in the last property tax assessment. Bonds were to pay 3 percent interest and were to mature at varying rates depending on the value of the property. Property worth Q100 or less would be paid for in two years, whereas property worth more than Q30,000 would be paid for in twenty-five years. In other words, the bonds would amortize at rates varying from 50 to 4 percent a year.

Land was to be distributed in various ways. It could be allocated as private property to peasants or workers, who were to pay 5 percent of the value of the harvest until the agrarian debt was paid. When not given to peasants directly, the land became national patrimony. In order to abide by the constitutional precept that the property of the state was inalienable, the law maintained that this land, if subsequently distributed, was to be given out in lifelong usufruct, for which the beneficiaries paid 3 percent of the value of the harvest. In addition, national finca property could be distributed, if the majority of the beneficiaries freely voted to do so, in the form of agricultural cooperatives. Although all three of these forms were used, most land was given out in usufruct.

The Agrarian Reform Law established a series of hierarchical organizations, presided over by the president. The implementation of the law was to be overseen by the National Agrarian Department (Departamento Agrario Nacional [DAN]), which was to be advised by the National Agrarian Council (Consejo Agrario Nacional [CAN]). Below these national organizations were departmental (Comité Agrario Departamental [CAD]) and local agrarian committees (Comité Agrario Local [CAL]). The DAN was answerable to and appointed by the president. The CAN was to have nine members named by the president from the Ministry of Agriculture, the Ministry of the Economy, the General Office of Statistics, the Bank of Guatemala, the AGA, the CGTG, and two from the CNCG, with the chief of the DAN presiding. Members could only be removed by the president. The CADs were to have five members named by the chief of the DAN and proposed by the DAN, the governor, the AGA, the CGTG, and the CNCG, and was to be chaired by the DAN representative. CALs were to be formed wherever there was property to be affected by the law. They were to have five members with one nominated by the governor, one by the municipality, and three by the local unión campesina or sindicato. Where these organizations did not exist, these three members were to be elected by a public vote with representatives of the CGTG and the CNCG present.

Expropriations were to be processed from the bottom up. Denunciations of land believed to be potentially affected by the agrarian reform were to be made to the CALs, usually by residents of the community. After the CAL verified the facts as presented in the denunciation, it was passed on to the CAD, which made the initial decision concerning the amount and value of land, if any, to be expropriated. Appeals could be made to the CAN and then to the president. Once an expropriation was declared, the CAL was responsible for distribution of the land, usually to those who had denounced it. In the case of a conflict between a comunidad and a municipality, the initial decision was to be made by the CAD after a hearing attended by the two sides.

The beneficiaries of the law were to be determined primarily by the denunciation process itself, but certain priorities were established. In the case of national fincas — and in practice in large private fincas as well — workers and mozos colonos on the fincas were given first consideration. They were to receive no less than five and no more than ten manzanas of cultivated land or between fifteen and twenty-five manzanas of uncultivated land. Once all the resident workers had received their parcels, workers and peasants from anywhere in the country could petition for land in usufruct.

Some special provisions were made. The DAN was to be guided by the consideration that general interests superseded private interests. In addition, decisions of the various agrarian agencies were declared to be beyond the jurisdiction of the courts; decisions could be appealed only through the agrarian agencies themselves, and the final decision rested with the president.[30]

The Agrarian Reform Law established an agency with two widely diverse foci of power. On the one hand, the DAN and all its agencies were the creation of and answerable to the president, who appointed DAN and CAN members as well as the departmental governors, who were important members of each CAD. The law significantly augmented the president's powers and allowed him, with certain limitations, to determine the speed and range of the application of the law. On the other hand, the CALs also became important centers of power and influence. To a great extent, they were able to control the allocation of the most important local resource, land, and enjoyed almost unlimited discretion in determining who would benefit from the law. The dominant place on the CALs of the CGTG and the CNCG, coupled with their presence on the CAN, insured that the law also greatly increased their strength.

The Application of Decree 900

Less than one year after he signed decree 900, Arbenz announced to congress: "The agrarian reform has until today determined the internal political struggle. The question of the agrarian reform has drawn the classic line in the sand: on one side those who are definitely with the revolution and on the other side those who are definitely against the revolution. There has been no place left for the middle ground as in all the great historic decisions. There is no family, there is no class, there is no person now in our country, who has not felt, in one form or another, . . . the impact of the commotions the agrarian question has caused in Guatemala."[31]

Arbenz was not overstating the impact of the agrarian reform. A large percentage of the Guatemalan population probably supported the law, but apprehension mounted as the CNCG and the CGTG steadily augmented their power and influence over the government. A series of land invasions occurred, property that the law did not affect was seized, and the government seemed unprepared to confront the spreading unrest in the countryside. It appeared to many that Arbenz lost control of the situation and was prepared to allow the peasant league and labor federation free rein in the countryside. Much of the urban middle class, which had supported the *results of the Decree* revolution through more than eight years of struggle, now deserted it. As more and more of the moderate political sectors abandoned the revolution, Arbenz relied more heavily on peasant and labor organizations and a few communist advisers, adding weight to the claims that communists were taking over the government. By 1954, there was hardly a pocket of the country untouched by unrest and unease associated with the agrarian reform. *The series of land invasions amplified the significance of communist advicers*

The agrarian reform proved immensely successful in its primary objective of transferring land from the hands of the large landowners to peasants and rural workers. The law was implemented remarkably quickly. Less than a month after its passage, the CNCG announced that 400 CALs had been formed around the country. Two weeks later, that number had almost tripled to 1,000, and by October 1952, Clodoveo Torres Moss, one of the CNCG members on the CAN, announced that there were over 3,000 CALs. These local committees rapidly began processing denunciations of land; by August 1952 the DAN reported that it had received almost 5,000 denunciations. The first land appropriated under decree 900 was parceled out to workers and some neighboring peasants from the national finca Bárcenas near Lake Amatitlán in early August 1952. By January 1953 the junta in charge of liquidating the national fincas announced that thirty-five fincas were ready to be distributed. In the same month, Arbenz expropriated land from four private fincas. By early February, parts of thirty-nine private fincas had been expropriated.[32]

In October 1953 the National Agrarian Bank was created with a mandate to supply credit to beneficiaries of the reform. The director of the bank, Alfonso Bauer Paiz, promised that over Q2 million would be extended in small loans before the end of 1953. By April 1954 the bank had granted credits of over Q6.5 million. In October 1953 the government began to pay off the agrarian bonds it had given out for expropriated land. By May 1954 it had paid Q163,825 to bondholders and had issued over Q6 million in bonds.[33]

The existing records of the DAN indicate that by June 1954, 745,233 manzanas of land had been expropriated from nearly 800 private fincas. Agrarian agencies at one level or another had issued rulings declaring a

TABLE 3. EXPROPRIATIONS UNDER DECREE 900 BY DEPARTMENT

Department	Number of expropriations	Total manzanas	Average size of expropriation
Alta Verapaz	74	152,633	2,063
Escuintla	105	78,444	747
El Quiché	63	53,589	851
Huehuetenango	35	37,374	1,068
Suchitepéquez	59	35,948	609
Guatemala	127	34,216	269
Santa Rosa	66	27,724	420
Baja Verapaz	43	20,615	479
Retalhuleu	19	15,508	816
Jutiapa	31	15,328	494
San Marcos	60	13,280	221
Izabal	7	11,705	1,672
Quezaltenango	30	9,732	324
El Progreso	6	5,883	980
Sacatepéquez	23	5,013	218
Jalapa	13	4,401	339
Chimaltenango	10	4,401	440
Sololá	12	2,063	172
Zacapa	8	1,470	184
Chiquimula	3	612	204
Total	794	529,939	667

Source: Carátulas para expedientes, in records of the Departamento Agrario Nacional, Instituto Nacional de Transformación Agraria, Guatemala City.

Note: United Fruit Company land and communal land is excluded. There were no expropriations in Totonicapán and El Petén.

further 189,803 manzanas subject to expropriation that had not exhausted the appeal process before the overthrow of the Arbenz government. Seventeen percent of all land held in private hands in the country had been expropriated or was in the process of being expropriated under the law. In addition, there was a huge backlog of denunciations on which no ruling had yet been made.[34]

The number of people who directly benefited from the law is more difficult to determine. DAN figures suggest that over 70,000 plots of land were given to beneficiaries. In addition, there were more than 22,000 beneficiaries on national fincas, either on private plots or in cooperatives. Close to 100,000 peasant families may have received land in some form under the reform, directly benefiting as many as 500,000 people out of a population of close to 3 million. This was the beginning of a remarkable transformation of the agrarian structure of the country. More than 19 percent of the people eligible to benefit from the law received land before the overthrow of Arbenz.[35]

Much of the process of expropriation and distribution was carried out as the law intended. The official newspaper, *Diario de Centroamérica*, and the communist newspapers, *Octubre* and *Tribuna popular*, emphasized the numerous expropriations that proceeded according to the law. The government publicly acknowledged owners who had abided by the rules of the decree and who had placed few obstacles in its way. It especially praised Erwin Paul Dieseldorf, a German/Guatemalan planter in the Cobán. In addition, the law was applied to everyone without exception. Arbenz lost fifteen caballerías of his cotton finca; Nicolás Brol, the minister of agriculture, lost eighty-five caballerías of his property; Guillermo Toriello, then the ambassador to the United States and later foreign minister, lost slightly over ten caballerías of his land in Escuintla; and relatives of most of the revolutionary activists, including Carlos Manuel Pellecer and José Manuel Fortuny, lost land under the reform.[36]

Agricultural production in the country seemed to suffer little from the dislocation and disruption of the reform. Guatemala's agricultural production increased steadily from 1951 to 1954. Significantly, this was true of both domestic-use agriculture and export crops. The economy was assisted by an increase in the prices for agricultural products in 1953 and 1954, particularly coffee. Still, Víctor Bulmer-Thomas has estimated that the value of Guatemala's export crops, expressed in constant 1970 dollars, increased from just under $97 million in 1951 to over $109 million in 1954. The production of all basic foodstuffs increased substantially from 1951 to 1954, and the production of corn, the most important staple, increased to such an extent that it was exported to Mexico and Honduras beginning in 1953. The 1953/54 coffee crop was the second best in the history of Guatemala.[37]

Glowing reports from the inspectors of the national fincas that had been converted into cooperatives stressed the abundant harvest they expected in 1954. The DAN estimated that the coffee crop from the cooperative on the former national finca Concepción would be worth Q600,000, one of the best harvests the finca had ever enjoyed and one that would give each member between Q3,500 and Q4,000. The *Tribuna popular* claimed, "Never has a peasant dreamed of making this much money." The newspaper reported that the members of the cooperative at the finca San Julian would also receive more money than they had ever imagined. Some were planning to buy "picops" or "yips." One thirty-five-year-old member was quoted as saying, "Before the 20th of October I earned 20 cents daily . . . , and to think that now I can even buy a truck with the product of our land." These stories were obviously communist propaganda meant to entice peasants, who had been disappointingly reluctant, to form cooperatives, but they cannot be totally discounted. In addition, of course, the bumper harvest was picked from trees that had been planted and nurtured long before the agrarian reform. It remained to be seen if the cooperatives and new land owners would continue to produce good yields.[38]

The director of the INFOP also praised the new agrarian regime. He admitted that he had been worried when the reform was initiated that laborers for the coffee harvest would be difficult to recruit. However, his fears proved groundless; as far as he knew, no finca had lacked workers for the harvest in 1953/54. The difference, he pointed out, was that in 1953 they received Q1.25 per quintal of coffee, some workers picking three quintals a day, compared to a daily wage of between 25 and 50 cents at the beginning of the revolution. The government planned to build on the success of the agrarian reform with new incentives benefiting those who had received land. In early 1954, the minister of agriculture announced an ambitious program to provide new types of seeds for a variety of crops, 40,000 breeding chickens, and 5 million tree seedlings to the beneficiaries of the Agrarian Reform Law.[39]

Besides this statistical evidence of success, there were personal stories of triumph. The newspapers that supported the government continually recounted tales of peasant communities finally acquiring land that had been taken from them under previous regimes. They dramatized the details of the decades of struggle the communities had endured attempting to regain possession of the land.[40] In addition, the Agrarian Reform Law prompted court cases involving agrarian issues not directly related to land tenure. With the abolition of unpaid personal service, cases were brought forward demanding retroactive wages, sometimes stretching back many years. In the most dramatic case, a man who had worked for forty years as a caretaker of a small finca for no salary was awarded Q78,000 by a labor judge.[41]

Much of the success of the agrarian reform can be attributed to the work of the CNCG and the CGTG. During the two years the reform was in effect, both organizations were inundated with requests for assistance in almost all matters pertaining to the law (and many other issues). This undoubtedly caused some friction. Many workers for both organizations complained regularly about not getting enough assistance or direction from the over-worked national offices. In addition, the numerous "petty" complaints that CNCG leaders took to DAN officials on behalf of their members caused problems. At one point, an inspector-general of the DAN petulantly re-sponded to the secretary of conflicts for the CNCG that it was about time the peasants learned to defend their own rights and stopped trying "to transform the National Agrarian Department into a justice of the peace."[42]

Nevertheless, workers for both the CNCG and the CGTG, especially Leonardo Castillo Flores, responded carefully and courteously to almost all requests for assistance. They explained the provisions of the law; sent commissions to investigate land disputes; held congresses to identify the further needs of peasants; were responsible for the formation of the Na-tional Agrarian Bank and the extension of easy credit to beneficiaries of the law; assisted in the distribution of seeds, tools, and literature concern-ing their use; and sent letters of support when local organizers felt over-whelmed by the difficulties they encountered. Their most important role was to insure that local officials upheld the law and to foster the formation of the CALs, which were essential for the application of the law.[43]

Like the peasants' and workers' organizations, the agrarian officials were flooded with a sea of correspondence as the agrarian reform was implemented. Occasionally, they drowned in confusion as they tried to make sense of Guatemala's complex land tenure structure and to apply the sometimes vague articles of decree 900. These officials exerted great effort in trying to apply the law legally. The agrarian agencies rejected 509 petitions for expropriation of property, almost as many as were approved. In the majority of cases, landlords took advantage of every opportunity for appeal offered to them by the law, which often led to a significant reduction in the amount of land expropriated. In 239 of the cases in which appeals were ruled on by Arbenz himself, the amount of land expropriated was reduced, often substantially.[44]

Petitions to have land expropriated were most often rejected because the property in question was under two caballerías. In addition, numerous fincas were kept intact because the owners cultivated or in some other manner used two-thirds of the property, as stipulated by decree 900. Land-owners frequently complained that they were not given sufficient oppor-tunity to respond to the decisions of the agrarian officials in time to meet the various deadlines established under the law. Certainly, this was true on a number of occasions, but there is no evidence that the agrarian officials purposely made it difficult for landlords to appeal decisions.[45]

Agrarian officials were confronted with numerous problems in enforcing the law. It was often difficult to determine the size of the property denounced. Those petitioning for the land rarely had any clear idea of the legal extent of the finca, and the inspections carried out by the CALs seldom helped. Agrarian officials were forced to engage in exhaustive and often bewildering investigations, going back decades, through the various land registers before they could give accurate estimates. Even so, it was not uncommon for the CADs to recommend expropriations larger than the property being denounced before subsequent investigation revealed the error. On at least one occasion, even the CAN recommended taking more land than the property actually contained.[46]

It was often just as difficult to determine the identity of the current owner. To prevent landowners from selling parts of their property to avoid the application of the law, congress had passed a law that froze the sale of land after 9 May 1952. Although this was a necessary supplement to decree 900, it often made it more difficult to determine legal ownership of property denounced a year or two later. Not surprisingly, landowners often refused to cooperate in the various investigations carried out by agrarian officials. For example, when the finca El Jocotén in Jalapa was denounced in January 1953, the CAD and the CAN had difficulty getting a response from the landlord concerning ownership of the property. The CAD finally determined that the property was co-owned by a number of adult members of the family and thus exempt from the law, as each individual had less than the minimum stipulated under decree 900. They still could get no response from the landowners, however. In May 1954, a DAN official scolded one of the owners, Francisco Pinto, saying, "Your policy of not providing the information already solicited three times is not very intelligent [as the property had already been declared exempt]. . . . We need to know the registration number of the property to send that decision to you. For the last time we ask you for it; the next time you will suffer a penalty under decree 900."[47]

Landowners often had good reason for their reluctance to provide information to agrarian officials. When the finca Santo Domingo Los Ocotes in San Antonio La Paz, El Progreso, was denounced and the whole property expropriated, the owners presented no defense, failing to take advantage of any of the appeal procedures available to them. After the overthrow of

Arbenz, when the owner, José Mejía, applied to the new government to have the property returned, only two of the fifteen caballerías in the finca were given back. The new agrarian officials decided that the former owners could not prove legal possession of the entire finca since testimony indicated they had acquired most of the property from the neighboring community on very questionable legal grounds.[48]

Agrarian officials faced many other problems in applying the law. While decree 900 declared property of less than two caballerías to be exempt from the law, it failed to take into account individuals who owned numerous properties or who tried to evade the law by dividing their fincas into smaller parcels. Most often, the agrarian officials considered multiple holdings to be one property, even if they were dispersed throughout the country. Even though this procedure was most often used to expropriate *fincas de mozos* (in which land was rented out to workers in return for work contracts) of less than two caballerías, it required the agrarian officials to keep complicated inventories of landlords and their holdings.[49]

The most famous of these cases involved Casimiro Gutiérrez. Gutiérrez owned more than seventy-three parcels of land in a number of municipalities in the department of El Quiché, most of which he rented to peasants. The agrarian agencies received more than twenty-five denunciations of his land, all involving parcels with less than the two-caballería limit. Some of these denunciations described efforts by the owner to frustrate attempts to denounce his land. One petition for land called Gutiérrez an "antiagrarista and falangist" and charged that "all the peasants that support the agrarian reform" were subjected to harassment by Gutiérrez and his "flunkies [paniaguados]." All those who had joined the peasant union were being thrown off the land they had rented from him. After listing the names of people who suffered at Gutiérrez's hands, the petitioner concluded by saying, "I could continue giving cases . . . of the *rabia* of this señor Casimiro," and asked for the immediate assistance of the agrarian officials. The CAN decided to consider all of his land as one property, and land was expropriated from thirteen parcels; five denunciations were pending when the Arbenz administration was overthrown, and four lots were declared unaffected.[50]

Decree 900 was also rather vague about what constituted proper use of land, a determination that was most important in the case of property used to raise cattle. Many landowners claimed to be fully utilizing their land by grazing a few head of cattle on it. Although the agrarian agencies occasionally accepted these arguments and declared the lands to be unaffected, they usually demanded evidence of significant capital investment, especially proof that large amounts of the property had been planted in grass. Agrarian officials exercised a significant amount of discretion in ruling on these cases, and decisions to expropriate cattle land often prompted bitter disputes. Clashes concerning forest reserves also occurred. The revolutionary governments had made the protection of Guatemala's diminishing forests one of their priorities, and the Agrarian Reform Law had stipulated that forest reserves with slopes greater than 30 degrees were exempt from expropriation. While some forestland was declared to be unaffected by the law, significant amounts of land with slopes greater than 30 degrees were taken by the law, most of it placed in forest reserves controlled by the state. It was in this area that the various agencies of the agrarian reform most often overstepped the bounds of the law.

Decisions by the agrarian agencies often appeared to be, and occasionally were, arbitrary, deepening many landowners' resentment of the law. But usually the problems associated with applying the law were the result of the difficulties entailed in creating and administering a huge bureaucracy. In general, the agrarian agencies attempted to abide by most of the provisions of decree 900. Landlords had substantial opportunity to appeal the decisions of the agrarian agencies, and most took full advantage of those opportunities.

"Whatever It Costs"

The appeal procedures and other protections given property owners under the Agrarian Reform Law did little to appease the majority of the landowners who lost or feared losing land under decree 900. Landowners like Dieseldorf notwithstanding, the AGA steadfastly opposed the agrarian reform from its inception. Its opposition to the law and the government continued to grow until the overthrow of Arbenz in 1954. Despite a number of invitations, the AGA refused to send the representatives it was entitled to have in the various organs of the DAN. Perhaps the association's perception of the law was best expressed in one advertisement it placed in *El Imparcial* that asked, "Can a cow give lemonade? The communists cannot make a *democratic* law" (emphasis added).[51]

Landowners also attempted to fight the decisions of the agrarian agencies through the courts, despite the provisions of the law itself. The most serious challenge came in the case brought before the Supreme Court by

— important Moment

Ernesto Leal Pérez in February 1953. Leal's finca, Las Conchas, had been *Specific Example* denounced by sixty-seven peasants in August 1952. The agrarian agencies declared that 5.5 of Leal's 7.5 caballerías should be expropriated. On 5 January 1953, in the final appeal allowed by the law, Arbenz agreed with the expropriation, despite Leal's claims that the property was a legal forest preserve. Disregarding the articles in the law declaring that the courts had no jurisdiction over decisions made by the agrarian agencies, Leal took the case to the Supreme Court. The judges ruled 4 to 1 that the expropriation had not been carried out properly. Perhaps more importantly, three of them also declared that Arbenz had "abused his authority" in making his decision.[52] *Explains why landowners opposed to Arbenz*

This decision prompted much concern among the revolutionary forces; the process of land redistribution could be delayed substantially if appeal to the courts were allowed. Moreover, the court's statement concerning the extent of the president's authority seemed to threaten the whole expropriation process. Arbenz moved decisively, removing the judges who had ruled against the expropriation. After thirty-nine hours of debate, congress approved the dismissals on 7 February. The government was supported in this decision by an avalanche of telegrams from the various revolutionary organizations and their local affiliates. Víctor Manuel Gutiérrez was one of the most forceful defenders of the president's actions, saying, "One can live without tribunals, but one cannot live without land."[53]

The dismissal of the judges prompted significant opposition to the Arbenz administration. To those already concerned about the influence of communism on the government, this action seemed to indicate that Arbenz would not be bound by the law. Perhaps the most important opposition came from the lawyers' association, representative of middle-class urban interests, which had previously supported the revolutionary political parties. A number of street demonstrations took place calling for the reinstatement of the judges and the resignation of Arbenz, in one of which a person was killed. Protest quickly subsided, but the opposition to the president's actions marked growing disillusionment with the government on the part of large sectors of the important urban middle class.[54]

Arbenz refused to back down. In a speech at a rally held to support his action, he vowed, "WHATEVER COMES TO PASS, WHATEVER IT COSTS, with the assistance of the army, and within the law, we will complete the application of the agrarian reform." He went on to warn landowners, "We are tired of the maneuvers of the reaction. Despite them, with the constitution in hand, we will continue fighting for our rights. . . . But, I want to say publicly, fully conscious that I am in front of you, representatives of the people, I want to warn the other side, that if they go outside of the law, if they provoke a civil war, we will also fight." It was Arbenz's harshest warning to date and marked a major escalation in the conflict.[55]

Conflict over the agrarian reform in the countryside was growing increasingly violent. Rural activists continually complained about the actions of landowners who attempted to avoid the law and who attacked peasants seeking to apply it. In many communities, peasants organized self-defense committees before sending official notification to local authorities that they had established a CAL. The peasant league and the rural workers' union were constantly requesting gun licenses for their workers in the countryside, usually to no avail. Numerous activists were imprisoned by alcaldes or the rural Guardia Civil. Many were killed. Peasant leaders were shot, hung, beaten, burned, and run over throughout the country. By 1954, after yet another peasant organizer was found hung in Ipala, Chiquimula, the communist newspaper denounced "a new wave of oppression against the peasants who are fighting for land" begun by the "feudal landowners." The violence was not completely one-sided, of course, and landowners, particularly in Escuintla, San Marcos, and Chiquimula, also complained about violent attacks by organized peasants.[56]

One community from which numerous complaints were received by the revolutionary organizations concerning the activities of the largest landowners serves as an example. Santo Tomás La Unión in Suchitepéquez was a small municipality with less than 3,000 inhabitants, over 75 percent of whom were Indian according to the 1950 census. One hundred and eighty-five Indian farm operators controlled slightly over 500 manzanas of land, while fifty Ladino operators controlled almost double that amount. Moreover, almost half of the 235 farm operators rented their land or were mozos colonos on estates in the municipality and controlled less than 100 manzanas. Almost 1,000 of the 1,554 manzanas farmed in the municipality were operated by eleven administrators for absentee landlords.[57] The Bonifasi family owned many of these estates. According to *Octubre*, the family had arrived from Spain near the turn of the century. They had opened a bar in the municipality and accumulated a considerable fortune "through the usual methods of this class of adventurers," primarily by lending money to drunk customers and then foreclosing on the loans. By 1951, they were the largest landowners in the municipality and controlled the production of coffee and bananas. Complaints to the newspaper noted that "almost two generations of Indians have been wickedly exploited at their hands." The

Bonifasi family had such tight control over the municipality that no peasants could successfully initiate actions against them through the law, although some of their property was taken in Sololá.[58]

Other problems emerged in the application of decree 900. There were constant complaints that landlords were bribing DAN officials to avoid or delay expropriation. Members of virtually every revolutionary organization involved in the agrarian reform were accused either of accepting bribes from landlords or of forcing peasants and workers to pay them to enforce the law in their municipalities. People also complained that officials favored friends or relatives in the distribution of land. While this clearly went on at the local level with the distribution of land through the agrarian reform (and will be discussed more fully below), it occurred on a grander scale with the expropriation of UFCo land. Hundreds of thousands of manzanas were taken from the company, many more than could be allocated quickly to peasants and workers petitioning for land. It was a vast reservoir of potential graft available to those with influence, and some took advantage of it. The records of the various organizations, particularly the CGTG, document numerous requests made of the CALs in the area of UFCo farms to find plots of land for friends or activists. Some were appalled by the corruption and not only refused the land offered to them but also spoke out against the practice. One woman on the PAR executive was particularly incensed when she was offered a parcel of land at Tiquisate. She informed Major Alfonso Martínez Estéves, the head of the DAN, that she had not asked for land and would accept none, and she warned that "the land must be for those who work it."[59]

There was also increasing conflict among the various revolutionary organizations surrounding the implementation of decree 900. This conflict began with the creation of the DAN, a highly centralized organization dependent on and answerable to the president. Given Arbenz's predilection for listening to a few close friends and advisers and the importance of the DAN in his economic plans, the choice for head of the DAN provided a good indication of who within the government had the president's ear. There were many rumors concerning possible candidates for the position, most naming Augusto Charnaud MacDonald and Alfonso Bauer Paiz. Finally, however, Major Alfonso Martínez Estéves was appointed to the post. While the U.S. embassy called his selection a "local surprise," there was good reason for his appointment. Charnaud, despite his closeness to Arbenz and his strong position as the head of the Socialist Party (which at the time had the support of the CNCG), was disliked by too many politicians to be an effective head of the department. Bauer Paiz had no support within the two major rural-based parties, and his position in the FPL made him suspicious to local PAR and peasant activists who saw the FPL as a conservative party.[60]

Martínez fit the bill rather well. He was a PAR deputy in congress and was reasonably influential within the party. On the other hand, he was not closely linked to the faction that had led to the resignation of Charnaud and the withdrawal of the peasant league, nor was he too closely linked to the party "radicals," considered by some to be influenced by the communists. Of equal importance, he had a long connection with Arbenz, who considered him to be a most trustworthy associate. Martínez had a distinguished career at the military academy. His support within the military was important given the army's traditionally strong position in rural areas and Arbenz's attempts to tie the military to his program of agrarian reform. Martínez had been one of the officers who had been with Arbenz when Arana was killed in 1949. Following Arbenz's election, Martínez became his private secretary. In that position, he was one of Arbenz's closest confidants and, according to the U.S. embassy, had a "quicker mind" than Arbenz and "great influence" on him. His appointment as head of the DAN gave Arbenz a trusted, efficient ally, who also had good political and military connections.[61]

The members of the CAN, as the major advisory body and arbiter of disputes under the law, also had an important influence on the way the law was implemented. The CNCG had the most members on the board and filled its two positions with the most powerful men in the peasant league, Castillo Flores and Clodoveo Torres Moss, the secretary of conflicts. The CGTG initially wanted Carlos Manuel Pellecer to serve as its representative on the board, but Pellecer declined, saying his work in the field kept him too busy. José Luis Ramos was eventually selected, but it was clear that Gutiérrez influenced him greatly. The other members of the CAN were moderate professionals without noteworthy partisan attachments. However, the deputy chief of the DAN was Wlademar Barrios Klee. Although not officially a member of the Communist Party, he was generally considered to be communist. His appointment, along with the strong position of the peasant league and the workers' federation in the CAN, heightened concern about communist influence over the agrarian reform.[62]

Arbenz had argued, and at times seemed to believe, that the agrarian reform could be carried out after sufficient preparation and in such a fashion to insure that a "violent confrontation" between classes and sectors in the country could be avoided. It became apparent quite quickly that many others involved in the reform did not share this belief or the desire to avoid a confrontation. A series of land invasions by peasants and rural workers began in January 1953 in response to the law. In some instances, invaders simply occupied land already denounced under the law and slated to be distributed. In many cases, however, they forcibly occupied land not affected under the terms of the law. Many people blamed peasant league and workers' federation organizers for the invasions, with some justification. Pellecer admitted to fostering invasions, and Arbenz subsequently blamed him for much of the rural unrest. Persistent rumors that the expropriation of some of Arbenz's property had been preceded by an invasion of his land served to confirm suspicions that the government had lost control of the countryside and that the communists were prepared to take over.[63]

Much of the alarm over the unrest in the countryside was couched in terms of ethnic conflict. The revolutionary organizations consciously sought to play down the importance of ethnic differences and distinctions in their correspondence and publications during the last few years of the revolution.[64] Nevertheless, many others continued to see the conflict in ethnic terms. The Canadian trade commissioner described the law as Arbenz "giving Guatemala back to the Indians." *El Imparcial* once again trotted out the specter of an Indian uprising, suggesting that the rural activists had unleashed a force that would take on a life of its own and "nobody knows where it will end." U.S. embassy officials observed the extent of this fear as well; one remarked, "If there is one thing the wealthy Guatemalan fears it is an Indian uprising. Nothing could be better calculated to bring this about than a fight on the question of agrarian reform once promised to them." Observers in the State Department went on to suggest the tension might "prove too hot for Arbenz to handle." The *Tribuna popular*'s attempt to link this struggle for land with an Indian uprising in Totonicapán in the early nineteenth century did little to calm these fears.[65]

While it is clear that a number of peasant invasions occurred in 1953 and 1954, it is difficult to distinguish between invasions and peasant occupations of land taken under the reform but opposed by the landowners. The expropriation of land from the finca of María Nieves Leal in Malacatán, San Marcos, is illustrative. The property contained thirty-nine caballerías, used primarily to graze a few head of cattle. The peasant union in the municipality, led by Florencio Bamac Gómez, denounced the property in the name of more than eighty peasants in the surrounding aldeas. The CAN ordered nine caballerías, forty-two manzanas, taken. The peasants appealed this decision, according to their right under the law, and on review, Arbenz ordered almost twenty-three caballerías expropriated. In testimony to the new agrarian officials after the "Liberation," the owner indicated that she believed nine caballerías had been legally expropriated but that peasants from the area "led by communist elements" invaded the rest of the twenty-three caballerías. Her testimony coincides with the general impression that was fostered in Guatemala — and repeated in later studies of the agrarian reform — of widespread peasant invasions. But Bamac and the others argued that they believed they were acting in accordance with the decision of the agrarian officials and settled down peaceably to farm their new property. It is not clear whether this was a genuine case of confusion on the part of the landlord, a peasant invasion subsequently given legitimacy by Arbenz, or another attempt to exaggerate the state of unrest in the countryside. Numerous similar cases make it difficult to determine with any accuracy the level of unrest in rural Guatemala during the application of the agrarian reform; however, they certainly heightened concern over the law in various sectors of Guatemalan society.[66]

Despite the condemnations leveled at Pellecer and others, many of the invasions were not prompted by national peasant organizers. Most of the invasions occurred in the early months of 1953 and 1954, at a time when peasants needed to obtain land to prepare it for seeding in the coming months. In both years all the organizations active in the agrarian reform put increasing pressure on the DAN and the government in January to speed the distribution of land. "Land in this month" was a rallying cry. It was partly this pressure that prompted Arbenz to begin the distribution of expropriations from private fincas and to announce that numerous national fincas were to be divided in January 1953.[67]

Despite the rapid alteration in land tenure caused by the agrarian reform, there were constant complaints to the DAN, the CGTG, and the CNCG that the distribution of land was taking too long. Some unions and sindicatos demanded to know why no action had been taken on petitions for land almost two years after they had been made. There were continual charges that local CALs, departmental governors, and even CNCG and CGTG representatives were sabotaging efforts to get land. The lack of action demoralized local unions and caused many to break up despite the best efforts of CNCG and CGTG organizers, who frantically tried to hold them together. Many CNCG and CGTG members in the countryside were in dire circumstances. Thrown off land they had rented or sharecropped for many years because of their involvement with the revolutionary organizations or because of the government's emphasis on eliminating such "feudal" practices, they were left with little or no means of gaining a livelihood and watched the planting season slowly pass by yet another year.[68]

Although there is little in the records of the major revolutionary organizations to indicate that they actively encouraged land invasions, no doubt certain individuals did. A cadre of people in the Communist Party and the CGTG briefly believed they could provoke unrest in the countryside to bring on increased class conflict and thus inspire a more "radical" bent to the revolution.[69] Just as important, perhaps, leaders of the various revolutionary organizations led the rural poor to expect too much from the agrarian reform. Gutiérrez was particularly guilty of this.[70] This partly explains why even after expropriations occurred peasants and workers expressed discontent with the amount of land given to them. Nonetheless, most of the correspondence from the CGTG and the CNCG to their local affiliates attempted to explain the legal provisions of the law and to detail how their members could apply for land under it. Most of the land invasions were the result of local initiatives; the national organizations were usually informed only after they had taken place. Gutiérrez and Castillo Flores often admonished local affiliates who had taken part in such invasions for acting outside the law.[71]

The rural workers' union and the peasant league trod a thin line between encouraging rural organization and controlling local affiliates that were chafing at the bit and demanding land they had been promised for years. These local affiliates had, throughout the revolution, proven themselves to be notably independent, rejecting organizers sent by the national office, not supporting candidates for local and national office backed by their federations, and continually refusing to pay their dues until they saw action on their behalf. From 1952 to 1954, once it became apparent that the sympathetic national government was not going to react vigorously against them, local peasant organizations led assaults on land they had coveted for generations. They needed little prompting from the CNCG and the CGTG.[72]

The reason for some of the invasions accompanying the agrarian reform can be traced to decree 900 itself. While many peasants and workers in the western highlands had been led to expect substantial changes with the agrarian reform, the amount of land in those departments subject to expropriation under the law was extremely limited. Decree 900 was interpreted by many in these regions to mean that finca land, often previously part of the patrimony of the community, would be divided among them despite the provisions of the law or the size of the fincas. The law itself did not provide

TABLE 4. LARGE ESTATES AND PERCENTAGE OF COUNTRY'S TOTAL RURAL
POPULATION BY DEPARTMENT

Department	Size (in caballerías)					% of rural population
	1–10	10–20	20–50	50–100	100+	
Alta Verapaz	267	58	53	16	17	8.4
Baja Verapaz	373	13	20	7	0	2.9
Chimaltenango*	237	32	11	1	0	3.8
Chiquimula	271	8	1	0	0	4.8
El Progreso	323	17	1	3	0	1.9
El Quiché*	342	22	20	9	0	7.6
Escuintla	315	65	50	25	9	4.6
Guatemala	536	35	14	5	0	5.7
Huehuetenango*	529	28	25	6	2	8.9
Izabal	39	7	12	4	8	1.6
Jalapa	363	15	13	0	0	2.9
Jutiapa	621	30	10	1	1	6.0
Quezaltenango*	258	25	17	6	0	6.7
Retalhuleu	137	23	23	7	4	2.5
Sacatepéquez*	52	8	2	0	0	1.0
San Marcos*	404	34	11	1	2	10.4
Santa Rosa	614	52	34	5	6	4.6
Sololá*	46	5	2	0	0	3.1
Suchitepéquez	334	60	28	4	3	4.9
Totonicapán*	10	0	0	0	0	3.9
Zacapa	396	28	11	4	0	2.8

Sources: *Censo agropecuario, 1950* (1954), 1:2–24; *Sexto censo de población, 1950* (1957), 23.
Note: El Petén had no estates larger than 1 caballería included in the census.
*Departments in which all or some of the territory is considered to be part of the highlands.

adequate mechanisms for transferring land held in large estates in the less-populated lowlands to peasants and rural workers who lived in the crowded western highlands.

"Not a Single Step Backward"

The question remains: why did Arbenz not take a tougher stand against the invasions, force the rural organizations to curtail the activities of their local affiliates, and/or allow the army to move in as it had done under Arévalo in the face of unrest in the 1940s? There is no simple answer. Martínez clearly tried to impose order in rural areas on a number of occasions. During the land invasions in January 1953, he publicly demanded that the invasions stop. This declaration was soon followed by rumors that he would be forced to resign from his post. After a series of land invasions in January 1954, he went to Escuintla for what many considered to be a showdown between Pellecer and himself. Much was made of the fact that Martínez left the country shortly afterward. It was generally thought that Arbenz had once again failed to support him in the confrontation and that Martínez's departure would lead to even greater concessions to communists and increased unrest in the countryside.[73] Martínez declared that he was going to Switzerland for a heart treatment and vowed that there had been no disagreement between himself and Arbenz, who did not seem overly concerned about the invasions. Others have claimed Martínez left to arrange the sale of arms later transported to Guatemala on the Swedish ship, the *Alfhem*. The U.S. embassy's explanation was that Arbenz had been completely won over by the communists.[74]

A more likely explanation for Arbenz's actions is more complicated. Arbenz's vow before 35,000 supporters in February 1953 that "whatever comes to pass, whatever it costs, . . . we will complete the application of the agrarian reform" became a slogan employed by many government figures and activists to end speeches.[75] In 1954, in the face of increasing calls to curtail radical reforms and move against the communists, the slogan became, "Not a single step backward." Arbenz clearly believed that, while there were some excesses accompanying the application of the law, the basic purpose of decree 900 was being achieved. To congress, he suggested that the "line in the sand" he had mentioned a year earlier had deepened and had more firmly divided the two sides. He warned that lately many reactionaries had "struck their breasts and declared they were with the agrarian reform, but 'with strict adhesion to the law' without radicalism and communist extremism. . . . These words really disguise a new position toward the agrarian reform: that it be as superficial as possible." Arbenz was determined that the reform would substantially alter landownership and agricultural production. In addition, he felt little threat from the communists and the rural unrest, believing that he could control the latter whenever he wished. With the army firmly behind him — as Arbenz and most knowledgeable observers believed — the greater danger to the revolution stemmed from violent conservative reaction and the invasion force being prepared in Honduras. There appeared to be little to gain and much to lose from a too precipitous restriction of rural organization.[76]

Nevertheless, there were indications that by the spring of 1954 Arbenz had decided to act firmly against the land invasions. Following the death of two landowners in Escuintla, he ordered an extensive investigation of the violence. His 1954 May Day speech warned against sectarian application of the Agrarian Reform Law and called for the law to be applied correctly. Martínez, upon his return to the country, declared that the law was to be applied properly and that the invasions would stop. Arbenz, like the CNCG and the CGTG, was determined to strike a balance between encouraging a true transformation of land tenure in the country and controlling unrest. Although there was a somewhat greater level of unrest than he had expected, the agrarian reform was doing exactly what Arbenz had hoped it would do and with quite remarkable alacrity. The basis of economic, social, and political power in the country was being altered in the space of a few years. Before Arbenz and Martínez could effectively quell some of the unrest associated with that transformation, however, they were confronted by an armed invasion from Honduras and an army mutiny that brought the revolution to an end.[77]

CLASS, ETHNICITY, POLITICS, AND THE AGRARIAN REFORM

You had better guard your ranks to insure
you don't let the venom of politics enter.
It in no way can resolve the problems
of the workers of the field.

—Leonardo Castillo Flores to

a local unión campesina, 1952

I n his address to congress in 1953, President Arbenz remarked that the agrarian reform had caused an "earthquake in the consciousness" of Guatemalans.[1] It was an apt description. The application of the Agrarian Reform Law prompted bitter conflict in many sectors of Guatemalan society. The most important of these was a struggle between landlords and peasant activists. To a certain extent, however, the Arbenz administration and the revolutionary forces that supported it had been prepared for this type of confrontation. Had this been the only source of unrest in rural Guatemala, the government may well have been able to ride out the storm, anchored as it was by widespread worker and peasant organization and the continuing support of much of the urban middle class.

However, many other sources of conflict emerged in rural areas during the revolution, some of them quite unexpected. Rural Guatemala was knit together by a complex interlacing of jealousies and feuds that lurked beneath the surface, at times strengthening, at other times deflating, the overriding class and ethnic divisions. The competing revolutionary organizations, intent on winning converts among the rural poor or imposing their own view of a redrawn rural landscape, often fastened themselves to these existing disputes. The result was a rural society seething with conflict — conflict the revolutionary organizations had trouble understanding and often unwittingly contributed to, and conflict that made it increasingly difficult to implement reform legislation in the countryside.

Caudillos, Factionalism, and the Revolutionary Organizations

Rural communities in Guatemala, often somewhat isolated and insular, were especially fertile ground for the growth of antagonistic cliques. Both Indian and Ladino communities were riddled with factions that battled each other through access to secular, religious, and supernatural authorities. These disputes were often the result of very real class and ethnic differences. Conflict often had a geographic or "community" basis as various entities (cantones or aldeas) within a municipality claimed competing loyalties. Feuds were often clan or family based, a division that in some villages could encompass much of the community. Factionalism was also more personal and grew around the activities of embryonic local caudillos. As many people began to struggle for power in new ways, using new institutions, during the revolution, conflict among these local bosses became more intense and more divisive.

The competing ambitions of local caudillos often tore apart peasant unions and political parties. A battle between the PRG organizer in the department of Jalapa, Daniel Vanegas, and the secretary-general of the local unión campesina and alcalde of Monjas, Jalapa, was particularly disruptive. The battle raged for the better part of two years and prevented any serious peasant organization from occurring in the region. The alcalde's apparently single-minded pursuit of power proved to Vanegas at least "the difficulty of working with peasant leaders." But Vanegas was not blameless.[2]

In Tucurú, Alta Verapaz, two native leaders fought a vicious battle for control of the peasant union. According to the alcalde, the feud engulfed the whole municipality, and the peasant organization was torn apart by it. The tattered remnants of the union only began to stitch themselves back together after the two protagonists were forced to take the conflict to the governor of the department to be arbitrated.[3]

One of the most serious such conflicts occurred in San Pedro Yepocapa, Chimaltenango. Two peasant leaders, Natzul Aguirre Cook and José Villatoro, fought for control of the local government and the peasant league using every tool at their disposal, including the agrarian agencies after the passage of decree 900. The struggle finally led to a violent clash involving more than 800 combatants when two competing peasant unions met to elect members for the CAL. While the communist newspaper, *Tribuna popular*, suggested that the struggle occurred because Villatoro was in the pocket of the "terratenientes" and was persecuting those intent on implementing the Agrarian Reform Law, other reports from the municipality indicated a fierce personal antagonism between the two that, at least, deepened the conflict.[4]

During the revolution, the municipio of Cantel was torn apart by rival political parties and revolutionary organizations. The local social structure was complicated by the existence of a large textile factory established in the late nineteenth century that employed 900 of the 8,000 people in the municipality. While the conflicts among the PRG, the PAR, a local comunidad campesina, and the workers' union at the factory were shaped partly by differing economic interests, neighborhood loyalties, and religious affiliation, personal connections determined the degree of success in the municipal power struggle. Revolutionary parties controlled the local government throughout the decade, and they were buttressed by active revolutionary organizations on the local level. But largely because of the intense factional disputes in the municipality, little progress was made toward reform during the decade.[5]

The type of caudillismo apparent in Monjas, Tucurú, San Pedro Yepocapa, and Cantel helped foster conflict between alcaldes and revolutionary organizations throughout Guatemala, a struggle that became increasingly apparent after the passage of the Agrarian Reform Law. Alcaldes in every department of the country were accused of being "antiagraristas" and of persecuting peasants between 1952 and 1954. Alcalde opposition to the agrarian reform often reflected deep-seated class or ethnic divisions within the municipality. But it also, at times, apparently had little to do with these underlying differences. In many municipalities, alcaldes were elected as champions of peasant interests but soon turned on their followers. The case of Gregorio Bajxac, the alcalde of San Martín Jilotepeque, Chimaltenango, who was elected with the assistance of the unión campesina and then began to persecute its members mercilessly (if we are to believe the reports of the CNCG), was a famous example. Native peasant leaders from all over the country, looking for CNCG support for their political ambitions, felt compelled to promise that they were "no Gregorio Bajxac" in correspondence with the peasant league.[6]

Gregorio Bajxac joined the company of the alcalde of La Democracia, Huehuetenango, in the collective memory of the CNCG. In La Democracia the alcalde, voted in with the support of the peasant union, increasingly opposed its attempts to get land under the Agrarian Reform Law. The growing conflict exploded in late October 1952 when the drunk alcalde encountered some members of the peasant organization celebrating a fiesta in the village cemetery. According to the union members, the alcalde shot and seriously wounded one of them and had the rest imprisoned. They were whipped to the accompanying cry, "Kill those communist thieves." The peasants blamed four teachers in the village for provoking the alcalde into making the attack.[7]

The problem with alcaldes was a serious concern for the CNCG, one they could not completely understand. After some study, Clodoveo Torres Moss, the secretary of organization of the CNCG, presented a long assessment of the reasons for these problems in an internal memorandum in 1952. He felt it was "apparently incredible that the alcaldes, men lifted to their posts by the vote of the peasants, forgot them to the point of denying them that which they solicit within the law." Torres Moss argued that the problem resulted primarily from trusting old caciques who treated the peasants "like sheep when the elections were near to gain these posts and from there legalize exploitation." Once in power, these caciques joined with the terratenientes in abusing the peasants. Although this assessment accurately described the situation in some municipalities, it reflects an incomplete understanding of the complexity of issues and alliances in rural Guatemala. More than anything else, it indicates the level of confusion apparent within the CNCG as it saw local affiliates torn apart by factional politics.[8]

Political parties and revolutionary organizations that were able to cooperate at the national level were often locked in bitter conflict in rural Guatemala as their local affiliates reflected various sides of local disputes. The peasant league and the workers' federation usually supported different revolutionary parties in municipal and congressional elections and were dragged, unwillingly, into political squabbles that helped disrupt their activities and weakened them substantially. This type of internecine conflict among the revolutionary stalwarts was clearly demonstrated in the strange triangle that developed among the CNCG, the PAR, and the PRG.

The national directors of the CNCG argued strenuously after its creation that it was not to be used as a political instrument. This proved to be an unrealistic stand considering the highly charged political atmosphere in Guatemala during the 1950s. The CNCG, primarily through three of its directors — Leonardo Castillo Flores, Clodoveo Torres Moss, and Amor Velasco — was an important part of the Socialist Party after it was formed by Augusto Charnaud MacDonald in 1951. Following the inauguration of the party, Castillo Flores and the others applied pressure on local peasant league affiliates to form Socialist Party branches in their communities. There was much opposition to this campaign; many union members refused to join the Socialists and even quit the peasant league to remain with the PAR. Nevertheless, it was due mostly to the efforts of Castillo Flores and the CNCG that the Socialist Party spread so quickly in rural Guatemala.[9]

In 1952, the Socialist Party, the PAR, and the RN joined to form the PRG. When the PRG began to unravel later that year, it occasioned more conflict within the CNCG affiliates. Castillo Flores briefly remained with the PRG but declared that the peasant league would be revolutionary but apolitical. Castillo Flores and most of the directors, with the notable exception of Amor Velasco, soon abandoned the PRG and rejoined the PAR. This caused some concern that the peasant league would be turned into a PAR tool.[10]

Despite these misgivings, Castillo Flores, for the most part, attempted to steer the CNCG along a nonpartisan line while at the same time he held a position on the national executive of the PAR. Most directors of the peasant league followed this potentially confusing course, continually warning local unions not to "carry politics into the union." On one occasion Clodoveo Torres Moss, the secretary of organization of the CNCG and a member of the national executive of the PAR, instructed a local peasant leader, "The unión campesina is an organization of workers of the field for the defense of their interests, for the study and resolution of their economic and social problems. The unión campesina is not a POLITICAL PARTY and . . . we must be careful not to bring politics into it."[11] On another occasion Castillo Flores warned the secretary-general of the local union in a small town in Baja Verapaz about the activities of politicians: "The visits that politicians are constantly making to you are for no other reason than to take advantage of the votes of the compañeros to get to Congress. It is not important to them that the peasants are suffering misery and imprisonment. Well, you had better guard your ranks to insure you don't let the venom of politics enter. It in no way can resolve the problems of the workers of the field."[12] The local affiliates most often agreed. On a number of occasions, local unions forced members from their ranks because of their politically partisan activities, and many of their letters to Castillo Flores emphasized their intention to keep political discord out of the associations.[13]

Nevertheless, some of the most bitter conflicts within the peasant league were the result of the political activities of its members. This occurred both on the local and national level. One of the most interesting disputes was with Daniel Vanegas in the department of Jalapa; it clearly illustrates both the political and personal dimensions of much of the conflict. Vanegas was a close friend of Charnaud and had been sent to Jalapa first as an agent for the Treasury Ministry when Charnaud directed that department. He was, naturally, also an organizer for Charnaud's Socialist Party and later for the PRG. In addition, Vanegas was involved with the CNCG and in 1952 began a campaign to link the peasant unions in the department to the PRG. Given the uncertainty of the CNCG's political affiliation at that time, Vanegas's activities prompted much criticism both from local unions and the national executive of the peasant league.

The issue reached a climax in late June and early July 1952. One union, in response to Vanegas's entreaties, bluntly informed him that it had no intention of joining a political party because Castillo Flores "has told us as organized peasants we must be apolitical." Vanegas took up the issue with Castillo Flores, arguing, "It is indispensable that they . . . take an interest in politics to protect their conquests as an apolitical entity." The CNCG executive refused to budge on the issue, but Vanegas also refused to curtail his political activities. He entered into a very public debate with Castillo Flores and was disowned by the peasant league. He was later accused of trying to organize rival peasant unions in the department. His activities plunged the peasant league in the district into a prolonged period of discord.[14]

Amor Velasco, one of the few CNCG executive members to stay with the PRG after the others rejoined the PAR, was also eventually expelled from the peasant league, ostensibly for his insistence on proselytizing for the party. Castillo Flores's explanation to the local unions for the expulsion was that "we are in a time of cleansing our movement and are not going to permit anyone to tarnish our peasant struggle with politics." Velasco's expulsion was a serious setback for the CNCG as he was a popular, experienced peasant organizer and, at one time, second only to Castillo Flores in power. His removal had much to do with the growing political rift between him and the other members of the peasant league and Castillo Flores's jealousy of potential rivals in the CNCG.[15]

Given the highly politicized nature of the issues affecting the peasantry, however, it became readily apparent that Vanegas had been essentially correct. Local government had too much power for the CNCG to remain indifferent to the outcome of local political contests. Castillo Flores was flooded with requests from local unions for guidance concerning which candidates they should vote for or how they should go about getting rid of unsympathetic alcaldes. The numerous alcaldes who were both leaders of peasant unions and secretaries-general of local party organizations reveal the intimate connection between peasant organization and local politics.

Realizing his original position was unrealistic, Castillo Flores adopted a different tack. Despite his position within the PAR, he encouraged the peasant unions to support those candidates who the members felt best represented their interests, no matter their political affiliation (as long as it was "revolutionary"). A pattern evolved nationally in which peasant unions usually supported PRG candidates in the Oriente and PAR candidates in much of the rest of the country. However, all sorts of local anomalies developed, with unions supporting RN and Communist Party candidates in many communities as well.[16]

This diversity suggests that there was a certain degree of local autonomy. Peasant unions increasingly became essentially local organizations with deep roots in the community, primarily intent on resolving local conflicts. They readily used this strong local organization to attempt to influence the national policies of the CNCG and even, on occasion, to oppose decisions made by the national executive. This was most clearly seen in the naming of peasant league representatives to agrarian agencies at the various levels after the passage of decree 900. Local peasant league affiliates insisted on representatives they trusted, and when they were able to join with neighboring affiliates and present a united front, they had substantial influence over the choice of representatives.[17]

As local unions began to develop more confidence in their own political judgment, they occasionally used the offices of the CNCG to gain more control locally over the political parties to which they belonged. On occasion, local party affiliates appealed to the CNCG for support in opposing the national executive of one of the revolutionary parties. For example, most of the members of the local PAR affiliate in Quiriguá were also members of the peasant league. When told that representatives of the national executive of the party were coming to organize candidates for the coming municipal elections, they complained to Castillo Flores that the executive had previously picked men who had "demoralized" them. They declared, "What we want is that the party be left in the hands of the peasantry, because that is the only way we can effectively carry out our revolutionary struggle." This was an argument that appealed to Castillo Flores, and he helped put pressure on the PAR executive to allow the local affiliate more say in the choice of candidates.[18]

Peasant unions also used the CNCG to oppose decisions made by the national executives of parties concerning candidates for congress. When the national executive of the PRG asked the members of the unión campesina in Chichicastenango to support José Francisco Silva Falla in the elections for deputies from the department, the peasant members of the PRG turned to the CNCG. They asked the CNCG to convince the party to "retire" Silva Falla because he was a traitor to the peasantry and because "all the Quiché hate him" and "consider him a political cadaver." They went on to suggest a native from San Juan Chajul for the position.[19]

Despite the cautious stance of the CNCG executive concerning political partisanship, this local independence was one factor that helped foster a series of conflicts in rural areas between the PAR, the PRG, and the CNCG. Castillo Flores's constant warnings to the political parties that it was "the peasant compañeros who suffer the consequences of the disorientation" caused by these internecine struggles had little effect. The conflicts grew in intensity with the application of the Agrarian Reform Law.[20]

The most common complaint was that the party controlling agrarian agencies at the departmental or local level favored party cohorts in the distribution of land taken through decree 900. In the municipio of El Quetzal, San Marcos, the secretary-general of the local peasant union complained to Castillo Flores about the activities of the CAD inspector, Oscar Bautista González. Bautista was in the region to explain the provisions of the Agrarian Reform Law and to coach peasants on how to denounce land under the law. But as a loyal member of the PAR, he refused to come to El Quetzal, where most of the peasants were members of the PRG. Instead, he explained the law to PAR-affiliated peasants in a neighboring municipality who then denounced a finca in El Quetzal. The PRG-affiliated peasants of El Quetzal had already begun proceedings against the finca and complained that Bautista "wants to disorganize us with the goal of taking from us the land we have already denounced to divide among strangers."[21]

The PRG in Escuintla also charged that Carlos Manuel Pellecer, in cahoots with the agrarian inspector of the department, insured that land from the finca San Sebastion Buena Vista was given only to PAR members of the workers' union, while other resident workers were ignored. Pellecer denied the charges, claiming instead that he had met with all the resident workers but that many, disoriented by the PRG, which was "antiagrarista," had refused to accept any land. The PRG's response was that it was not at all against land distribution but simply wanted to see the land distributed more equitably, without political partisanship.[22]

As these examples indicate, the PRG regularly complained about political sectarianism in many aspects of the application of decree 900. This extended to the organization of the DAN. On one occasion after the PRG-PAR split, the PRG asserted that all its party members who had been working for the DAN in the departments of Chiquimula, Zacapa, El Progreso, and San Marcos were being fired. It warned that this kind of political warfare was a serious threat to the revolution. Pointing to Castillo Flores's hand in the dismissals, the PRG suggested that his involvement was particularly disturbing because "we are so tired of reading his declarations concerning the apolitical nature of the CNCG."[23]

PAR members had their own criticisms, however. They complained that the PRG had control of the National Agrarian Bank in many areas and gave money solely to party cohorts. They also suggested that many of the PRG workers in the bank lacked revolutionary zeal and were only after the impressive salaries they collected. PAR members especially criticized the bank's "enormous bureaucracy that in a short time will swallow all the funds dedicated to national liberation and the effective completion of the agrarian reform."[24]

These periodic skirmishes between nationally allied political parties and organizations were terribly disruptive. Instead of working to reduce unproductive conflict in rural areas and concentrating their forces on the application of decree 900, the revolutionary parties heightened tension through the sectarian application of the law. Therefore, they often failed to unite in combating the very real opposition that agrarian change faced in many parts of Guatemala.

Workers and Peasants

One other source of tension not foreseen by the revolutionary activists developed along with the realignment of land tenure begun by decree 900: disputes between finca workers and peasants from neighboring communities over land. It was a conflict that often tore revolutionary organizations apart and befuddled agrarian agency administrators.

Despite the initial bitterness between the CNCG and the CGTG, the two national organizations, one representing peasants and the other workers, were able to cooperate effectively on most issues. This cooperation was made easier by the sincerity of the two leaders, Leonardo Castillo Flores and Víctor Manuel Gutiérrez, in their approach to peasant and worker concerns. It was also assisted by Castillo Flores's decision to sever his close connection to Augusto Charnaud MacDonald. An essential component of the relationship between the two federations was that they agreed not to compete for adherents in areas already organized by one of the federations. Gutiérrez and CGTG representatives were invited to most of the peasant league's public meetings, and the same courtesy was extended by the workers' federation. When the CGTG decided to send representatives to the World Federation of Trade Unions meeting in Vienna, it invited peasant league members along. Both leaders repeatedly stressed the "fraternal alliance of Guatemalan workers and peasants."[25]

Conflict soon developed in rural areas, however. There were regular complaints that one organization was infringing on territory staked out by the other. In particular, the CGTG was worried about the number of members leaving its ranks to join the peasant league. As more people received land through the agrarian reform, former members of the CGTG flocked to the peasant league banner. As the leader of the CGTG sindicato in San Martín Jilotepeque informed Gutiérrez, "Because we are campesinos we must affiliate with the Confederación Nacional Campesina."[26]

As the situation in San Martín Jilotepeque, which had much to do with the aggressive actions of the local unión campesina leader, Genaro Julian Reyes, illustrated, conflict between the two organizations was often the result of overexuberant efforts at recruitment by local organizers. The two national organizations did their best to dampen these tensions. On a number of occasions, local peasant unions, upset for a variety of reasons at the CNCG, requested affiliation with the workers' federation. Gutiérrez invariably replied that "fraternal considerations" prevented him from allowing the transfer of allegiance but passed on their complaints to the CNCG. Similarly, Castillo Flores was constantly assuring Gutiérrez that the CNCG was not proselytizing among CGTG parishioners.[27]

The strain of maintaining effective cooperation showed most clearly in the application of the Agrarian Reform Law. Workers on the national fincas were the greatest strength of the CGTG in rural areas. The Agrarian Reform Law threatened to turn these workers into landowners (or at least farm operators), making the peasant league more appealing to them. It was partly this concern that prompted the workers' federation to champion the idea of cooperatives on the national fincas. However, these workers, finally presented with the opportunity to control land of their own, were unsympathetic to the idea of full-producer cooperatives. Only 9 were established out of the 110 national fincas.

Even in the fincas where cooperatives were established, many workers refused to join, instead demanding land of their own. *Co-operativistas* and *parcelarios* on these fincas often clashed. Tension was most apparent when the division of land and equipment from the national fincas was being decided, when costs for the maintenance of roads and schools were allocated, and when the parcelarios organized peasant unions following the division of land. Very often the two groups allied with different political parties as well. Despite attempts by the *Tribuna popular* to paint glowing pictures of the success of the cooperatives, requests flooded in from cooperativistas who had changed their minds and wanted individual parcels of land. Occasionally these changes of heart were greeted with threats of violence from the sindicato leaders.[28]

The most serious conflict between peasants and workers occurred as a result of competition for land under decree 900. The Agrarian Reform Law gave preference in the division of land to resident workers and those who rented land on fincas. It was only after they had received certain minimum amounts of land that peasants from neighboring communities could receive a share. This appeared grievously unfair to many peasants since often fincas had been carved out of community land in the first place. In most highland departments, there was only enough expropriated property for the resident workers. In addition, in many areas the redistribution of land on the fincas reduced the opportunity for occasional labor that had been available to some peasants from communities near the estate. In these cases, peasants viewed the good fortune of the finca laborers with increasing resentment as it became clear that they were not going to benefit from expropriations in their vicinity.

The provisions for CGTG and CNCG representation on the CALs fostered competition between the two for control of these important local institutions. Despite continual calls from Castillo Flores and Gutiérrez for cooperation, tension continued to build. Rivers of paper flowed between the two federations, and convoys of joint commissions crisscrossed the country trying to resolve the various disputes engendered by the formation and decisions of the local committees.[29]

A few examples will illustrate more clearly the varieties of conflict that developed between the two groups. In San Marcos, 99 resident workers of the finca El Naranjo denounced the finca and were initially awarded 200 *cuerdas* (one cuerda was approximately .3 acres, although in practice the size varied somewhat throughout Guatemala) by the CAD. However, the inspector for the DAN brought 315 peasants from two uniones campesinas in two aldeas of neighboring Tajumulco onto the expropriated finca. The amount of land given the workers was reduced to 88 cuerdas. Each worker still received more than three times the amount of land given each peasant. Nonetheless, the workers of El Naranjo were not pleased with the decision of the DAN and continued to petition for the return of the initial grant until the end of the revolution.[30]

The records of expropriations on numerous other fincas document that preferential treatment was given to workers and that they were granted land allotments many times the size of those given peasants from neighboring communities. Nonetheless, workers often expressed grave concerns about whether their rights to land had been upheld or lodged complaints about their treatment under the law. When the finca Rabinala was denounced in June 1953 by peasants from the neighboring municipality of Cubulco in Baja Verapaz, workers on the finca were concerned. In a petition expressing their alarm, 67 mozos colonos on the finca protested to the CAN, saying: "We are aware that the denunciantes are trying to have the major part of the finca given out to them in lifelong usufruct. This would cause severe harm to us and the other residents of the finca. Because we are 'criollos' and natives of this place, with cultivations for many years, we have more right than the denunciantes who are only seeking to appropriate for themselves our cultivations and long and constant efforts." The petition went on to complain that those who denounced the finca already owned plots of land and lived thirty kilometers from the finca. In this case, the CAN met many of their concerns, dividing the 15 caballerías that were expropriated among the mozos colonos, renters on the finca, and those who had denounced the finca. It also insured that the workers' homes and gardens, which had been left out of the original expropriation, were given to the workers as private property.[31]

In the national finca Bárcenas in the department of Santa Rosa, finca workers protested that much of the land was given to neighboring peasants. An inspector for the DAN visited the finca and ruled on behalf of the workers, declaring that the peasants now located on the finca would be removed. While the reaction of the peasants who had been given land and then deprived of it was not recorded, it can be imagined.[32]

The division of the finca Westphalia in Baja Verapaz involved even more complexity. During the initial expropriation, the finca was divided between resident workers and peasants from the neighboring village at a natural geographic boundary: the Polochic River. However, the U.S. owner of the finca had also owned a farm in Alta Verapaz. Workers from this farm had been accustomed to traveling to Westphalia every year to plant corn. With the expropriation, the land these workers had farmed was given to the peasants in the union. While no violence among the various competing sides was reported, the expectation of problems was apparent in the decision to send a delegation to the workers in Alta Verapaz to inform them "peaceably" of the decision.[33]

From the perspective of peasants struggling to get access to land in the often crowded highlands, many of the decisions of the DAN favoring workers seemed unfair. Sometimes even the *Tribuna popular*, which was closely linked to the workers' federation and suspicious of the peasant league, agreed. In September 1953, it ran a story on the village of San Miguel Dueñas detailing the village's struggle to reclaim land that had been taken from it in 1722. Its last attempt to acquire the land in 1936 failed when President Ubico ruled in favor of the "owner," Salvador Falla Santos. In December 1952 the finca was denounced under decree 900. Twelve caballerías and fifty-three manzanas were expropriated and distributed to resident workers. As the newspaper pointed out, however, justice had still not been served since the 417 peasants of the comunidad agraria campesina of San Miguel, who had also petitioned for the land, were no better off. They asked Arbenz to reverse the DAN decision, pleading, "We have documents that prove our ancestral right over these lands and therefore we are asking President Arbenz, in order to do justice, to return these lands, finally, to us. We are 417 peasants who need these lands that have always been ours."[34]

In many places there was an attempt to combat the built-in bias of the agrarian reform by rushing to denounce land. There was a tendency to favor those who had made the earliest denunciation in the subsequent allocation of land, despite provisions of the law. It was this competition, as much as any factor, that led to the land invasions beginning in January 1953.

The most common complaint in this struggle between workers and peasants was that one side or the other had stacked the CAL, which was thus making biased decisions. There were also complaints, but little evidence, that Castillo Flores had bribed agrarian committees to favor the peasant unions.[35]

Other groups used more ingenious means. The case of the finca Santa Rosa Caníbal near Cuilco, Huehuetenango, became quite complex. It also demonstrated how quickly some groups learned to use the various and often conflicting entities established by the revolutionary governments in rural areas to oppose the extension of the Agrarian Reform Law. In this instance, the owner of the finca, Dolores Laparra de Barrios, had arranged to sell it to a small group of workers on the finca to avoid expropriation. To try to get around the provision of the law restricting the sale of land after 7 May 1952, these few workers — perhaps no more than three families — registered themselves officially as a *comunidad agraria* (a term often applied in correspondence to comunidades campesinas or comunidades indígenas). The law allowing for the establishment of such comunidades, for very different reasons, had been passed during the Arévalo administration (see chapter 6). Their ploy appeared to work and the CAD accepted the sale and declared the finca unaffected by decree 900. The local alcalde strenuously protested this action to Castillo Flores, but since the DAN had accepted the sale, he was unable to suggest any means by which the peasant union could get part of the land.[36]

However, peasants and workers interested in getting part of the finca were not easily dissuaded. The finca was denounced by three different groups: the other workers on the finca, a peasant union from the neighboring San José Ojetenán, and a union from the aldea of Sajquim in the municipality of Tacaná, San Marcos. The workers were particularly anxious to denounce the finca because after the sale of the land, the new owners were intent on forcing them from the finca. Their anger is apparent in a letter to the DAN stating: "It is not possible that more than forty-eight families will be thrown in the streets, suffering from the depravity of a bad patrón. After having served her all my life, a life we have lived miserably, she wants now to evict us. . . . I hope the Agrarian Reform Law will be a reality in our case. . . . We want to live freely and not as we are under the talons of the patrón." Eventually, the CAN ordered forty of the forty-six caballerías in the finca expropriated. After much deliberation and many petitions, it was decided that the 140 mozos colonos would be accommodated before peasants from either of the peasant unions. More conflict developed between workers and peasants after the overthrow of Arbenz when the land was returned to the few families of the comunidad agraria of Caníbal. They insisted that the new government remove the parcelarios, who were to be resettled on land from the ejido of Cuilco, prompting a new set of disputes between the workers and the neighboring peasants.[37]

The case of Caníbal illustrates another cause of tension in the implementation of decree 900, one inherent in the structure of the law, which called for expropriations to be initiated from below. Most fincas subject to expropriation under the law were denounced by more than one group of potential beneficiaries. Not only did workers and peasants struggle for the same land, but peasant unions from various locales also petitioned for land from the same fincas. This did not always lead to conflict. In the case of the finca San José Calderas in San Andrés Itzapa, Chimaltenango, the mozos colonos on the finca and peasants from the municipality who were also temporary workers on the finca, each of the two groups having organized a different unión campesina, cooperated in sending one denunciation of the finca to the CAL to insure that there would be no problems in the expropriation.[38] This was, however, an exceptional case. In most instances, substantial conflict accompanied the competing claims for land.

One of the major problems in insuring equitable distribution of land was that the bulk of the land subject to expropriation was in the Pacific piedmont, the Pacific and Atlantic lowlands, and Alta Verapaz, while the majority of the rural population lived in the western highlands. Much of Castillo Flores's energy was spent trying to arrange for land in the lowlands for peasant unions from villages in the highlands. This often prompted opposition from workers on lowland fincas. The concern this caused on both sides was demonstrated in numerous letters to the CNCG.

The unión campesina from the municipality of Tacaná in the *zona fría*, or highland region, of San Marcos wrote Amor Velasco in August 1952 inquiring about getting land from the finca El Porvenir in the lowlands of the department. In an emotional plea, the peasants described the conditions of the land they were forced to farm in the highlands, where they could only grow potatoes and a little wheat and where, as likely as not, the crop froze before it could be harvested. The letter had a palpable sense of urgency about it as the peasants questioned Velasco as to whether any other unions had requested the same land and sent along Q5 to register their union, which they clearly saw as some kind of down payment on the land.[39]

On the other hand, workers on the finca San José Real Alotepeque in Chiquimula expressed their alarm on learning that the CAD had ordered the expropriation of five caballerías from the finca in response to a denunciation from peasants from another locale. They wrote the DAN that most of the twenty-six people named in the letter had been planting milpas for twenty-five years in the mountains of the finca, "the mountains which are now being expropriated." They argued that if the expropriation was to take place, they had more right to the land. They ended by reiterating, "The denunciantes of these lands are completely foreign to the finca and for this reason WE MUST HAVE PREFERENCE over them." The dispute was never completely resolved before the land was returned to the owner in 1956.[40]

In a somewhat similar case, the secretary-general of the unión campesina of Chicazango, San Andrés Itzapa, Chimaltenango, explained to Castillo Flores that the peasants had denounced the neighboring finca, where they all worked regularly. He expressed concern that the land be given out to "honorable workers, not lazy men of bad conduct who do not know how to respect our different customs." The letter proceeded to twist Castillo Flores's repeated warnings that peasants needed to organize to protect themselves from those who would do them harm, saying that on the basis of this advice they had talked to the owner of the finca, who told them "as old renters who had fulfilled their duties, they should denounce the finca as soon as possible before it was invaded by other people from afar who have never served the finca." Castillo Flores carefully explained to them that they would receive first consideration for the land and "in this manner you should have no worry that as workers of the finca you will get your parcel, even if it is denounced from some other place."[41]

This struggle between workers and peasants, sindicatos and unions, spread throughout Guatemala in 1953 and 1954. In finca after finca, both legal skirmishes and physical battles broke out between the two sides. With peasant unions and worker sindicatos scrambling for insufficient land, each side worrying that the other would get access to property it coveted, each group represented by a different national organization concerned about expanding its membership in the countryside, and both groups fighting the reaction of landowners and nervously eyeing the Guardia Civil and the military, a headlong rush for land developed in many departments. In the scramble, combatants at times paid little attention to the provisions of a law that was vaguely understood. In the process, tension and violence mounted, and much of the countryside was engulfed in conflict.[42]

Class and Ethnicity

One popular account of rural Guatemala during the revolution has suggested that class distinctions among peasants accounted for much of the unrest that was associated with the agrarian reform and was an essential element in the overthrow of the Arbenz government.[43] This overstates the case. The prevailing division between Indian and Ladino in Guatemala, the articulation of peasant production with export agriculture, and the defensive institutions erected in peasant communities all insured that class differentiation was weak and that class conflict among rural inhabitants was most often subordinated to other types of tension. This does not mean that there was no class differentiation in peasant communities or that conflict between "nascent" classes in rural areas did not occur.

Land in Guatemala was distributed in a dramatically inequitable fashion. Most often this benefited those who had been able to take advantage of the opportunities afforded by the expansion of export agriculture in the nineteenth century — coffee finqueros primarily. Beyond this, the most obvious inequity was between Indians and Ladinos; Indian farm operators averaged less than 4.5 manzanas each, while Ladinos averaged close to 35.

Nonetheless, significant differences in the amount of land controlled by Indians and Ladinos throughout the country helped to determine the way they would react to the reforms of the revolution. These differences were evident from region to region, from municipality to municipality, and within each municipality (the only situation in which nascent classes among peasants becomes apparent or important). Average landholdings in the central highland and largely Indian departments of Totonicapán, Sololá, and, to a lesser extent, Sacatepéquez were less than half the average holdings in the peripheral peasant areas of Huehuetenango and El

Quiché, both largely Indian, and in the Oriente of Chiquimula, Jalapa, and Jutiapa, with larger Ladino populations. In addition, within each of these departments, the amount of land available to each municipality varied considerably.

There were also substantial differences in the amount of land available to Indians in the same municipality. Two farm owners classified as Indians in the 1950 census controlled fincas larger than 100 caballerías, one in Alta Verapaz and one in Chiquimula. These were probably communal lands registered individually to avoid Liberal laws, but inequity was evident in other ways. Slightly over 1 percent of the Indian farm operators controlled 25 percent of all Indian land. Even in the land-hungry departments of Totonicapán and Sololá, this inequity was apparent. In Totonicapán, 5.3 percent of the Indian farm operators controlled 32 percent of all Indian land, while in Sololá 13 percent controlled 46 percent of the land. In the peripheral peasant areas, where there was slightly less land pressure, even greater inequities existed, with 1.3 percent of the Indian farm operators in Huehuetenango owning 26 percent of Indian land, while in El Quiché, 2.5 percent controlled 31 percent of Indian land. While these inequities do not necessarily point to class distinctions within individual villages, it is clear that no number of community structures designed to legitimize differences in wealth would have been able to assuage completely the jealousies created by these inequities.[44]

Conflict between wealthier and poorer peasants became apparent in many municipalities as the Agrarian Reform Law began to be applied. In Chinautla, 90 percent of the population was Indian but only 30 percent had enough land for subsistence. This group dominated the local government structure, both through its influence in the traditional village hierarchy and, in the 1940s, through its control of the local FPL affiliate. A peasant union affiliated with the PRG was later organized by a *mujer brava* from Guatemala City, joining both poor Ladino and Indian peasants. After careful preparation, its members invaded a neighboring finca. Although the union never threatened to attack the land of the wealthier peasantry, its illegal activity sufficiently frightened the village elite that they formed an opposition political party and opposed both the local peasant union and the Arbenz administration.[45]

A similar type of class conflict afflicted Magdalena Milpas Altas, a predominantly Indian municipality near Antigua. The municipality had long been divided between a somewhat wealthier upper barrio and a poorer lower barrio, whose members on average had access to less land. The majority of members of both barrios were soon organized into two compet-ing political parties, the upper barrio organizing an anticommunist civic committee and the lower barrio an affiliate of the PAR. By 1952 the PAR candidates supported by the lower barrio were able to win the municipal elections. But the alcalde, once in power, shifted allegiance. He opposed the extension of government reforms favored by the poorer members of the municipality and increasingly opposed the Arbenz administration.[46]

In some localities landownership and class relations were such that many people, perhaps the majority, opposed the spread of revolutionary organizations. In the Indian community of Jutiapa, most Indians owned land, with very few landless laborers reported in the census. While the average holdings for the community were slightly below the national In-dian average of 4.4 manzanas, there seems to have been little obvious in-equity in the amount of land owned by individual members of the comuni-dad indígena organized in the municipality. As early as 1951, 248 members of the comunidad petitioned the president and the Guardia Civil to stop the "agitation" in the community caused by an organizer for the CNCG. They urged that he be arrested for vagrancy. In a letter to *El Imparcial*, they asserted: "As owners and workers of our own property . . . we don't need sindicatos, we don't have anyone to defend ourselves against, nor anyone to organize against, nor do we want or need agitators or directors. . . . The comunidad indígena of Jutiapa is a conglomerate of people who work and possess land of which they are owners, with clean titles and registrations. We wish to dedicate ourselves to honorable work."[47]

While there is little indication of substantial support for the CNCG in Jutiapa, in the neighboring municipality of Yupiltepeque, the formation of the peasant union caused significant conflict between the comunidad indí-gena and the union. The organizer for the CNCG suggested that the tension was caused by a struggle between richer and poorer peasants. He asserted that Indians in the municipality were equally divided between the two organizations, but that the comunidad indígena was controlled by a few wealthier peasants who enjoyed the support of the *cura*, who used his religious position to foster opposition to the union.[48]

A similar complaint from San José del Golfo indicated how pervasive fears of losing their land were among the more wealthy peasantry, despite the substantial protection given under the Agrarian Reform Law. Members of the municipality urged the minister of gobernación to take action against the CAL that had denounced their land. They argued that "our small par-cels of land are not nor can they be affected by the agrarian law. Nonetheless, the committee has all the protection of the departmental government and the CAD and so considers itself superior to the law."[49] Numerous other complaints from groups of wealthier peasants protesting the actions or threatened actions of political parties or union members flooded various government offices during the revolution. It is clear that at least in some municipalities the agrarian reform fostered conflict among various levels of the peasantry, despite the intention of the government that the law would be applied only to extremely large landholdings.[50]

In many instances conflict between richer and poorer peasants was fought through the medium of the traditional village structures, primarily the church, and involved a battle for control of municipal land (discussed at greater length in chapter 6). But despite the differences in landholding and the concerns among better-off peasants caused by the spread of revolutionary organizations in some municipalities, surprisingly little of the struggle in the countryside during the revolution was shaped around this type of class conflict. More often than not, class conflict was subsumed by a much more prevalent ethnic division or community orientation.

Of Guatemala's 2,937,748 people in 1950, 53.5 percent were classified as Indian. They were a disadvantaged majority. Of the 348,647 farm operators of various types in Guatemala, the almost 65 percent who were Indian possessed less than 20 percent of the land. Just over 35 percent of the farm operators were Ladinos, and they possessed 81.3 percent of the land. Of the 54 fincas larger than 100 caballerías, only 2 were registered to Indians.

These figures disguise some very substantial regional variations. In the heavily Indian departments of the western highlands, Ladinos owned a lower percentage of land and their landholdings were smaller than elsewhere. In Totonicapán, for example, few Ladinos farmed. They owned only 2 percent of the land, and their landholdings averaged only 2.9 manzanas. In Sololá, also predominantly Indian, Ladinos owned 34 percent of the land and their landholdings averaged 34 manzanas. However, in the department of Alta Verapaz, which was also predominantly Indian, Ladinos made up approximately 5 percent of the farming population but controlled 78 percent of the land, averaging 367 manzanas. In Escuintla, Ladinos owned or operated an average of 74 manzanas apiece, while Indians only operated slightly more than 2 manzanas on average. However, Ladinos made up almost 83 percent of the farming population in the department.

Variations within departments confused the issue even more. In Escuintla, the average Ladino holdings included the huge expanses of Compañía Agrícola (a subsidiary of the UFCo) land, inflating their totals. In a department like San Marcos, where Ladinos controlled on the average 23 manzanas and Indians (who were 72 percent of the operators) averaged slightly above 5 manzanas each, quite remarkable differences existed between the *zona fría* and the *zona caliente* of the department. Given these variations, relations between Ladinos and Indians concerning land differed dramatically throughout the country.[51] *Not uniform so difficult to say*

Nonetheless, some basic similarities existed in ethnic relations throughout the country. By and large, Indians were poorer and possessed less land than the Ladinos who surrounded them. Partly as a result, most Ladinos had a different attitude about land and agriculture. In much of the country, Ladino landowners seldom worked the land themselves; they employed Indians instead. In the western highlands, ethnic differences fairly accurately reflected class distinctions as well. On the other hand, in the Oriente, with a larger percentage of Ladinos and numerous Ladino peasants, ethnic relations appeared to be even more strained and bitter. Tension between Ladinos and Indians pervaded all other aspects of the revolution, despite revolutionary organizations' attempts to play down ethnicity, but the degree to which other struggles were overshadowed by ethnic tension varied from region to region and municipality to municipality.[52]

The constitution of 1945 and the Municipal Law that followed it provided for substantial local autonomy and a certain amount of administrative flexibility in order to accommodate local variations. In addition, the Electoral Law granted male illiterates the vote. This combined to provide a stimulus to Indian attempts, largely successful, to gain control of local government. By 1948, of 45 municipalities surveyed by the Instituto Indigenista Nacional in the western highlands, 22 had elected Indian alcaldes. This was a significant change and demonstrated a readiness and ability to use the new political opportunities offered by the revolution to grasp power from a clutching local Ladino elite. Nonetheless, despite an immense numerical superiority on the part of Indians, in many municipalities Ladinos continued to dominate local government.[53]

The unfolding of the revolution in San Luis Jilotepeque, Jalapa, provides a good example of the important role of ethnic differences in heightening unrest during the revolution. San Luis Jilotepeque was a combined Ladino/Indian municipality with approximately two-thirds of its 10,000 people Indian. Although many Ladinos were poor peasants and the wealthiest Indians owned more land than the poorest Ladinos, Ladinos dominated landownership. One anthropologist working in the municipality during the revolution estimated that Ladinos controlled 70 percent of the agricultural land, while the 1950 census puts that figure at slightly over 65 percent. The average Ladino landholding was ten times the average Indian holding. Small Ladino farmers frequently hired Indian laborers, but no Indians ever hired Ladinos.[54]

During the revolution the municipality was initially divided into a "conservative" party and a "democratic" party. Indians were the majority within the latter, although the party was run by a "progressive" Ladino. The "democratic" party won the municipal elections in 1948, and for the first time, Indians won a majority of posts on the municipal council. The alcalde was the Ladino leader of the party. By 1952 a local unión campesina was organized, primarily composed of Indians from the outlying aldeas. When they began to pressure for land and to talk aggressively about altering landholding in the municipality, even though little property would be legally subject to expropriation, the majority of Ladinos in the municipality closed ranks. The "democratic" alcalde turned against the organized peasants, and "ydígoristas" and anticommunists dominated the local government. Attacks on the union were persistent and resulted in the killing of at least one Indian leader before the overthrow in 1954. Despite the existence of a sizable population of Ladino peasants, the majority of them refused to make common cause with their slightly worse off Indian neighbors. Rather, they were the most vehement supporters of the reaction.[55]

Most of the national organizations made a concerted attempt to minimize ethnic divisions in their activities and literature, stressing instead the favored dichotomy of "reactionary" versus "revolutionary." But this did little to reduce the very real ethnic tension that existed. Ethnic divisions hampered the growth and consolidation of revolutionary organizations in many areas. In municipality after municipality, class allegiances were forgotten in the face of an all-encompassing fear of Indians and Indian unrest.

In most instances, it is impossible to distinguish ethnic conflict from struggles between municipalities or among different entities within municipalities. As the Agrarian Reform Law began to alter landownership, Indian communities either saw the law and the agrarian agencies associated with it as a way for the "community" to reclaim land lost to Ladinos or feared the law would be used in yet another Ladino assault on native land. Thus the struggle for land in the agrarian reform became one more stage in the history of Ladino encroachment on Indian land and community response. This communal aspect of the struggle for land and of ethnic tension, the most essential part of the revolution in the countryside, is discussed next.

Regional Variation

This study focuses on the Guatemalan revolution as it was experienced on the local level. But Guatemala is a country of regions; climate, geography, ethnic composition and conflict, agricultural activities, and the level of land scarcity vary dramatically from region to region. It is not surprising, then, that the revolution was felt differently in different regions. While some of these variations have already been mentioned, it would be valuable at this point to explore a brief summary of the regional experience before proceeding, in the next chapter, with a discussion expanding on local complexities.

Regional variations in the experience and implementation of reform and in the responses to it stem from differences in geography, agricultural practices, ethnicity, and the degree of isolation from the capital. These factors all helped determine the way worker and peasant organization and agrarian reform were accepted.

As a general pattern, heavily Maya regions organized less quickly around revolutionary institutions than regions with a larger percentage of Ladinos. This occurred partly because many Maya, for good reason, tended to be more suspicious of government initiatives. In addition, organizers for revolutionary organizations, especially in the early years of the revolution, were usually Ladinos, less comfortable in and less accepted by predominantly Maya communities. Restrictions on rural labor organization that were in place until 1948 also helped determine regional variations. "Rural" workers around Guatemala City tended to organize more quickly as a result of their more intimate contact with urban colleagues. The 1947 Labor Code allowed organization on UFCo plantations, on national fincas, and on a few other farms. For this reason, labor organization and the implementation of government reforms occurred earlier and more energetically in Escuintla, where the Compañía Agrícola had a plantation at Tiquisate, and to a lesser extent in Alta Verapaz, where many national fincas were located. Many of the early peasant league organizers were Ladinos from the Oriente. Partly because it was more active in that region and because it was more readily accepted there, the CNCG grew most quickly in the Oriente.

There were major exceptions to these generalities, however. San Marcos, distant from the capital and predominantly Maya, was the scene of early and intense labor organization. As recent work by Cindy Forester has shown, it was also a scene of significant unrest and most of those involved in the rural unions were self-consciously "indígenas."[56] Similarly,

forest products

milpa

Río Chixoy

coffee

potatoes

bananas

milpa

sheep

potatoes

milpa

milpa

citrus

coffee

fruits

Río Motagua

milpa

sugar cane

pasture

milpa

coffee

cotton

coffee

bananas

cattle

MAP 3. MAJOR CROPS IN THE 1940S

parts of Sacatepéquez, although predominantly Maya, organized early and experienced significant labor- and peasant-related unrest throughout the revolution.

The terms of the Agrarian Reform Law determined in many ways where it could be applied most successfully. Large areas of the country, particularly in the central highland regions, had very little privately held land falling under the terms of the law. But despite attempts to "mobilize" campesinos in their search for land — that is, to help them petition for land in regions distant from their home communities — attempts to get land expropriated had a very local complexion. Many regions with large amounts of potentially affected land had few people petitioning for the land. In some areas, as well, especially parts of the south coast that were heavily involved in the production of "new" crops, most significantly cotton, landowners were more "capitalist," used the land more intensely, and were more prepared to combat expropriation of their land. Thus, it was in those regions, such as Alta Verapaz and to a somewhat lesser extent San Marcos, where a large, active population of campesinos were presented with a substantial amount of privately held land in large estates, much of which was not used, that the agrarian reform was applied most successfully.

There is no indication that Maya were more reluctant than Ladinos to use the Agrarian Reform Law. The extent to which they could use the law on privately held land was restricted in much of the western highlands, however. Partly because of this, and partly because Maya tended to view land from a more "communal" perspective (as chapter 6 will discuss more fully), predominantly Maya regions experienced relatively more conflict over communally owned land as a result of the Agrarian Reform Law. This pattern is tempered, however, by the scarcity of communal land in the central highland departments, such as Totonicapán, or in regions of intense coffee development, such as Alta Verapaz. Thus, it was in "peripheral" highland regions, such as the department of Huehuetenango, with strong but land-hungry Mayan communities and a substantial amount of community-controlled land, where the most conflict over communal land occurred within municipios. In some more densely populated highland regions, such as in the department of Sololá, conflict over land erupted more often among different municipios.

The importance of population density, land concentration, degree of reliance on agriculture for a living, and degree of isolation from the capital in determining the extent to which the agrarian reform could be applied in any region is illustrated in the departments of Totonicapán and El Petén. Neither Totonicapán nor El Petén had a single successful denunciation of private land.

The revolutionary organizations that were active in the countryside during the course of the revolution were determined to confront the political, economic, and social power of the large landowners. But the "fraternal solidarity" between the revolutionary organizations and the various sectors of rural society that stood to benefit from the reforms, a solidarity desperately needed in order for the reforms to take place, collapsed in a welter of conflicting claims and allegiances. Instead, the agrarian reform opened a Pandora's box of conflict in rural Guatemala. The revolutionary organizations fought each other for rural converts; nascent classes within rural municipalities had varying reactions to the changes occurring in rural areas; and ethnic tension heightened every other source of conflict.

Possessing little clear understanding of rural society, the revolutionary organizations were not prepared for these bewildering sources of antagonism. Agrarian officials scrambled to douse the flames of factional disputes and ethnic tension. Unrest and violence heightened as various sectors of society grew increasingly opposed to the agrarian reform and the revolution. The revolution's opponents gathered their forces.

weakened from within allowing the opposition to gain strength

COMMUNITY AND REVOLUTION

6

Each one of the political changes that has occurred in our nation has filled us with anxiety and dread because we know that individuals who say they represent the interests of the state rush to our community to fill our peaceful existence as agriculturalists with confusion and disorder. . . . Now . . . we are looking for the justice that is required to reach a solution to the numerous problems that arose with the implementation of the sadly famous Agrarian Law.

—Comuneros of the comunidad indígena
of Santa María Joyabaj, 16 January 1955

T he all-encompassing ethnic tension evident in rural Guatemala during the revolution embittered the struggles between workers and peasants, between wealthier and poorer peasants, and among the revolutionary organizations that flourished with the passage of the Agrarian Reform Law. These conflicts aggravated the confrontation between rural activists and peasants on one side and large landowners on the other that the revolutionary officials had expected with the agrarian reform. But it was the continuing strength of community identification that most complicated the revolutionary organizations' activities in rural areas.

The changes that had come to rural Guatemala with the spread of coffee cultivation and the application of liberal/positivist ideology in the late nineteenth century had varying effects on rural communities. Many of these changes had reduced community independence and had prompted increasing connections between the community and national society. On the other hand, some changes had heightened community identification and prompted inhabitants of rural communities, especially Mayan communities, to shun interaction with national society whenever possible. Of course, to many in Indian communities, this also meant shunning Ladinos.

The revolutionary administrations had an ambiguous relationship with these at least partially closed and corporate communities. The 1945 constitution provided for increased autonomy and power of Guatemalan municipios. The changes in voting regulations and the more democratic electoral process that was followed in most municipalities during the revolutionary decade insured that in many areas the majority of citizens had been able to wrest control of local politics from members of the local elite. In predominantly Indian municipalities, this very often meant that Indians had been able to take control of local politics, displacing the local Ladino elite that had dominated the municipality since the Liberal revolt of the 1870s. The abolition of the vagrancy law, which had been applied almost exclusively to Indians in the western highlands, guaranteed that Indians were no longer compelled to work outside of the community. The Agrarian Reform Law seemed to be the major initiative in favor of peasant villages, promising residents the opportunity to acquire land and to augment their production, thus strengthening the village economy.

However, the revolution also produced a strong current of national consolidation and sought to inspire the extension of capitalist relations of production throughout Guatemala, both of which might be perceived as threatening to peasant production and to the existence of closed corporate communities, which had distinct cultures and noncapitalist relations of production. The agrarian reform, which led to an incredible expansion of national institutions throughout rural Guatemala (especially the peasant league, the rural workers' union, and political parties) and which openly advocated strengthening the "capitalist agricultural economy" of Guatemala, might well be seen as the greatest challenge to the continued existence of these communities.

This ambiguity is reflected in the literature dealing with rural Guatemala during the revolutionary period and in the various descriptions of the effects of the revolution on communities in rural Guatemala. One view suggests that the revolution challenged and eventually shattered the structure of villages in rural Guatemala, bringing "disastrous and rapid destruction of many Indian communities." Another argues that the revolution prompted conflicts in communities that should be seen primarily as struggles between "nascent classes" in rural areas. According to this view, the revolutionary organizations failed to recognize the nature of this struggle and did not support the poorer peasantry, which not only tore the communities apart but helped lead to the overthrow of the revolution. A third approach merges these two arguments to suggest that both the reforms of the revolution and the struggle between "nascent classes" that they helped inspire weakened the institutions that defended the corporate community and left many rural, particularly Indian, communities in Guatemala unable to withstand more repressive government policies in the decades that followed the revolution.[1]

However, much of the unrest that exploded in rural Guatemala during the revolution was a function of the continuing strength of community identification. The reforms of the decade placed some pressure on the elements most often associated with community in Guatemala: the traditional religious/civil hierarchy, the cofradías, and, most importantly, community-controlled land. But throughout the revolution, community members were able to shape local affiliates of national organizations to meet their own needs as well. Most often this meant that the majority of residents were able to gain more control over community affairs, not less, and to obtain stronger representation in national government for their interests. The process of agrarian reform did remove some land from community control, although this was not its intent. On the other hand, many communities used the agrarian reform to regain control of land that had been lost years earlier to large landowners, neighboring communities, or the local elite. In many instances, this also meant that Indians were reclaiming land from Ladinos. In the process, however, the agrarian officials were confronted with an

extremely confusing panorama of ancient claims and long-standing conflicts that they found difficult to comprehend and almost impossible to
settle equitably. These conflicts rarely fit easily into the "reactionary/revo-
lutionary" dichotomy favored in their view of rural conflict.

The Revolution and the Village Hierarchy

Given the power and autonomy granted to municipios by congress in 1946,
the revolutionary political parties quickly became involved in municipal
elections throughout rural Guatemala. The peasant league also took an
intense interest in insuring that those sympathetic to the agrarian reform
process gained control of municipal governments. Municipal elections not
only prompted intense struggles between political parties as they sought to
strengthen their position within the revolutionary pantheon but also caused
conflict between the revolutionary parties and the organizations that supported them on the one side and the traditional hierarchy on the other.

Village government in Guatemala had a complicated and organic structure. It varied significantly from region to region and from village to village. Generally, villagers had adapted the Spanish institutions of the alcaldía (elected village officials consisting of various regidores or councillors,
a municipal secretary, and one or two alcaldes) and the cofradías (brotherhoods organized to care for and honor various important village saints),
mixing them into one civil/religious hierarchy. A male member of the
municipality in good standing usually worked his way up the various levels
of the religious and civic ladder. Those who reached the position of alcalde
or majordomo of a cofradía, or both, often joined an informal group of elders or principales, who were consulted when important decisions needed
to be made.

In the late nineteenth and early twentieth centuries, Liberal administrations attempted to place Ladinos in positions of authority within municipal
governments. They were largely successful, and even in predominantly
Mayan municipalities, Ladinos dominated the highest positions in municipal government for much of the seventy years before the revolution. In
many municipalities, an informal, mainly Indian, government developed
alongside the formal government controlled by Ladinos. While this kept
intact some of the structures of Indian village government, it meant that
official power was in the hands of a local Ladino elite. President Ubico
had tampered with this system by appointing *intendentes* to oversee munic-

ipal government. Although this somewhat weakened the authority of the local Ladino elite, it did not return power to the traditional civil/religious hierarchy.

After decades during which the civil/religious hierarchy had functioned only intermittently, if at all, the importance of the hierarchy had been weakened in many municipalities. The survey of fifty-six municipalities conducted by the Instituto Indigenista Nacional in the 1940s and 1950s revealed the varying strengths of the traditional village structures. Few municipalities had elected an Indian as first alcalde for decades before the revolution. In many, the cofradías no longer performed an important function and the principales no longer met, nor were they consulted when major decisions needed to be made.[2] Thus, in discussing the relationship between these traditional structures and the revolutionary organizations from 1944 to 1954, it is important to note that these structures had been under intense pressure for decades and that in many municipalities they were no longer an obvious or important part of the community.

As indicated earlier, many predominantly Indian municipalities had taken advantage of the opportunities provided by the revolution to elect Indian alcaldes. The relationship of these alcaldes with the traditional structures of the municipality differed from place to place. In a number of municipalities, at least in the early years of the revolution, the elected officials had first been approved by the traditional hierarchy and no conflict occurred. However, as the political parties strengthened their position in rural Guatemala, and as the peasant league and the rural workers' union developed into more powerful entities in many municipios, it became more important for potential local politicians to pay their dues by serving in these organizations rather than in traditional village structures. This prompted some conflict and was an important element in creating unrest surrounding municipal elections during the revolution.[3]

This conflict must be seen in perspective, however. It is clear that in some municipalities the traditional hierarchy had been a local wealthy elite who had used their positions for their own advantage. The conflict engendered by the growing importance of the political parties in some municipalities was thus not simply between the traditional structure and new, disruptive elements but also between the traditional elite and poorer sectors of the peasantry.[4] In addition, the new elements that gained power in municipalities through their participation in revolutionary organizations did so only with the approval of the majority of the municipal population, otherwise they would not have been able to win the position of alcalde in increasingly democratic political contests. While the activities of political parties may have created conflict within the municipality as the parties competed for positions, these new leaders reflected the widespread desire of community members to take advantage of the opportunities provided by the revolution.

The revolution also challenged the traditional structures of rural municipalities in other ways. The dual civil/religious hierarchy required residents, usually young men, to fill the many unpaid positions in the alcaldía and the cofradías. With the spread of revolutionary organizations to rural areas, some young men refused to serve in these positions. A number of such cases made their way to local and regional courts, and the revolutionary organizations usually supported this challenge to the traditional hierarchy as part of their campaign against unpaid labor.[5]

A more important challenge to tradition emerged during the revolution concerning the place of the cofradías and the honoring of saints. While this conflict was caused partly by the spread of revolutionary organizations, it was not the result of revolutionary opposition to traditional religious practice. The hierarchy of the Catholic church had always demonstrated an ambiguous attitude toward traditional religion and the cofradías. The Spanish had originally encouraged the adoption of the cofradías as a means of Hispanicization and to help distance Catholicism in the Americas from the emerging Protestant challenge in Europe during the sixteenth century. Periodically during the colonial period, however, sectors of the church became alarmed at the growing divergence between native Catholicism and that promoted by the church. This concern was occasionally expressed in campaigns designed to purge native religion of its nativist characteristics. However, these efforts were inevitably unsuccessful and often provoked a violent response.

During the 1930s, Protestant missionaries had enjoyed some limited success in rural Guatemala, often because the Protestant churches proscribed the use of alcohol and because turning away from folk Catholicism allowed individuals to avoid the financial burden of participation in religious festivals. While generally small in number (in 1950 almost 97 percent of the population was Catholic), these converts constituted a wedge of community members who refused to participate in many of the structures of the village.[6] Partly because of increasing concern about Protestant success, partly as another campaign against nativist practice, but mostly as an attempt to combat the influence of revolutionary organizations, which the church saw as Marxist, the archbishop of Guatemala, Mariano Rossell y Arellano, encouraged the spread of Catholic Action in Guatemala.

Archbishop Rossell later observed, "Our small Catholic Action was one of the greatest comforts in those hours of enormous distress in the presence of Marxist advance that invaded everything."[7] In the villages, however, Catholic Action was felt as another attack on the traditional religious structures and it heightened unrest. The best-known example of this conflict during the revolution was caused by attacks by the bishop of Sololá against Maximón, the village "saint" of Santiago Atitlán. The struggle surrounding Maximón dominated politics in the village during the revolution.[8] Similar types of conflict occurred in numerous villages during the revolution. In the village of San Agustín Acasaguastlán, El Progreso, the new village priest attempted to stop holy week celebrations because of the "pagan" customs associated with them. The angry response forced him to flee the municipality, but he locked the church and took the keys with him. It took the intervention of the governor before the priest agreed to give back the keys. In San Miguel Chicaj, Baja Verapaz, the new priest forbade cohabiting unmarried couples from participating in religious ceremonies, an action apparently intended as the initial encounter in a battle to get rid of the cofradías, which the priest believed "insult the saints." His activities brought an emotional response from many in the community, resulting in conflict that dominated local politics for many years. In Cantel in 1953, Catholic Action adherents broke into the church, dragged out the figure of San Simeon (a local "saint" like Maximón), and burned it as part of the campaign against the traditionalists. Similar unrest occurred in Concepción, Santa María de Jesús, and San Antonio Sacatepéquez. Given the strength of religious sentiment in rural Guatemala, these threats to traditional religious structures caused a great deal of unrest and provoked angry responses.[9]

However, this conflict was not primarily the result of the activities of revolutionary organizations in rural Guatemala. Indeed, in most cases the revolutionary organizations supported the traditionalists in their struggle against Catholic Action. In San Agustín, the peasant league helped intercede with the governor, and the communist newspaper, *Octubre*, portrayed the return of the keys as a victory for the whole village, describing the shouts of "Viva el pueblo" and "Viva el pueblo que manda" that punctuated the subsequent meeting to complete arrangements for holy week. The paper described the priest's actions in San Miguel Chicaj as an attack on the poorest peasants, members of the unión campesina, who often could not afford marriage ceremonies, and sprang to their defense. The situation in Cantel was more complicated as many of the Catholic Action adherents were members of the local affiliate of the PRG. Nonetheless, they were

Communist newspaper portraying itself as the voice of the people

opposed by the equally "revolutionary" PAR and PGT, who occasionally supported the traditionalists.[10]

The Limits of "Community"

The local affiliates of political parties and revolutionary organizations were shaped by residents into weapons used in fighting long-standing local conflicts. Very often this tension reflected a fundamental disagreement over the very essence of what entailed "community" within the sometimes broader concept of "municipality." Traditionally, "community" has been viewed in Guatemala as being synonymous with the officially recognized "municipio." Sol Tax probably presented this view most explicitly in the 1940s when he observed: "The Indians of the municipios think of themselves as distinct groups of people, biologically and socially. Each municipio typically has its own costume different from those of its neighbors and this costume is a label wherever the Indians go. Each has, moreover, a relatively exclusive set of customs and practices. . . . At the same time all of the Indians typical of one municipio are strictly part of that community."[11]

While this may have been an accurate description of some of the municipalities around Lake Atitlán that Tax studied, it clearly was not true of many others in Guatemala by the time of the revolution. Guatemalan municipalities were created as political constructs and recognized by national governments. The roots of many municipalities can be traced back to the *congregaciones* of the sixteenth century, but many others had been formed in the intervening centuries as a result of population increases or petitions from residents. The formation and dissolution of municipalities often prompted intense battles over the geographic limits of the municipality and the power of the municipal capital or cabacera. Very often the conflict was between Ladinos and Indians, as Ladinos sought to carve out their own municipios in rural Guatemala or attempted to dominate predominantly Indian municipios through control of the cabacera.

One example of this process was the formation of the municipality of San Marcos, by the time of the revolution the capital of the department of San Marcos. San Marcos had originally started as a Ladino barrio of the predominantly Indian municipality of San Pedro Sacatepéquez. By 1754, the Ladinos had formed a distinct village with its own elected government. In 1832, it was made capital of the department. Relations between the Ladinos of San Marcos and the Mam Indians of San Pedro were strained. In

1793, for example, when San Marcos purchased some land claimed by the inhabitants of San Pedro, the latter protested to the colonial government, suggesting, "The inhabitants of the *barrio* [San Marcos] want to thrust us out and deprive us of our own town and lands. They want to be owners of all the lands. Indeed, they have us surrounded and in a few days they will want to put their haciendas in the San Pedro cemetery."[12]

Although ethnic conflict as evidenced between San Marcos and San Pedro helped heighten tension within and among municipalities, it was not a necessary ingredient. In many predominantly Indian municipalities, significant tension often prevailed among a number of long-standing geographically defined entities claiming primary loyalty. Indeed, even in those municipalities that originated in the congregaciones of the sixteenth century, there was conflict between the various components of the community. George Lovell's description of Sacapulas in the sixteenth and seventeenth centuries as being characterized by "various social groups . . . in almost constant collision as each . . . sought to gain control of as much land in the vicinity of the town site as possible" is at least in some ways applicable to many other communities in Guatemala during the decade of the revolution.[13] In many cases the perceived importance of the municipality obviously stemmed primarily, and perhaps solely, from the official recognition granted it; the smaller geographic units (aldeas and cantones), which more often represented "community" to many within the municipalities, lacked this official recognition and thus could not "communicate" with the national government. During the revolution, with the spread of revolutionary organizations to the aldea level, this changed fundamentally.

The process of elections and the application of the agrarian reform during the revolution demonstrated the extent to which many inhabitants in rural municipalities sought to redefine "community" or to end the domination of their community by the cabecera. With the creation of the new Municipal Law in April 1946, the government was confronted with numerous petitions from aldeas for recognition as distinct municipalities. These requests were often attempts by aldeas to regain municipal status lost at some time in the past, but many were from aldeas that felt little connection to the municipality in which they had been located for over a century. This conflict influenced many aspects of the extension of revolutionary organizations and national government in rural Guatemala.

For example, the initial election campaign of the revolution, that between Juan José Arévalo Bermejo and Adrian Recinos for president, was a lopsided affair. Arévalo was clearly the choice of the majority of the young politicians who dominated politics in Guatemala City following the October Revolution, and their efforts insured that he easily won a large majority of votes in all parts of the republic in the fairest elections Guatemala had ever held, defeating Recinos by approximately 260,000 votes to 20,000.[14] But in many rural areas of Guatemala, local concerns superseded these national trends, even in the presidential elections. Both Arévalo and Recinos visited the municipality of San Pedro Necta in the department of Huehuetenango. Santiago Chimaltenango, at that time an aldea of San Pedro Necta, had previously been a separate municipality, and with the presidential elections, the *chimaltecos* saw an opportunity to regain that status. Recinos, who had a long-standing connection to Huehuetenango, received most of his support from that department. Nonetheless, Arévalo had made vague promises to the chimaltecos, and they voted for him en masse. They even sought to convince the inhabitants of other aldeas to vote against the predominantly recinista cabacera. Arévalo did not disappoint the chimaltecos, and Santiago Chimaltenango was once again awarded municipal status.[15]

The Community and Agrarian Reform

While the conflict among the various components of municipalities and between different municipalities took on a variety of aspects during the revolution, the most bitter contests were reserved for struggles over land with the passage of the Agrarian Reform Law. The Arbenz administration had intended that decree 900 foster the development of capitalist relations of production in rural Guatemala. Thus, the law focused on improving the lot of *individual* peasants and rural workers; it was not intended to strengthen community or even to promote cooperatives. Only nine cooperatives were formed on a few national fincas. While peasants and rural workers were encouraged to organize in order to effect the application of the law, they were to receive the benefits of the law, both in terms of land and loans from the National Agrarian Bank, as individuals. But not everyone petitioning for land under decree 900 abided by these principles.

Numerous denunciations of land under decree 900 reflected the continuing perception of land as a community resource, although it might be owned individually, and the determination of those petitioning the agrarian agencies to use the law to strengthen the community. This determination was most clearly expressed when members of uniones campesinas, com-

unidades campesinas, or comunidades indígenas justified their denunciation of land from neighboring fincas by attempting to prove that it had
originally been part of the patrimony of the village and had been taken
illegally in the past. For example, the comunidad campesina of San Miguel
Dueñas, Sacatepéquez, denounced land in the neighboring finca owned by
Salvador Falla Santos in 1953. The members of the comunidad argued that
the land had been taken from the community in 1722 and declared, "We
have documents that prove our ancestral right over these lands and therefore we are asking President Arbenz, in order to do justice, to return these
lands, finally, to our power."[16] Similarly, in 1952 the representatives of the
aldea of Santa María Cacique in the municipality of Santiago Sacatepéquez petitioned to have land taken from a finca owned by Carlos Monteros.
They justified their request by reporting, "According to the tradition of
[our] people these lands pertained from time immemorial to the aldea."
The people of Santa María got slightly over two caballerías of the land in
November 1953.[17]

On many occasions, people attempted to use decree 900 to protect community land from further encroachment from the outside. In Alta Verapaz,
members of the unión campesina of Chiquin Guaxcux, representing the
comunidad indígena of that aldea, asked for the return of ten caballerías of
land from the finca Guaxcux, owned by Raymundo Lascoutx. They reported that the land had been part of the aldea since 1885, when they had
paid 50 pesos a caballería for it. However, over the years a few wealthy
landlords had forced people to give up their rights to the land through a
variety of means. They now asked that some of the land be returned and
that the rest of the communal land in the aldea be given them through
decree 900 to protect it in the future.[18]

Certainly the most bitter conflicts within and between municipalities
over the application of the Agrarian Reform Law concerned municipal
land. Municipally controlled land was probably the most cherished and the
most important community resource. The Liberal governments had attacked community-controlled land based on their belief that private ownership was the best means to promote agricultural development and possibly
in an attempt to drive highland peasants to work on coffee fincas. The
seven decades of Liberal efforts to reduce community control of land had
only been partially successful, however. By the time of the revolution,
municipalities controlled 721,613 manzanas of land. In addition, 420,654
manzanas of land were controlled by communities not constituted as municipalities, that is, cantones or aldeas. Fifty-six thousand comuneros had

access to the land in some form of rental arrangement. However, much of this community-controlled land was used as common woodlots or grazing areas and was not under cultivation. As the surveys of municipalities conducted by the Instituto Indigenista Nacional indicated, the importance of community-controlled land varied dramatically from place to place. In many communities, it was of little importance; indeed, in some whole departments, there was little community land. This was especially true of the most congested highland departments, such as Totonicapán, and those that had been the site of significant agricultural export production, such as Alta Verapaz and Retalhuleu. On the other hand, the marginal peasant areas — both predominantly Indian, such as Huehuetenango, and mostly Ladino, such as Jutiapa — had significant amounts of municipal or community-controlled land. In some communities in these regions, *vecinos* were free to rent cultivable land from the municipality or aldea for often nominal sums.[19]

The control and disposition of municipal land were a constant source of concern and unrest during the revolution. The Arévalo administration's first significant land measure was the 1946 Law of Agricultural Emergency, which attempted to regulate the disposition and rental of municipal land. The government passed two Laws of Forced Rental in 1949 and 1951, intending them to be used by campesinos to obtain land for reasonable rent from large landowners. But the law soon became a source of conflict between the national government and municipalities as residents of rural municipalities attempted to use the law to demand access to municipal land or to force the municipality to lower rents. In Santa Ana Huista, Huehuetenango, for example, a report of the agrarian inspector in 1952 indicated that since the passage of the law there had been serious agrarian troubles. A number of vecinos who rented municipal land had refused to pay rent, citing the Law of Forced Rental. One fellow in particular, Luis López Mazariegos, had inspired much opposition from other members of the municipality because of his refusal to pay rent, to the point of having his life threatened. Variations on this type of conflict developed throughout rural Guatemala. Once the administration began to involve itself in the constant conflicts that occurred over access to land in rural municipalities, it was entangled further and further in a web from which it became increasingly difficult to extricate itself.[20]

Most of the tension in rural municipalities over land was not, however, the result of the intervention of the national government. Rural municipalities had been torn apart time and time again in the past in struggles over land. These became more frequent during the revolution as community residents perceived that with the changing of the government the ownership of municipally controlled land might be altered. In San Pedro Soloma, Huehuetenango, this tension exploded in a violent struggle in 1947. The municipality had slightly over 8,000 inhabitants, 90 percent of them Indian. Almost half of the land was controlled by 129 Ladinos. In addition, the municipal capital, with a population of 900, 60 percent of which was Ladino, dominated municipal government and controlled the fifteen caballerías of municipal land. Indians from outlying aldeas had successfully regained title to the land in 1901 but had lost it to the town again in 1942. On 24 August 1947, according to newspaper reports, "hundreds" of Indians marched to the town to petition once again for the land to be returned to them. They were met by a crowd of armed Ladinos who tried to prevent them from entering the cabacera. The Indians attacked them and forced their way into the municipal building, where they tried to find the deeds to the property. They were driven from the building only after a squadron of the Guardia Civil rushed to the municipality.[21] Obviously, this action had done little to resolve the festering conflict over land, and Soloma was torn apart later in the revolution with the application of the Agrarian Reform Law.

Municipios and Comunidades

There was a slowly emerging perception on the part of the Arévalo administration that the municipality in many cases did not represent "community" and that, even after the extension of revolutionary political parties into rural areas, municipalities were not always "democratic" entities. This prompted the government to begin to act on the provisions of the constitution that called for special laws to benefit the Indian population. In 1946 the government provided for the legal recognition of comunidades indígenas and comunidades campesinas as separate entities within municipalities. These comunidades were clearly designed, and functioned in most places, to strengthen the democratic and popular nature of municipal government. The regulations for the foundation of the comunidad campesina in San Agustín Acasaguastlán, established on 28 December 1946, demonstrate this purpose. The comunidad was formed as "an association for mutual aid to better the cultural, economic, and sanitary conditions of its members." All vecinos who were natives of the municipality, who were given rights to municipal land under the regulation of the government on 25 May 1890, who were "working class," and who agreed to abide by the bylaws of the comunidad could join. It was to be run on a democratic basis with decisions made in open assemblies. The founding charter expressed the comunidad's desire to cooperate fully with the state and the municipal government. However, as the activities of the comunidad in the 1950s under the auspices of the agrarian reform made clear, it also acted as a democratic and community-focused counterweight to the municipal government.[22]

In a number of cases, residents of largely Indian aldeas in municipalities controlled by Ladinos used comunidades indígenas to regain a type of legal status for their "community." The population of the municipality of Patulul, Suchitepéquez, for example, was almost 63 percent Indian. The Indians were clustered in the outlying regions, however, and the municipal capital was predominantly Ladino. Some Indians in the aldeas had been able to purchase land in common in 1878. At some point before 1940, the land had been taken over by the municipality of Patulul. The original comuneros continued to assert their right to the land. In 1949, they used the new law to form a distinct comunidad indígena and tried to have the land granted to the comunidad. In this case, conflict was heightened by the ubiquitous political intrigues among the revolutionary parties. There were many complaints, some apparently with justification, that after the comunidad regained control of the land, it had been divided among a restricted group of Indians who "subscribed to the politics of the official parties" and had been refused those who were "contrary to their political ideology."[23]

The Agrarian Reform Law, under article 33, declared that municipal land could be expropriated in favor of a legally recognized comunidad campesina or comunidad indígena in the case of conflict between it and the municipality over the ownership of that land. The Arbenz administration did not advocate the expropriation of all community land, nor was it interested in promoting a wholesale transfer of municipal land to comunidades or the state. Nevertheless, substantial municipal land was denounced during the revolution, and 297,460 manzanas were taken. Much of this land was given out in usufruct to those who had denounced it, but a substantial portion was kept as forest reserves in the hands of the state.[24]

Attempts to expropriate municipal land angered residents in many municipalities in Guatemala and turned many of them against the agrarian reform process and the Arbenz administration. Conflict between the state and municipalities often emerged as the result of insensitive decisions on the part of the agrarian officials. These decisions were often tied to the

Arbenz administration's attempts to enforce measures to protect Guatemala's diminishing forest cover, which had been one of the stated priorities of both governments of the revolution. The Municipal Law compelled alcaldes to enforce provisions of the new forestry law, resulting in intense conflict in some municipalities and growing opposition to alcaldes in some areas. Residents were angered by increased fees for taking wood from communal lands and by the fines that were levied when they did not abide by the new laws. In San Martín Jilotepeque alone, for instance, there were twenty-six people in prison for forestry offenses in 1954.[25]

The desire to protect Guatemala's forest reserves led the agrarian agencies to attempt to use decree 900 to place much of the land in Guatemala that was covered in forest and on slopes greater than 30 degrees in the hands of the state. As indicated earlier, this was one of the areas in which the agrarian officials often exceeded the bounds of decree 900 when dealing with private fincas, expropriating forest reserves with slopes of over 30 degrees despite the provision in the law that exempted such land. This was also true when dealing with municipal land; the agrarian officials regularly expropriated municipal land falling in this category, placing it in state-controlled forest reserves. While this seldom led to any immediate change in the municipality's access to such land, the expropriations were deeply resented. When the unión campesina of Patzicía denounced over twenty caballerías of municipal land, most of which was in forest cover, over 100 people in the municipality responded with an impassioned petition against the expropriation. They explained that the land was in the municipal forest, "where all the widows go to look for the little bit of wood and in that way earn a few centavos."[26]

The operations of the Agrarian Reform Law also caused much concern when denunciations of municipal land were made by restricted groups of residents attempting to monopolize this resource unfairly. In Alotenango, Sacatepéquez, Juan Paxel, a local organizer for the PAR who had led the denunciation of several private fincas in the region, also formed a comunidad campesina that was given official recognition by the government. When its 106 members denounced the municipal land, they sparked intense opposition from various groups within the community. A letter signed by 300 vecinos and sent to the chief of the DAN expressed their anger on learning that "a tiny group of people has solicited the partition of community forest of this village, the only place where the population of Alotenango can get wood for their necessities. If this is distributed and we are deprived of it, it will occasion grave prejudice. We . . . are not against the Agrarian Reform Law . . . but we do believe that general interest should prevail over private interest and that one should not favor a few by prejudicing the great majority of the population of Alotenango." They went on to ask that if the cultivated part of the property was taken, at least the community forest, which made up the bulk of the five caballerías, should be maintained. The CAN tried to appease them somewhat by ordering that although the cultivated land should be parceled out, the remainder should remain as a forest reserve in the hands of the state. This ruling had little positive effect, however. Many in the municipality were so angered that an antigovernment party, headed by an alliance of the traditional hierarchy and Ladino merchants, won the municipal election in 1953 and promptly began to try to take back the municipal land given out to Paxel's followers. The resulting violence continued to plague the community until the end of the revolution and led to a further perceived attack on village autonomy when a brigade of the national police was stationed there.[27]

Not all attempts to take land from municipalities were fostered by legally recognized comunidades. In a number of localities, various types of revolutionary organizations petitioned for municipal land. These petitions almost invariably prompted a vehement response. In Mazatenango, Suchitepéquez, eleven caballerías of community land in the aldea of San Rafael were denounced by a sindicato linked to the CGTG. Those renting plots of this land grew a variety of crops on small parcels and paid 25 centavos a cuerda to the municipality a year. In 1952, some of these renters, linked to the sindicato, tried to get possession of the land to avoid paying rent to the municipality. Although 181 people had petitioned to have the land appropriated, many of the renters opposed the action and responded with a petition of their own signed by 95 people. Their letter expressed the unrest that was afflicting many municipalities. The alcalde wrote that the members of the sindicato had threatened to throw the others off the lots they had been farming for years. The letter went on to explain that the most serious aspect of this conflict was that the leaders of the sindicato "arrived armed with revolvers and threatened to shoot our compañeros. . . . You know, Sir, that if they commit crimes against us, we are going to have to defend ourselves. We are peaceful people and we do not want to have to bloody our hands through pure necessity. Why don't the authorities impose the order necessary?"[28]

More often, it was the CNCG that inspired denunciations of municipal land, partly because it was intent on helping its affiliates, many of whom were involved in struggles with the local elite that controlled municipal government, and partly because it was under pressure to provide positive benefits to campesinos who joined the league. In many areas of Guatemala, particularly in the western highlands, there were few private fincas of sufficient size to be affected by decree 900. (In the highland departments of Sololá, Totonicapán, Quezaltenango, Huehuetenango, Chimaltenango, Sacatepéquez, and El Quiché, there were only 221 fincas larger than ten caballerías.) Peasant league representatives often turned their sights on municipal land. As uniones campesinas spread to represent aldeas within municipalities, the pressure to provide increased land for their members, as return payment for the monthly membership dues if nothing else, increased dramatically.[29]

While these attempts to obtain unjust control over municipal land prompted significant unrest, they resulted in expropriations that represented only a small proportion of the municipal land that was denounced during the revolution. The agrarian agencies turned down most of the denunciations for expropriation of municipal land, primarily because it *was* communally owned and its expropriation would have done little to further the administration's goals of increased production in agriculture and more equitable distribution of land. Not all such decisions were easily made, however, and many members of municipalities were seriously concerned about disturbances that took place while the decisions were being debated at various agrarian agencies. In Rabinal, Baja Verapaz, the scene of significant unrest from the beginning of the revolution, a small group of people denounced what they described as a private finca of about forty-two caballerías. Upon investigating the denunciation, the CAL discovered that in reality the land was communal land farmed by the comunidad campesina of El Pilar and had been registered in the name of the seventeen principales of the aldea. The CAL then demanded to know by what right the small group had denounced the land. They had no explanation, and the CAL wisely decided that no expropriation should take place. In order to protect the property, the CAL registered an official document in the agrarian records declaring that all members of the comunidad campesina had equal right to the property and that they would pay an equal share of the taxes, insuring that it would be recognized as communal property. It also pressured the members of the comunidad to form a unión campesina, arguing that this would protect them further. Although the property was thus never affected by the Agrarian Reform Law, the original petitioners did take the case through all of the stages of appeal and kept the community in a state of anxiety over the land until after the end of the revolution.[30]

In a number of cases concerning municipal land, the municipality appears to have supported the expropriation and distribution of its lands to the people who had denounced it. It is often difficult to determine if, in fact, a majority of people in the municipality had agreed to such appropriations or if the alcaldía at the time simply happened to be in the hands of a "revolutionary" who did not want to oppose the application of the law. In San Luis Jilotepeque, for example, the unión campesina denounced much of the municipal land of about twelve caballerías, located in a number of distinct "fincas." The petition explained the action by saying that "in spite of the fact that we have been cultivating the land for many years, the lands are currently registered in the name of the municipality and we have been worried about our possession of them." The alcaldía, recently won by the PRG, which was linked to the unión campesina, expressed its agreement with the expropriation.[31]

When nearly 200 members of the unión campesina in Santiago Atitlán denounced the municipal land, the alcalde supported the denunciation. He expressed his belief that the appropriation would help "all the peasantry of the municipality, especially the poor class," as was the responsibility of the municipality, and he asked only that sufficient land be left in a forest reserve. After the "Liberation," even the inspector for the General Office of Agrarian Issues (Dirección General de Asuntos Agrarios [DGAA]), which almost invariably suggested that land taken under decree 900 be returned, argued that this expropriation had been beneficial and recommended that the land not be returned. It is doubtful, however, that all community members were happy about the transfer of close to 200 caballerías of forest reserve to the state.[32]

Despite the troubles that accompanied the application of decree 900 to municipal or other communally owned land during the revolution, in many cases decree 900 was used to insure a more equitable or just distribution of the resource to members of the community. In some areas, it was clear that a privileged elite had used their power and prestige to gain preferential access to communal land. Poorer members of the municipality used the Agrarian Reform Law to regain control. In Granados, Baja Verapaz, the unión campesina of Llano Granados denounced municipal lands known as Las Balas in August 1952. The petitioners complained that "in the course of years, various people emerged who have appropriated grand extensions of this land. For this reason, as well as reducing our possessions to infinitely small amounts, we have had to rent from these people." In response, those in possession of the land claimed that they were the rightful owners and that it was not municipal land at all. A thorough search through land titles and numerous testimonies from peasants in the community convinced the CAD that the current owners had gained title to the land illegally. One statement given to the agrarian commission complained that "people without scruples . . . , taking advantage of the public offices they filled during the tyrannical and despotic governments of those times . . . and their advantageous economic conditions, in an easy but illegal manner, have expropriated great amounts of . . . Las Balas and appear now to be the legitimate owners. We mention the tyrannical governments because there still exist those who simply because they are police, harass [colgaran] humble people in order to force them to give up their rights to the land." Fifty-eight caballerías were taken and distributed to the petitioners, who were all described as "legitimate sons of the pueblo, burdened with great numbers of dependents and excessively poor."[33]

In many other municipalities, comunidades used the Agrarian Reform Law to guarantee their access to lands that had been threatened in the past by powerful individuals. In Quesada, Jutiapa, the comunidad campesina of Santa Gestrudis denounced the communal land. In this case it was not trying to gain possession of the land but was intent on insuring that the "terrenos comunales" were not taken by nineteen "señores usurpadores" who were named in the denunciation. The denunciation, which was signed by more than 150 people, claimed that "these señores came, disturbing the public order, attempting to take our land from us, damaging us by doing so, damaging us with rumors and scandals, and causing us to lose time in court." These people responded to the denunciation by saying that they had purchased the land from the community. The municipality itself did not protest the expropriation, and the DAN, as it did in most cases of this sort, ordered that the thirty caballerías be turned over to the peasants in the municipality.[34]

In many instances, the decisions concerning what was most equitable and who was most deserving were not so easily made. In San Lucas Tolimán, Sololá, municipally controlled land was denounced by the unión campesina. The municipality opposed the expropriation and submitted a list of 378 people who already rented land on the property. An agrarian commission was sent to the municipality, and it decided that those who denounced the land had a legitimate claim. However, the commission did not want to dispossess peasants who had access to only a small amount of municipal land. Thus, it carefully determined who among the petitioners had access to land elsewhere, eventually arriving at a list of 500 people who were to be given five cuerdas each in usufruct. This angered a few recipients who had been renting more than this amount previously. As one man who had rented 6.5 cuerdas from the municipality for years expressed it: "What was my surprise when the alcalde indicated to me that I now did not have the right to a cuerda and a half of this parcel. This is unjust because in this parcel I sow my corn and beans that are food for my children." However, there were only five people in similar circumstances among the original 378 renters, and the decision of the commission appears to have been both reasonable and just.[35]

Agrarian officials were often completely befuddled by the various claims and counterclaims that flooded their offices concerning municipal land. They sent commissions to investigate claims in municipality after municipality. Given the political balance in Guatemala at the time, these commissions were necessarily composed of representatives of the peasant league, the workers' union, the PAR, the PRG, the DAN, and the governor. They often reprimanded local officials who appeared to have made politically biased decisions, but they also often found it difficult to make equitable judgments. In a number of cases, they never reached a decision. For example, after six months of listening to claims concerning a small amount of land in Cubulco, Baja Verapaz, the agrarian officials had still not been able to determine who owned the land or even how much land was in dispute. Instead of ruling on the matter, they passed the buck, telling the contestants that the case needed to be settled by the courts.[36]

The DAN's decision in San Pedro Pinula, Jalapa, was no easier. The unión campesina of San Pedro Pinula denounced on 23 September 1952 what was first considered property in private fincas comprising 185 caballerías but that later turned out to be municipal land. This denunciation prompted significant protests, both about the attempted expropriation and other activities of the union. The most serious came from the members of the comunidad indígena of San Pedro Pinula, who feared that their land would be included in the denunciation. They pointed out to the agrarian officials: "We consider our land to be our only patrimony, our parcels are small, formed by the sweat and blood of our grandfathers, our fathers and ourselves and they are all we can leave our sons so they can continue working."

In defending the action of the union, Castillo Flores wrote to the chief of the DAN claiming that the municipality had accumulated hundreds of caballerías of territory and that a few large landowners had taken the best part of it. This latter claim seems to have been true, for a number of people admitted to the DAN that they each had control of more than two caballerías of the best municipal land. One fellow in particular claimed to have bought his land from the municipality and considered it to be private property even though it was still officially registered as municipal land. The case eventually made its way to Arbenz himself, who tried to balance the conflicting claims and to reduce the tension in the municipality in his judgment. The land was expropriated and given out in usufruct to all peasants, mozos colonos, and renters in the municipality who wanted it. While this angered some people, the lands used by the majority of Indians in the municipality were never touched by the expropriation. It was the large landowners, such as Ignacio and Francisco Berganza, who "owned" hundreds of manzanas of "municipal" land, who led the opposition to the expropriation and attempted to have the land returned to them after the Liberation.[37]

Aldeas and Cabaceras

While all of these cases caused some concern within municipalities, the majority of denunciations concerning municipal land reflected more clearly the "community" orientation of many of the conflicts over municipal land that occurred under the agrarian reform. Very often this struggle was for control of land among aldeas within the same municipality or between an aldea and the cabacera.

Aguacatán, Huehuetenango, had a long history of conflict among the various aldeas that made up the municipality. Early in the revolution, this conflict emerged in the shape of struggles concerning the boundaries of the aldeas. In addition, a number of aldeas sought to increase their autonomy by organizing as comunidades indígenas. Under the agrarian reform, campesinos in two aldeas, Xenacecul and Majadas, denounced land in the neighboring aldeas of Pichiquil and Xisbiac. On 25 August 1953, the DAN agreed with the denunciation and transferred some of the land. The members of the latter two aldeas protested vehemently. The DAN felt compelled to send an agrarian commission to the municipality to attempt to resolve what was rapidly becoming a problem. It reported that the agrarian inspector for the region had been acting improperly and described the "just alarm felt by the campesinos of the aldeas Pichiquil and Xisbiac" after the denunciation against their lands had been confirmed. The agrarian officials were in the process of reversing the decision when the Arbenz administration was overthrown.[38]

In Momostenango, Totonicapán, two comunidades indígenas, representing more than 1,000 people, used the Agrarian Reform Law to try to regain control of two caballerías of land in 1954. They claimed that they had "for many years and in succession from our ancestors been the legitimate owners of these lands." Some time in 1947, however, people from other cantones in the municipality had illegally begun to take possession of the land. The DAN had not yet ruled on the denunciation when Arbenz was forced to resign.[39]

San Pedro Pinula, already disturbed by tension within the cabacera over the control of municipal land, was rocked by further conflict between the aldeas of Río Blanca and Achiotes over communal land.[40] In Zacapa, the residents of the aldea of Santa Rosalia claimed that peasants from three neighboring aldeas had invaded their land in 1953. In Cobán, Alta Verapaz, members of the peasant union from the aldea of Senahú claimed that their lands had been invaded and their crops destroyed by residents of a neighboring aldea in 1954. In Amates, Izabal, the conflict between the aldea of Juan de Paz and its neighbors over communal land became so intense that armed battles broke out on a number of occasions and the DAN was unable to even begin to mark off the boundaries of the aldeas.[41]

Despite these examples of struggles among aldeas over land, most conflict within municipalities appears to have occurred between the aldeas and the cabacera, an indication of the continuing resentment by the aldeas of the cabacera's domination of municipal politics and the privileges it entailed. Throughout much of 1952, peasants in the aldea of Santa Bárbara fought with the municipal capital of Chuarrancho, Guatemala, demanding the return of land they claimed had been taken from the aldea during the presidency of Ubico. The ethnic mix in this municipality was the reverse of that in most of the municipalities in which aldeas battled the cabacera: the cabacera was almost completely Indian while the aldea of Santa Bárbara had a higher percentage of Ladinos, who resented the control over the municipality exerted by the Indian alcaldía. In the majority of cases, however, it was Indians in the aldeas who used the Agrarian Reform Law to wrest control of municipal land from a Ladino-dominated cabacera.[42]

This conflict occurred most often in municipalities that had a history of tension between aldeas and the cabacera. In two municipalities in which violent outbursts had occurred at the beginning of the revolution, the

Agrarian Reform Law provided an avenue for continuing the struggle. In San Pedro Soloma, Indian peasants from the outlying aldeas who in 1947 had failed in their bid to reclaim by force the land controlled by the municipality were more successful using decree 900. On 24 October 1953, five uniones campesinas representing five different aldeas in the municipality joined together to denounce the municipal land, "which is for the most part abandoned." They received over fifteen caballerías, which they divided among the peasants who needed land "to extend their cultivations of potatoes, wheat, and other articles of primary necessity." The municipality later blamed this action on "communists" who had provoked the Indians in the aldeas, but it was quite clear that it was yet another battle in the conflict between the Ladinos in the cabacera and the Indians in the aldeas that had being going on for nearly a hundred years.[43]

The Indians in the outlying aldeas of Patzicía were even more explicit in their attempts to get control of municipal land. The municipality had been the site of perhaps the bloodiest rural conflict in the early years of the revolution: the Patzicía revolt in 1944. What the Indians had failed to do with machetes in 1944 they accomplished in the 1950s when they won control of the alcaldía in elections. Uniones campesinas representing aldeas then denounced the municipal land without opposition from the municipal government (but, as mentioned earlier, with opposition from some individuals within the municipality). They berated the former municipal governments for exploiting the peasants, charging them "twig by twig" for the use of municipal land and forcing them to work on public projects without payment. The meeting to decide whether to denounce the land was occasionally interrupted by shouts declaring that they "could not continue being slaves of the owners, of the authorities and of all those that still believe we are in the times of the dictatorship." The CAD agreed with them and gave them control of over six caballerías of municipal land.[44]

Similar conflicts occurred in San Jerónimo, Baja Verapaz, and Santa Cruz Muluá, Retalhuleu; peasants from the aldeas who were organized into uniones campesinas or comunidades indígenas successfully denounced land controlled by the municipalities. In both municipalities, Ladinos dominated the cabacera while Indians constituted a much larger percentage of the population in the outlying regions.[45]

These conflicts were common enough that a number of agrarian officials began to take a dim view of the activities of many municipal governments. After an investigation of a denunciation of municipal land in San Miguel Petapa, Guatemala, the CAD decided to divide the land up among the "trabajadores campesinos" of the community. It explained its position by arguing, "While it may be true that at one time the municipality represented popular interests, today . . . the control of these lands by the municipality . . . serves at times to cement the economic and political power of the antipopular groups that can be currently found in command in many municipalities."[46]

Municipio versus Municipio

The most serious community conflicts over land occurred between municipalities. Guatemalan municipalities have a history of struggle with neighboring areas for possession of land, a history that stretches back to the preconquest battles between rival Mayan groups. Because of the huge decrease in population due to the European epidemic diseases that accompanied the Spanish conquest, throughout much of the colonial period this conflict was less apparent. As population levels increased in the eighteenth century, however, these struggles intensified. They were accentuated by the Liberal policies of the late nineteenth century as the governments "rationalized" municipal land and gave parcels to those municipalities, usually predominantly Ladino, that assisted the Liberal armies. From the 1870s to the beginning of the revolution, these simmering conflicts erupted whenever residents felt they might be able to alter successfully municipal land boundaries.

Even before the October Revolution, this tension became apparent when the Ponce administration proposed altering the municipal boundaries of Patulul, Chicacao, Santa Bárbara, and San Juan Bautista in the department of Sololá in response to local unrest. In 1948, a more violent expression of the tension occurred when, according to newspaper accounts, 200 "Indians" from the mountains of Jalapa invaded land controlled by the municipality of Sansare, El Progreso. The land had been taken from various aldeas in Jalapa by Sansare under the government of Estrada Cabrera in the first decade of the century. After some alarm in the capital concerning spreading unrest in the countryside, the invaders were allowed to stay on the land.[47]

With the passage of the Agrarian Reform Law, these conflicts bubbled to the surface throughout Guatemala. Despite the clearly stated intentions of decree 900 that it was to be used primarily for the expropriation of unused land from large fincas, many municipalities tried to use the mechanisms of the law as another weapon in their battle with neighboring municipalities. Once again, the agrarian officials and the revolutionary organizations found themselves sinking deeper and deeper into the quicksand of conflict over land among the various entities that make up "community" in rural Guatemala. The records of these revolutionary organizations and the DAN indicate clearly how befuddled officials often became.

Conflict between municipalities over land, fought through the medium of decree 900, raged in almost every community in Guatemala at some point after the passage of the law. There were struggles between San Pedro Pinula and Jalapa, between Zaragoza and San Andrés Itzapa, between Santa Eulalia and Santa Cruz Barillas, and between San Miguel Uspantán and Chinique. Indeed, the concerns about municipalities denouncing land in neighboring municipalities became so widespread that in a number of places municipal land was denounced from within the municipality with the sole purpose of preventing it from being denounced by people from outside of the municipality. In August 1953, for example, people in San Rafael La Independencia denounced land in eight properties controlled by the municipality. The report from the agrarian inspector stated, "These lands were denounced by people from San Rafael La Independencia to prevent them from being taken by people from outside of the municipality because neighbors in Soloma and San Miguel Acatán were interested in denouncing the land."[48]

In 1952, the 429 caballerías of municipal land controlled by San Juan Ixcoy were denounced in the name of the "campesinos of the municipio of Concepción" and by "cowboys" from a neighboring hacienda in two separate actions. The municipality lost seven caballerías of the land. Fearful that there would be other applications, members of the municipality organized into a number of uniones campesinas representing more than 500 people and denounced the remaining municipal land. The municipal government agreed to the expropriation, clearly concerned that the land might be given to outsiders if it refused. Following the overthrow of the Arbenz administration, the concerns this incident had created in the municipality were expressed by the new alcalde, who blamed the original expropriation on the "communist" organizer of the unión campesina in Concepción and warned that it would "completely ruin the economy of the municipio."[49]

The crowded area around Lake Atitlán had always been the site of tension between municipalities over land. One of the most interesting cases was the conflict described by Juan de Diós Rosales between San Pedro La Laguna and San Juan La Laguna during the 1940s that led to the burning down of the San Pedro courthouse allegedly by residents of San Juan in an effort to destroy the records of land transfers from San Juan to San Pedro. Santa Clara La Laguna was involved in a similar conflict with Santa María Visitación. The report on the municipality for the Instituto Indigenista Nacional in 1949 recorded that the inhabitants of Santa Clara were disliked by the vecinos of Santa María because "they want to get possession of the land of Santa María" and recounted a long conflict between the two municipalities over land.

In 1953, the unión campesina of Santa Clara denounced what it claimed was municipal land. The municipality expressed its complete agreement with the expropriation. A commission of agrarian officials that was already in the region around Lake Atitlán reviewed the case and suggested that the cultivable part of the land be taken and divided among the members of the union and other landless workers in the community, with the current renters of the land getting first consideration. Within a month, however, other municipalities became involved in the conflict.

A letter of protest from the unión campesina of Santa María in 1953 destroyed the agrarian commission's previous careful recommendations concerning the expropriation of Santa Clara's municipal land and gave some indication as to why the municipality of Santa Clara had agreed so quickly to the expropriation. The union of Santa María argued that the bulk of the land was in reality municipal land of Santa María and asked that it not be expropriated. The secretary-general of the union explained the history of the land in a petition: "For many years we have faced [frontando] difficulties with the vecinos of the municipality of Santa Clara La Laguna over the limits of the municipal lands that we have not, up until now, been able to resolve. Without understanding the spirit of chapter 4 of decree 900, they denounced the lands that pertain to Santa María . . . , creating since then difficulties among the campesinos that have possession of these lands." The agrarian officials still had not been able to resolve the case when the Arbenz government was overthrown.[50]

One of the most interesting conflicts between municipalities occurred between Indians in Cantel and Ladinos in neighboring Salcajá. In 1952, the unión campesina of the cantón of Estancía in Cantel denounced municipal land controlled by the municipality of Salcajá. The property, which was about eleven caballerías, was known by its previous name of Chicua in Cantel, whereas in Salcajá it was known as the finca Justo Rufino Barrios, and for good reason. The union, which claimed to represent more than half of the people of Cantel, from five cantones, argued that the land had been taken from Cantel and given to Salcajá in the 1870s because Salcajá had provided soldiers for the hated Liberal armies under Barrios and that Cantel had received no consideration whatsoever for the land. The land, which was almost completely surrounded by the municipality of Cantel, was used by individuals from Cantel, but they were subject to a "series of abuses from the forest guards of Salcajá."

The municipality of Salcajá opposed the expropriation, arguing that it would effectively transfer title for the property to Cantel, which already had enough land. A letter signed by the "vecinos" of Salcajá reflected their alarm about the denunciation: "We begin by expressing to you Mr. President, that as concerned citizens, we are the first to appreciate the benefits of the agrarian law, and we will not place ourselves in opposition to your wise decisions. But in this case we present to you, we consider that applying it would profoundly damage the economy of the entire village of Salcajá." The letter went on to argue that the only reason Barrios had given the land to Salcajá was because he had been aware that its residents had no other land and that the 4,000 residents of Salcajá now used this land as their only source of wood. There appeared to be some justification for this argument as only 8 percent of Salcajá residents owned their own land, whereas 16 percent of Cantel residents did. However, the average size of landholding in Salcajá was almost double that in Cantel. The CAN sent a commission to the area, which investigated the case for over a year before deciding in favor of the union from Cantel.

The case was not over, however. Shortly after the land was officially transferred to the control of Cantel, the unión campesina of Salcajá denounced it, claiming that it was not being used by the peasants from Cantel because "the vecinos of Cantel have enough land" and thus was subject to reexpropriation. The DAN, out of patience by this point, refused to deal with the case any further. After the overthrow of Arbenz, the peasants of Salcajá applied to have the land returned. They explained their misfortune under decree 900 as the result of the coming elections for congress, claiming that "as Salcajá was always a town 100 percent aligned with the opposition, and in Cantel there were many communist leaders, the political parties of the government offered Cantel the community forest of Salcajá if they would vote in these men of the same political beliefs as them." The land was returned to Salcajá in May 1955.[51]

While agrarian decisions concerning denunciations of municipal land often angered people in rural Guatemala, in most cases the agrarian officials clearly attempted to make equitable and just decisions in the disputes. Most often the DAN's decisions meant little alteration in access to land in the community; those already renting small parcels of land were always given first priority when the land was distributed. The land was never given out in ownership; rather, it was assigned in lifelong usufruct, and 4 percent of the harvest was to be paid in rent to the municipality in most cases. Often the agrarian officials showed substantial wisdom in reaching their decisions. For example, San Pedro Soloma, which had suffered through bitter land conflicts throughout the revolution, was shaken by more conflict in 1952 when 125 people denounced municipal land. The property was registered in the name of the municipality, but Antonio Gaspar Pablo reported in the denunciation that he and the other petitioners had bought the land, which was about two caballerías, between 1941 and 1946 and that they farmed it "en forma comunal agraria." They wanted to register it in their own names to prevent the municipality from taking it from them. The CAL reported that, in essence, the land belonged to four aldeas of the municipality and that the heads of families in the aldeas were represented by the 125 people involved in the original purchase. The CAD supported the attempts to prevent the municipality from taking land from the aldeas because it was aware of the various conflicts that other aldeas had had with the cabacera, but it also wanted to insure that all residents of the four aldeas had access to the land. Thus it ruled that the denunciation should be accepted and that the property should be given in lots to the original 125 petitioners as well as all the vecinos of the four aldeas.[52]

In a similar conflict in Tejutla, San Marcos, the agrarian officials were faced with a petition from the unión campesina of the aldea of Tojuchoco for land in the aldea of Venecia. Seventy people in Venecia complained about the denunciation. On the other hand, the forty-five members of the unión campesina of Tojuchoco desperately needed land, and there was cultivable land in Venecia that was not being used. The CAD decided that the land should be expropriated and divided among the forty-five people from Tojuchoco, thirty-four people from Venecia that did not have any land, and forty-seven people from Venecia that had only small plots of land.[53]

The agrarian officials demonstrated similar caution in Comitancillo, San Marcos, where municipal land was denounced by members of the aldea of San Luis, organized into a unión campesina. More than 200 members of the union asked that five caballerías of municipal land be given to them since the land "had been purchased by our ancestors and for more than 100 years our great grandfathers, our grandfathers, our fathers, and now we have been working the land. In 1925, because of a lack of caution on the part of our fathers, these five caballerías were titled in favor of the municipality of Comitancillo, which has constantly threatened us with wanting to give the land to another aldea that used to be part of San Luis and won recognition as an aldea on 27 May 1951." The CAD suggested that the property be given out in usufruct "not only to the petitioners, but also to the inhabitants of both aldeas San Luis and Tuijmuj." It then asked that a complete census be taken of the two aldeas before the distribution so that it could be done with "complete impartiality." The CAD's decision did not satisfy either side, however, and conflict continued over the issue past 1958.[54]

One of the most difficult cases for the agrarian officials to decide occurred in Parramos, Chimaltenango. Eight caballerías of municipal land were denounced by the unión campesina headed by Maximo Cinto Yuc, which represented more than sixty-three people. The denunciation provided substantial proof that those soliciting land were poor and deserving. However, some of the people already renting land from the municipality complained in a letter to the governor that they were equally poor and stated, "It is sure that if you take this land from us our situation and that of our families will be grave for we have no land of our own." The municipality reported that 326 people rented land from the municipality, paying 30 centavos a year per cuerda. Some of those opposing the expropriation argued that the peasants seeking land should not be favored because they had joined into a unión campesina, which the letter writers described as a political party. They claimed that since they were military commissioners and therefore could not join a political party, they were being treated unfairly. The agrarian officials recommended going ahead with the expropriation but ordered that a commission be established among all the vecinos of the municipality to work out the dispute in the process of granting land. Those already renting land from the municipality were to be given first priority. The CAD suggested that they should be allowed fifteen manzanas each. This ruling, in fact, led to many of those already renting land obtaining larger plots to farm.[55]

The extension of revolutionary organizations and the application of revolutionary decrees in rural municipalities did not, as has been suggested, lead to the "destruction" of Guatemalan Indian communities. While there was some challenge to the traditional structures usually associated with the closed corporate community in Guatemala, it did not always come from the revolutionary organizations themselves, and in some instances revolutionary organizations supported traditional structures. During the revolution, political parties linked to national organizations eventually won control of local governments in many municipalities, but most often this represented a victory for the bulk of the inhabitants over a local elite that had traditionally controlled local politics. In many predominantly Indian municipalities, this often meant Indians taking control of local politics from a Ladino elite that dominated the municipal capital. The rural poor in Guatemala, Indian and Ladino alike, willingly, at times eagerly, embraced these new revolutionary organizations and used them to alter conditions in their communities and to bargain with the national government and national institutions.

The greatest potential challenge to the community and the greatest source of conflict was the struggle for control of municipal or community land. The agrarian officials during the Arbenz regime were, at times, heavy-handed in their dealings with municipalities over land. They expropriated a substantial percentage of the communally owned land in the country, placing much of it in forest reserves controlled by the state. The activities of revolutionary organizations, especially the peasant league, in helping to prompt denunciations of communal land caused much unrest and conflict within municipalities. But the expropriation of municipal land was not as harmful to rural communities in Guatemala as it might at first seem to have been. The expropriation of municipal land usually resulted in little alteration in land tenure in the community. Those already renting land were given first priority in its distribution; land was always given out in lifelong usufruct, not ownership; those who received the land could not sell it and thus could not alienate it from the community; and recipients continued to pay a portion of the harvest to the community for the land. In addition, in many municipalities the denunciation of municipal or other communally controlled land reflected long-standing conflicts within the municipality. Its expropriation often represented a victory over a small elite or over the Ladino-controlled cabacera by campesinos and Indians in the aldeas or in legally recognized comunidades. Very often the conflict over municipal land was the result of continuing tension among various parts of the municipality or between municipalities based on traditional claims to land. Throughout rural Guatemala, vecinos of municipalities used the Agrarian Reform Law, despite its intentions, as a weapon in age-old conflicts specific to their communities.

Despite the care the agrarian officials often used in deciding disputes over the disposition of municipal land, they seldom satisfied all sides in the argument. Rural Guatemala seethed with conflict with the application of the agrarian reform, much of it generated by the challenges, perceived or real, that the revolution brought to the structures of community in Guatemala. The comuneros of the comunidad indígena of Santa María Joyabaj described that unrest movingly to the new agrarian officials that came to the area after the overthrow of the Arbenz administration. The community had been forced to allow 200 Indians from San Martín Jilotepeque access to its communal lands during the revolution. In 1955, the comuneros explained:

> Each one of the political changes that has occurred in our nation has filled us with anxiety and dread [zozobra] because we know that individuals who say they represent the interests of the state rush to our community to fill our peaceful existence as agriculturists with confusion and disorder. It would take a long time to enumerate all the material sufferings our fathers endured to defend our ejidos and to give us the happiness of feeling we are on our own land. It would take a long time as well to describe the vexation and disgust we felt when others planted among us constant conflicts and litigations to reduce the size of our land. . . . Now . . . we are looking for the justice that is required to reach a solution to the numerous problems that arose with the implementation of the sadly famous Agrarian Reform Law.[56]

COMMUNISM AND THE MILITARY

Our dear Patria, Guatemala,

always hopes that you, loyal soldier,

will guard the blessed liberty

that the red breast of the Quetzal breathes.

—Enrique Laparra Espinosa, "Himno al Ejército,"
Alerta!, 10 December 1944

If tomorrow your sacred soil

is menaced by foreign invaders

shout to the wind your glorious banner

"to conquer or to die" declare

That your people with fiery will

will choose death before slavery again.

—CNCG poster

A few days after the "Liberation" army crossed the border from Honduras into Guatemala on 17 June 1954, President Arbenz spoke on the national radio station. It was his greatest speech, a fighting call to the nation and an indictment of the invaders. Calling the Liberation cohorts "greedy servants of foreign companies," he stated:

> Our attackers have been disappointed. They told their masters and mentors the entire population of Guatemala would rise up as soon as they had arms. . . . But, . . . the population has not rebelled. . . . Think of what would happen if, on the other hand, the skies over Nicaragua rained arms and ammunition. . . . And this is so because the people not only do not forget what they were, but because they remember what they can lose. Every worker, every peasant, every employee, every teacher, every member of the army and every Guatemalan of good heart knows what he stands to lose. . . . The National Army of the Revolution is a new army. This has been forgotten by our enemies. . . . There exists in our army a clear awareness that the patria is to be defended. . . . History and the right of the people are on our side. . . . Today more than ever we put our confidence in the unity of the people, in the national army and in victory.[1]

Why were the new army, history, and the right of the people not enough to keep the revolution from collapsing? By 1954 the Arbenz administration was beset by myriad pressures, including an intensely antagonistic U.S. administration; the threat of an invasion force trained, organized, and assisted by the CIA; and effective diplomatic isolation in much of Latin America. But these external sources of pressure, as important as they may have been, were less important than internal tensions. The Arbenz administration was overthrown primarily because of the increasing antipathy of a large sector of the Guatemalan military and the urban middle class. The officers' concerns were sparked largely by their fear of communism and the activities of rural activists associated with the agrarian reform. With the threat of invasion looming, organized peasants and rural workers declared their willingness to fight for Arbenz and the preservation of the revolution. However, this was exactly what the top military officers, already concerned about their diminishing power in rural Guatemala and the growing strength of peasant organizations, did not want. They demanded Arbenz's resignation, and Arbenz, unwilling to risk civil war and disillusioned, succumbed. He left office on 27 June 1954, and the revolution rapidly fell apart as the leaders of revolutionary organizations sought refuge in embassies and peasant leaders fled their communities.

Guatemala Out of Step

In 1951, Assistant Secretary of State Edward Clark, in a hastily written postscript to a personal letter to Milton K. Wells, at that time the chargé at the U.S. embassy in Guatemala, commented on the latest meeting of Latin American foreign ministers in Washington, D.C. His parting line was, "I suppose you have seen by now the picture of the Foreign Ministers in the latest edition of *Life*. All of the Foreign Ministers, that is, except one. I have yet to see the time when everyone isn't out of step except Guatemala."[2]

Clark's wisecrack says much about the relationship between Guatemala and the United States during the revolution. In the full bloom of its post–World War II military and economic might, the United States demanded uncritical accord from its most dependent Western allies. Nowhere was this more apparent than in Central America, and in that delicate region, no one broke ranks like Guatemala, on both the economic and political parade grounds.

The tempestuous relationship between the revolutionary governments and U.S. companies in Guatemala caused immense concern in the Arévalo and Arbenz administrations. The "unholy trinity" of the UFCo, the IRCA, and the UFCo Steamship Lines had grown accustomed to privileged treatment from Estrada Cabrera during the dictator's rule from 1898 to 1920 and to immediate and unrestricted access to the president during the long reign of President Ubico. The nationalist policies of the Arévalo and Arbenz governments shocked them. The other major monopoly concern, the Empresa Eléctrica, was treated no more gently by the revolutionary administrations and was no better prepared for their policies. Government attempts to renegotiate contracts, break monopolies, tax profits, collect back taxes, and inspect company accounts all prompted deep and bitter disputes between the companies and the government.

The freedom allowed Guatemalan workers during the revolutionary period after the companies had enjoyed decades of quiescent labor "relations" was also troublesome, particularly since the workers' federations saved their most hardy actions for foreign companies. As early as 1946, the CTG resolved to support "the liberation of Guatemala, as a nation, from its dependence on imperialism." Both labor federations struck U.S. companies more often, over more diverse issues, than national firms. The government-appointed labor inspectors tended to be less sympathetic to U.S. companies' protests. The application of the 1947 Labor Code, which allowed union organization in rural areas only on farms employing more than 500 people, caused particular resentment since only the government-controlled national fincas, the UFCo, and two other fincas fit that category.[3]

By 1951, Arbenz's first year in office, the relationship between these companies and the government was markedly hostile. Facing increasing government and labor demands, the UFCo threatened to leave the country altogether when its plantation at Tiquisate suffered severe storm damage that year. It drastically reduced its passenger service on the steamship lines and began to remove inventory from company stores. That same year, 5,000 railway workers struck the IRCA, and when the company refused to pay back wages demanded by the workers, the government intervened in the operations of the railroad. The government also began investigations into the operations of Empresa Eléctrica in what many people believed was a prelude to nationalization. Guatemala also led a protest by coffee-producing nations against the prices set by the United States under the coffee agreement. While the 1951 crisis passed — due primarily to efforts by the government to curtail worker demands — the relationship between the Guatemalan government and U.S. companies operating in the country remained extremely strained for the duration of the revolution.[4]

However, the most serious attack on the position of the largest U.S. company in Guatemala came with the Agrarian Reform Law. With huge amounts of land, much of it uncultivated, the UFCo was a natural target for decree 900. The first expropriation of UFCo land began in early 1953, and by August of that year close to 250,000 of its 350,000 manzanas had been taken.[5]

The expropriations of UFCo land were accomplished in a more orderly fashion than was common on much of the other land taken under decree 900. There was little pressure from competing peasant unions in the immediate vicinity of UFCo operations clamoring for restricted amounts of land, as was evident elsewhere in the country. Along with its land planted in bananas and other crops, the company was left with substantial forest reserves and thousands of acres in pasture. It was offered Q609,572 in compensation.[6]

The company fought the expropriations vehemently. Its protests were based on a number of points. The most substantial complaints focused on according to UFCo the compensation offered to them by gov. did not equate to the land taken

the amount of land taken and the compensation offered. The Agrarian Reform Law called for the expropriation of only land that was not in cultivation, in pasture, or in specified forest cover. The UFCo claimed that much of its appropriated land was actually used for pasture or forestland and should not have been subject to the law. More importantly, the company asserted that because of the prevalence of banana diseases, requiring that the afflicted land be rested and flooded, UFCo land should not be affected by the law at all. The company also disagreed with the compensation. For the purposes of decree 900, the value of rural property was based on a long-standing practice of self-declared assessment for tax purposes. As the last rural property assessment had been done in 1935, the Arévalo administration called for new assessments in 1945. The new value had to be registered by November 1948. The UFCo submitted its assessment in September 1948, but by April of the next year, perhaps in response to the discussions of an impending agrarian reform, the company asked to have the declared value of its property changed. The government began inspections to rule on the request in June 1951, but the new assessment was never completed. The company declared, therefore, that the money offered in compensation for the land, based on the 1948 assessment, was not adequate. It claimed that the value of the appropriated land was Q15,854,849, almost twenty-five times the amount offered by the government.[7]

The U.S. State Department and the embassy acted as steadfast allies of the UFCo in all of the company's difficulties with the government of Guatemala. The attitude of the State Department was aptly summed up by Milton Wells when, commenting on labor court rulings concerning a strike at a Guatemalan cement company, he noted, "If the Guatemalans want to handle a Guatemalan company roughly that, again, is none of our business. But if they handle an American company roughly it is *our* business" (emphasis in original).[8] Despite opposition from some people within the embassy, the embassy and the State Department soon became the principal negotiators for the company over the agrarian reform rulings.

Guatemala reacted as would be expected. The Arbenz administration had stressed from its inception that it had the right and the obligation to adopt a program of nationalist economic development and warned that foreign investment must be subject to Guatemalan laws. It was not prepared to broaden its discussions concerning decree 900 to include the U.S. government. Responding to a petition from the assistant secretary of state for inter-American affairs, the Guatemalan ambassador to the United States,

US involvement not stated as concern, protection of American business

Guillermo Toriello, noted: "The Agrarian Reform Law is a general law, applicable equally to natural or juridical persons, whether nationals or foreign, possessing rural property in the national territory. Its application constitutes an act of inherent sovereignty, for which reason the government of Guatemala could not consider . . . the possibility of making this case a matter for international discussion."[9]

The continuing conflict with the UFCo had an important effect on Guatemala's relations with the U.S. government. The tentacles of "el pulpo" reached into the heart of the State Department and the Eisenhower administration. The secretary of state, John Foster Dulles, and the director of the CIA, Allen Dulles, were intimately connected with the company. They had both been lawyers for the firm that drew up the 1931 and 1936 contracts between the UFCo and Ubico and had both been personally involved in framing those contracts. Allen Dulles accepted a gift of substantial stock from the grateful company. The UFCo also embarked on a powerful and effective public relations campaign against the Guatemalan government directed both at U.S. government officials and at the U.S. public.[10]

The communist mission first should...

By 1953 it was apparent that the UFCo was intent on getting rid of the Arbenz administration any way it could. Early that year, a group of conspirators launched an uprising in Salamá, Baja Verapaz. The tiny and ill-planned rebellion was quickly controlled, and the conspirators were arrested. Under questioning, they alleged that the UFCo had paid them $64,000 for their efforts. Also, rumors continually circulated throughout Guatemala of the UFCo's links to exile forces in Honduras preparing for an invasion.[11]

There is, however, some question concerning the impact of the UFCo's troubles in Guatemala on the Eisenhower administration. As Blanche Wiesen Cook has pointed out, Eisenhower had great respect for "men of finance" and "accepted their self-appointed role as his tutors." Moreover, a large amount of the United States' trade in the 1950s was with Latin America. Guatemala's "Iranian mentality," as Edward Clark described it, was quickly becoming a dangerous symbol of economic and political independence throughout Latin America.[12] Nonetheless, the Eisenhower administration was, without a doubt, more concerned about the importance of communism in Guatemala.

The question of the influence of communists on the Guatemalan president had become the dominant internal political issue in Guatemala by 1951, at least among the urban elite and middle class. Opposition newspapers were filled with articles condemning communism and the government's acceptance of it. Opposition political parties organized around the issue. Protest marches against the government focused on it.

There was, of course, a self-serving aspect to this obsession. Opposition political movements had proved throughout the revolution that they could not compete with the revolutionary political parties at the polls. The opposition was irreparably fragmented and could not offer a policy or a vision of the future. As a consequence, opposition parties fared remarkably poorly in elections. By the 1950s, these movements reduced their focus to a condemnation of communism, hoping in this way to forge a workable coalition of opposition groups and to win votes. In some municipios, they were temporarily successful and "civic committees" were occasionally able to win local office. Nevertheless, they were unable to translate their obsession into victory either in any significant number of local contests or in congressional elections.

The most prominent opposition leaders soon abandoned these attempts and concentrated on violent overthrow of the government, "dreaming of dramatic Hollywoodesque rescue by the Marines," in the words of Kalman Silvert, rather than working seriously to win electoral contests. In order to justify their violent attempts to grasp power, they emphasized the communist dominance of the Arbenz administration and created a myth concerning its imposition through electoral fraud and a reign of terror perpetrated by the director of the national police and the Guardia Civil. Although there were isolated incidents of electoral fraud and cases of civil rights abuse, they were neither systematic nor widespread. A careful study of the reported civil rights violations indicates that they were isolated occurrences perpetrated by individuals connected to the government who were not adequately supervised or controlled by the beleaguered administration. Even the first secretary of the U.S. embassy from 1951 to 1954, William Krieg, probably the person in the embassy who best knew Guatemala, declared that these accusations had little substance, with the exception of a brief period of panic immediately before the invasion of "Liberation" forces in 1954.[13]

Increasing concern about a perceived hovering communist menace was reflected in a growing number of anticommunist civic organizations that held periodic rallies, often with thousands of people in attendance. This concern was fueled by the major Guatemala City newspaper, *El Imparcial*, and the church. *El Imparcial* published constant warnings about communism and horror stories concerning the atrocities of communist regimes elsewhere and provided free advertising for meetings of anticommunist leagues throughout the country. It was not the only paper to take this tack; the editor of *La Hora*, Clemente Marroquín Rojas, directed a letter to Arbenz on the front page, warning: "With communism, Colonel Arbenz, there is no room for equanimity or justice. Communism does not accept the middle road of impartiality; it does not accept a place in the sun for everyone, nor is it of the opinion that to govern is to seek to attain the well-being of all inhabitants of a country. Communism must be served unconditionally or it must be fought all along the line."[14]

The church continued the criticism of government programs it had maintained throughout the Arévalo administration. Despite regular warnings from the government that the constitution forbade the church from mixing in politics, the archbishop, Mariano Rossell y Arellano, kept up a constant barrage through pastoral letters and the church paper, *Acción social cristiana*. The paper ran satirical columns on government figures that, among other things, attempted to link the leader of the PGT, José Manuel Fortuny, to the devil. Rossell even suggested that democracy, in itself, was not beneficial to Guatemalans. He argued, "Sad experience shows that liberty left to the caprice of each individual only disorganizes [our people] into opposing bands, weakens them, and begins to destroy them." Finally, in 1954, as anticommunist protest was reaching a fever pitch, he called on the people to "rise up as one man against the enemy of God, of our fatherland," against "the worst of the atheistic doctrines of all time, anti-Christian communism."[15]

The anticommunist campaign had a significant effect. Opposition to the government grew, becoming more vocal and influential. Unrest in the countryside associated with the Agrarian Reform Law, exaggerated and distorted by the urban media, only seemed to prove to many, particularly the urban middle class, that the country was indeed in danger of being taken over by communist cadres. Ironically perhaps, in response, the Arbenz administration and the revolutionary parties found it more difficult to distance themselves from the communists. The revolutionary parties continually asserted that they were not communists, but they refused to join the anticommunist chant, claiming that it merely "hid the face of reaction." Arbenz, opposed by an increasingly violent reaction, was prompted both to continue to provide support for the PGT and to rely more heavily on some of its members and the more dedicated reformers in the other revolutionary organizations. This, in turn, fostered charges that Arbenz was either a communist or a "fellow traveler."

Nonetheless, no admitted communist occupied a cabinet post, and the PGT was the smallest of the parties in the government coalition; by 1954 it had only five of fifty-eight deputies in congress. There was also some question concerning the political ideology of those few people who declared themselves communists. Guillermo Toriello, Arbenz's ambassador to the United States and foreign minister in the final days of the government, responded to the U.S. State Department's constant questions about communist influence by arguing that the few proclaimed "communists" in the country had little knowledge of communism. He suggested that their leader, José Manuel Fortuny, had become a communist "only after getting mental indigestion reading Marx." In some ways, this was a perceptive comment; the momentum demonstrated by the PGT and the support given to communist adherents like Carlos Manuel Pellecer and Víctor Manuel Gutiérrez came from their leading roles in implementing such nonsocialist legislation as the Agrarian Reform Law, the social security system, and the Labor Code. Most members of the PGT, like other communist parties throughout Latin America, believed there was no contradiction in the party's position at the head of a movement toward a more "modern" capitalism.[16]

However, a recognition of the limits of communist influence and ideology in Guatemala should not lead either to a denial of their importance or to a too hasty judgment that U.S. concern over communist influence was a calculated smoke screen to hide economic imperialism. Despite Arbenz's cautious cabinet appointments, there had been significant radicalization in the major government parties following his election. The most moderate of the reform politicians — that is, those who saw the revolution as an effort to bring about electoral democracy and some very minor economic and social reforms — had been forced out of these parties. Even some quite committed reformers had resigned from the government parties, complaining of the increasing influence of the communists. The dominant party, the PAR, forged an unofficial alliance with the PGT; the CGTG and, with less reason, the CNCG were considered by many to be communist controlled; and some key government agencies were run by people widely assumed to be communists, including the IGSS, the labor courts, and, most importantly, the DAN, headed by Wlademar Barrios Klee. Many of the most powerful members of congress adopted a rhetoric of class conflict and historical determinism that most U.S. observers saw as communist.[17]

Arguments that the PGT was small and that affirmed communists had little influence in Guatemala did not convince the U.S. State Department that there was no communist threat. Its chief concern was a perceived "underground" movement through which communists or communist sympathizers were quickly gaining power. In 1950 the CIA reported that the presence of a few communists in Guatemala was not particularly troublesome and did not constitute a threat to U.S. security interests. Slightly more than a year later, the State Department reported that it "considers the success with which the Communists are capturing the Government machinery of that country to be a serious element in the threat to our national security." By 1953 the CIA warned, "The current political situation in Guatemala is adverse to U.S. interests. The Guatemalan communists exercise a political influence far out of proportion to their small numerical strength. Their influence will probably continue to grow as long as President Arbenz remains in power." Although Arbenz was not considered to be a communist, he was thought to rely heavily on communists in a "working alliance . . . in the pursuit of leftist and nationalist policies," which included the "persecution of foreign economic interests . . . especially the United Fruit Company [and which enjoyed] the support or acquiescence of almost all Guatemalans." However, the report's strongest concerns centered around security interests and warned that "detriment to Hemispheric solidarity would not deter Guatemala from any course of action suggested by its own interests."[18]

CIA and State Department assessments of the influence of communists in Guatemala were not totally unreasonable. However, they did concentrate on a few quite restricted examples in drawing their conclusions about suspected communist affiliation. They were most concerned about Guatemala's independent stance in foreign affairs. Eisenhower himself said that he became convinced of the communist nature of the Guatemalan government by the arguments of John Moors Cabot, assistant secretary of state for inter-American affairs, who pointed to Guatemala's opposition to the Korean War and to the number of government officials who had signed a petition condemning the use of bacteriological warfare by the United States in Korea. U.S. officials were also concerned about the "peace campaign" that developed in Guatemala after 1950 as part of an international movement opposed to the war in Korea. Headed by Luis Cardoza y Aragón, it quickly gained the allegiance of many powerful government-aligned politicians, the first "big fish" being Roberto Alvarado Fuentes of the PAR. The U.S. government saw the peace campaign in the 1950s as a communist front and seemed to believe that affiliation with the campaign by any Guatemalan politician indicated communist sympathies. Numerous Guatemalan politicians not directly linked to the PGT supported the campaign. Its adherents were able to swing congress to issue a number of appeals for international peace, and a demand for peace was one of the rallying cries of May Day celebrations in the 1950s. It was partly as a consequence of the growing power of the peace movement that members of congress engaged in symbolic gestures such as a minute of silence after the death of Joseph Stalin in 1953, which the U.S. government found extremely objectionable.[19]

The major objection on the part of the U.S. administration to the Agrarian Reform Law was not that land was appropriated from the UFCo, although the importance of that action should not be ignored. Its greatest concern was that "communist" peasant organizers were using the Agrarian Reform Law to win adherents in rural areas. This fear was expressed clearly by Krieg in a memorandum of a conversation he held in 1952 with Ricardo Castañeda Paganini, a Guatemalan writer on Indian culture. Castañeda had remarked that it was fortunate that the communists did not have trained anthropologists among them because "they could use anthropologists to manage the Indians very skillfully." Despite the lack of anthropologists, it soon seemed apparent to many in the U.S. embassy that reformers they had already branded as communists were using the agrarian reform to win support in rural communities throughout Guatemala.[20]

All of these considerations affected U.S. assessments of the Guatemalan situation. U.S. actions were determined by a mix of economic and security interests, with an overwhelming concentration on the latter. U.S. concerns about communist influence in Guatemala were exaggerated but understandable given the nature of U.S. politics at the time, the people who were in positions to advise the U.S. government at the embassy and the State Department, and the activities of many Guatemalan politicians and the Arbenz government. Arbenz's increasingly close ties to known communists and growing reliance on their advice were especially troublesome for the U.S. State Department. There appears to be little justification for the oft-repeated accusation that the State Department acted against the Arbenz administration because of a UFCo-inspired conspiracy.

By late 1953, the stage was set for U.S. intervention. Guatemala had been effectively isolated in Central America, having been forced to resign from the Organization of Central American States in response to the organization's concerns about communism in Guatemala. The United States signed defense treaties with Honduras and Nicaragua in 1954. A growing chorus of U.S. journalists and politicians openly called for intervention in Guatemala. The arrival of a cargo of Czechoslovakian arms on board a

Swedish ship, the *Alfhem*, early in 1954, labeled "the Red Bloc's first public display of big brotherly trust and confidence in Guatemala" by *Time* magazine, provided the final prompting and a convenient excuse for the Eisenhower administration to unleash an invasion orchestrated by the CIA and the State Department. As a final step, the United States sought and received — although not without numerous reservations and restrictions, which it proceeded to ignore — a veiled "go-ahead" from Latin American states at the Organization of American States meeting in Caracas in March 1954.[21]

Shortly thereafter, the Liberation army, in training since 1952, invaded the country, seizing a number of small towns in the Oriente. Planes supplied by the United States and flown by U.S. pilots strafed Guatemalan towns, and a U.S.-installed "free" radio station bombarded residents with propaganda. Guatemalan attempts to have the United Nations rule on the invasion were thwarted by the United States in a heavy-handed manner that very nearly prompted the resignation of the United Nations secretary-general, Dag Hammarskjöld. By 27 June 1954, Arbenz had resigned and the revolution had effectively ended.[22]

The Military and the Intervention

Most discussions of the intervention and the overthrow of Arbenz concentrate on the U.S. decision to intervene; from that point on, the collapse of the revolution is generally seen as having been inevitable. This outlook, however, does not appear to be justified. Despite the fact that the intervention was widespread and carefully planned, U.S. commitment to it, in terms of manpower and especially public admissions of involvement, was severely limited. There certainly were no plans for extensive use of U.S. troops. Only a few days before Arbenz finally resigned, Raymond Leddy, the officer in charge of Central American affairs for the State Department, was predicting defeat for the Liberation army. There had been no signs of the hoped-for internal uprising, and the Liberation forces on their own were a tiny, unimpressive, rebel band. All chance of success rested on the actions of the Guatemalan military.[23]

However, most knowledgeable commentators stressed that the military was loyal to the government and would defend it, an analysis supported by the public statements of the top military commanders themselves. In March 1954, the chief of the armed forces promised congress, "The army is with and will always be with a government that, like the one presided over by our illustrious comrade, Jacobo Arbenz, permits the free play of all liberties and guarantees." He went on to assure the deputies, "The army makes clear before the people its unbreakable promise to comply with its duty to defend national interests and to repudiate with great firmness all that menaces the sovereignty and integrity of the nation."[24] Yet it was the military command's inaction in the face of intervention and, finally, its refusal to defend Guatemala unless Arbenz resigned that signaled the end of the revolution. The military's actions in the tension-filled days of June 1954 cannot be divorced from the revolution occurring in the countryside with the implementation of the Agrarian Reform Law.

The Guatemalan military had an ambivalent relationship with the revolution. Much of this ambivalence emanated from the character of the institution itself. Article 149 of the constitution declared the army to be "apolitical, essentially professional, obedient, and nondeliberative." Nevertheless, the army, through the chief of the armed forces, was to swear it "shall never be an instrument of arbitrary action or of oppression and that no one of its members shall respect orders that imply the commission of a crime." In addition, the army was to "defend the integrity of the territory, the constitution of the republic, and the rights and liberties of the people." It was a contradictory mandate, placing the military in the position of being the final arbiter of constitutionality and legality, while admonishing its members to be nondeliberative and obedient.[25]

In reaction to the string of dictators who had dominated the military and used it to maintain themselves in power, the revolutionary army was made into a rather decentralized and "democratic" institution. The president of the republic was the commander in chief, but the real heads of the army were the chief of the armed forces and the defense minister. The chief of the armed forces, responsible for promotions and assignments, was the most powerful, but the defense minister was an impressive counterweight; the constitution specifically called for the president's orders to be issued through both officers. The intent was obvious: to prevent challenges to an elected president from the military by dividing the highest authority between two positions, while making it more difficult for the president to dominate the military. This intention was perhaps best expressed by Colonel Ramiro Asturias, who, in an interview for a Mexican newspaper in 1948, commented, "The army is no longer an instrument at the service of the president. Today, the army serves the nation."[26]

There was also an attempt to create a democratic internal structure within the military while not unduly weakening the hierarchical chain of command necessary for an army to function. The Superior Council of National Defense, the main duties of which were vaguely defined as "the resolution of questions connected with the functioning of the army," was to have a significant number of its no less than fifteen members elected in a secret vote by all senior officers. The council's most important function was to suggest three officers to the president for the position of chief of the armed forces, who would hold office for six years. This effectively prevented the president from selecting the officer to hold the most important position in the military throughout the president's term in office. The council was also intended to prevent the accumulation of power in the military by one man. However, it also encouraged the formation of internal cliques within the army favoring one candidate or another for positions on the council.[27]

The Guatemalan army was divided at the beginning of the decade of the revolution and remained so throughout. The overthrow of Ponce had been accomplished primarily by "young" officers, and their youth was subsequently celebrated in song and poem. These officers made common cause against the geriatric cluster of generals who surrounded Ubico, kept him in power, helped stifle all democratic dissent, and — in the view of the young reformers — tried to hold back time itself in the country. A group of these aging officers was forced from the country along with Ubico and Ponce. But among the "young" officers, two distinct currents were readily apparent, clearly symbolized by Captain Jacobo Arbenz Guzmán and Major Francisco Arana.

Arana was a military loyalist, a respected figure in political and military circles although somewhat stolid, and, as described by the CIA, "a competent and persevering mestizo officer who had risen from the ranks."[28] For most of the Arévalo administration, he was the most powerful officer. Colonel Elfego Monzón claimed that it was a group of fifteen senior officers held together by Arana that protected the Arévalo administration from overthrow in the face of the almost constant coup attempts during the first few years of the revolution. It was abundantly clear, however, that there was a price to be paid for this protection, which often bordered on holding the president hostage. Arana stifled government policy during the first few years of the revolution. He was particularly insistent on curtailing labor and peasant activism in the countryside and frequently ordered the military to intervene in strikes in the countryside despite Arévalo's opposition.[29] Conflict between Arana and Arévalo became more apparent after the revisions to the Labor Code in 1948 that allowed union organization on fincas. The tension was so apparent that at one point Arévalo complained, "In Guatemala there are two presidents and one of them has a machine gun with which he is always threatening the other."[30]

Arana's only major opponent in the military was Arbenz, made minister of defense by Arévalo. Arbenz and Arana were close to the same age — they were certainly of the same generation — yet Arbenz very quickly became the representative of the "young" officers. Arbenz was unlike Arana in every respect except in his attachment to the military institution. Described by the CIA as a "brilliant, cultured graduate of the Military Academy of upper class European ancestry," Arbenz had an unparalleled record in the Escuela Politécnica, returned to teach there, and commanded the cadet company. At least through the early years of the revolution, Arbenz was most firmly linked with the young officers at the academy and those people with whom he had developed connections while he commanded the cadet company.[31]

Arbenz remains a shadowy figure throughout most of the Arévalo administration, leaving the impression that during the five years between Arévalo's assumption of the presidency and Arbenz's announcement of his candidacy for the position Arbenz was developing political connections. It was also probably a period during which he was constantly questioning unformed political ideas. Perhaps it is the nebulous quality of his political ideas during the first administration of the revolution that has led most observers, even the relatively impartial economist George Britnell, to label Arbenz a "thorough opportunist."[32]

Arbenz appears to have been somewhat of an outsider among the top military commanders. He did not attend the meetings of the Superior Council of National Defense regularly, nor, according to Monzón, was he part of the circle of officers who had pledged with Arana to support Arévalo. Nevertheless, he was clearly Arana's major opponent in the army. According to Colonel Carlos Paz Tejada, it was Arbenz who effectively prevented Arana from imposing a new defense council in 1949 that would be favorably disposed to Arana. This conflict precipitated a series of events in which Arana threatened Arévalo with a coup if he did not dismiss his cabinet (a dismissal that would, of course, have included Arbenz). Arévalo turned to Arbenz for support, and Arana was killed in a fight with Arbenz's supporters in the military.[33]

Although the circumstances surrounding Arana's death are still somewhat obscure, it did precipitate the most serious split within the military since the October Revolution. A major revolt erupted following the announcement of his death, a revolt only barely put down after intense fighting and the arming of workers and revolutionary politicians by Arbenz. Arana's death and Arbenz's actions during the revolt cemented his position in the military and paved the way to the presidency. The revolt served to purge the military of its most conservative officers. Approximately one-quarter of the active officers were relieved of their commands, and many were forced out of the country. A further coup attempt led by Colonel Carlos Castillo Armas during the election campaign in 1950 also assisted in pruning the army of those most opposed to the reforms of the revolution.[34]

Following his election, Arbenz attempted to insure the loyalty of the army through a variety of means. He promoted his most trusted officers to sensitive government positions, many of them younger officers connected to him through the military academy. He also continued the previous government's policy of rewarding the military with increased salaries and perquisites such as access to duty-free commissariats (despite intense merchant opposition), subsidized housing, and preference for government posts. Castillo Armas even claimed Arbenz was in the habit of secretly sending extra money to zone commanders every month. There was also an intense publicity campaign that endeavored to foster army identification with major government reforms; at one point, nearly half the workers involved in building the government-sponsored Atlantic highway were soldiers.[35]

Arbenz's efforts to maintain army loyalty had only limited success, however. His appointment of junior officers to government positions angered more senior officers not close to Arbenz. On the other hand, because of the 1945 constitution, Arbenz was unable to name the officers who held the most important positions within the military itself. Most of these officers had graduated from the Escuela Politécnica before Arbenz, the majority coming from *promoción* twenty-four and twenty-five while Arbenz came from twenty-six. As a consequence, Colonel Carlos Enrique Díaz was named chief of the armed forces in 1951. Díaz was not an Arbenz loyalist, nor was he considered to be an opponent, but he surrounded himself in the highest ranks of the army with cohorts from his years in the academy. It was primarily through Díaz and his coterie of officers that Arbenz had to negotiate for the support of the institution. Given the intense loyalties among members of the various promociones, they formed a group of linked, powerful officers who resented the privileges given to the *presidenciales* (officers linked to the president) from more junior years. In the

senior officers

end, it was Díaz and his promoción cohorts who forced Arbenz from office.[36]

Moreover, the revolution in the countryside was beginning to seriously concern many of the senior officers. The Guatemalan military always jealously protected its control over rural Guatemala. From independence to the revolution, it was the preeminent — and often the only — national institution that stretched its tentacles into rural areas. Under Ubico, with his mania for centralizing power, military influence in rural areas had increased. In the process, the military became not only an instrument of control but also the most obvious embodiment of the state.[37]

The military's influence was exerted primarily through a system of military commissioners, rural militias, and the rural police force, the Guardia Civil. The military commissioners were the army's watchdogs in rural areas; usually residents with some army experience, they controlled conscription and commanded the local militia. They had significant local power, and were influential members of the community. However, they were often feared and resented by other residents. Especially in the western highlands, the military commissioners were notorious for their brutal treatment of Indians. The Guardia Civil commanders were also disliked and feared by the rural poor. A worker at the Labor Day celebration in Monjas, Jalapa, in 1951 gave this description of the activity of the Guardia Civil before the revolution: "The terrible rural guard terrorized the people immensely because if one turned pale it was imagined that he had committed the crime they were investigating, [and] they beat him and choked him, or if one was a personal enemy of theirs, they frequently made him flee [the village] or killed him." Pointing to the emphasis on military control and the fostering of racial hatred that permeated the western highlands, Robert Carmack has argued that the local power structure in one community he studied during the Cabrera and Ubico period was "fascist" in nature.[38]

Following the October Revolution, steps were taken to increase the influence of other state institutions in the countryside and to reduce the strength of the military presence there. Representatives of a whole range of national institutions began to penetrate rural areas: agricultural extension workers, cultural missions, forestry guards, labor inspectors, teachers, and political party and labor organizers. They all to some degree challenged the dominance of the military in rural areas. On the other hand, the rural militias were disbanded. The Guardia Civil was substantially reorganized after Ponce's overthrow and then reorganized again and nominally demilitarized in 1949 following an attack by three of its members on a cabinet minister. While its top commanders were still army officers and the links to the military were still strong, the head of the Guardia Civil was now named by the president and not the military command.[39]

The army responded to these changes by dramatically increasing the number of military commissioners in rural areas; Arbenz has argued that their number grew from 2,000 to 7,000 by 1947.[40] During the first few years of the revolution, the military was still the dominant agent in the countryside, and Arana used it to keep union activists closely in check. However, after the passage of the Agrarian Reform Law, as both the CNCG and the CTCG developed into powerful national organizations, conflict between them and the military in rural areas heightened.

The CNCG, the CGTG, and the political parties realized the need for Guardia Civil commanders and military commissioners sympathetic to their goals and in agreement with the broad ideas of the agrarian reform. There was some attempt to promote this cooperation through a national rapprochement between the military command and the DAN. A provision was included in decree 900 specifying that peasants and workers serving in the military be granted land under the law, a serious concern if local land tenure arrangements were altered while a peasant was away in the army. The military was given representation on most of the government organizations in rural areas, including the cultural missions and the CAN, where Major Rafael Arreaga was the army's representative. Also, the president of the DAN was an officer, one of Arbenz's closest military associates, Major Alfonso Martínez Estéves. In addition, the DAN regularly promoted army/peasant cooperation under the law through a series of advertisements. The most striking featured a picture of a soldier lighting a cigarette for a rural worker as the two looked over a field, under which the caption read, "THIS WAS IMPOSSIBLE UNDER THE TYRANNY OF UBICO! TODAY THE FRIENDSHIP OF THE ARMY AND WORKERS is founded in the common interest in the land, in democracy, and in the dignity of the patria."[41]

Nevertheless, conflict between the revolutionary organizations on one side and the military through the military commissioners and the Guardia Civil on the other emerged almost immediately after the passage of decree 900. The CNCG, the CGTG, and the national executives of the political parties received frequent reports from their local affiliates detailing violent attacks on their members by military commissioners and guard commanders.[42] However, the CNCG and CGTG executives gained increasing influence over the director of the Guardia Civil and the departmental governors who helped command it. By 1953, the support they received from Arbenz and the director of the guard, Major Cruz Wer, meant they were able to control the posting of guard commanders throughout much of the country. Local commanders even began writing to the leaders of the peasant and labor federations, especially the former, when seeking transfers or special considerations. Cruz Wer's support of these organizations was obvious. The CGTG was invited to attend the graduating ceremonies for the guard cadets in 1953. Later that year, he issued a circular warning commanders they would be disciplined if they stood in the way of the "proletarian masses" in the implementation of the agrarian reform. The U.S. embassy interpreted the circular as "clearly a warning to the regular army officers who command the police that their careers would suffer if they resisted the Arbenz administration's leftist program . . . [and] attempted to oppose the communist oriented CGTG and CNCG which were stimulating land seizures." While Ambassador Rudolph Schoenfeld admitted Cruz Wer was not a communist, he believed his opportunism and corruption turned the guard into an "effective instrument in achieving the aims shared by the Communists and the administration."[43]

In the early years of the Arbenz administration, military commissioners were often the most vigorous opponents of local agrarian organizers. In community after community, they were accused of leading attacks on peasant league members, helping landowners avoid the agrarian reform, and being in league with the reactionaries. There were also regular complaints that the commissioners were conscripting all the peasant league members into the military in attempts to break up the unions. Both the CNCG and the CGTG intervened regularly on behalf of their members with the military commissioners. However, Colonel Carlos Enrique Díaz was not Cruz Wer; he was much more powerful and independent, and he represented an institution that was increasingly concerned about rural unrest. Although requests for action against military commissioners were always couched in the most polite terms, they were often dismissed by Díaz. Nevertheless, with Arbenz's support, Gutiérrez and Castillo Flores were able to have the military commissioners removed in many communities and began to interfere in the assignment of replacements.[44]

By late 1953, sporadic measures to remove troublesome Guardia Civil members and military commissioners turned into an orchestrated campaign. Castillo Flores asked local unions to send lists of guard members and commissioners whom they suspected were sympathetic to the "reaction." Requests to Díaz for their removal became more frequent and insistent. The military command became increasingly concerned about its loss of control in rural areas. There were rumors that the military planned to move on its own in defiance of the president against those who were believed responsible for land invasions. In 1954, the Superior Council of National Defense appointed a commission to study the situation in the countryside, with a special emphasis on re-forming the local militias. The report of the commission was alarming; it stated, "We encounter at this date the following panorama: TOTAL LACK OF CONTROL AND ABSOLUTE MILITARY DISORGANIZATION of the militias." The commission went on to suggest that the military would be unable to mobilize effectively in the face of attack. While the report focused on assessing the possible response to outside aggression, it was also obviously partly concerned about the military's rapidly diminishing control over rural communities.[45]

The concerns of the top officers were heightened in the final years of the revolution by the Arbenz government's inability to keep the military supplied with arms and by Arbenz's halfhearted attempts to arm peasant and worker militias. The Guatemalan military tried with little success to obtain new arms and equipment throughout much of the revolutionary period. Although U.S. military missions continued to operate in Guatemala and Guatemalan officers were still trained by U.S. advisers, the U.S. government consistently refused to sell arms to Guatemala. It also blocked Guatemalan arms purchases from Denmark, Mexico, Sweden, Britain, Argentina, and Cuba. During the Arbenz administration, Guatemala's search for weapons became quite desperate as existing weapons deteriorated, the government felt more isolated diplomatically, and the military began to put pressure on the government to keep it supplied. The most pressing need was for airplanes, which Guatemala had been attempting to buy since 1949. In 1950, the Guatemalan air force only had four fighters in service. As the revolution wore on, these planes were often grounded waiting for parts the government could not obtain. The government eventually turned to private arms dealers and Eastern bloc countries. Finally, it was able to arrange a shipment of weapons from Czechoslovakia.[46]

Arbenz meant the arms to be used for a popular militia, but this purpose would almost certainly have been opposed by the military command. Throughout the decade of the revolution, the army had been determined to retain an effective monopoly on arms in Guatemala. In 1946, when the CTG asked for weapons to help defend the revolution against the continual attacks on the president, Arana refused, saying Guatemala had not yet "reached that state of civic responsibility — like Switzerland — where arming the workers would not be counterproductive." In 1948 another request from the FSG for weapons was also turned down. After Arbenz armed civilians to help defend the government against the rebels following Arana's killing, the military insisted on recovering the arms. Tension mounted until the labor federations gave in, declared their trust in the army, and turned in the weapons. Sensing this opposition and unwilling to provoke a confrontation with the army, Arbenz reluctantly allowed the military to take control of the Czechoslovakian arms delivered on the *Alfhem*. However, he continued with his plan to have worker and peasant militias trained by *presidenciales*. The military high command became increasingly uneasy about these militias.[47] These concerns, involving matters about which the military had traditionally been extremely jealous, helped prompt a burgeoning opposition movement against the president among officers not aligned with either conservative or radical factions. These officers, somewhat ambivalent about the revolution but devoted to the military institution, easily made up the majority of military commanders.

In his call to the nation in the face of the U.S. intervention, Arbenz reemphasized his trust in the "new army." This trust appears to have been shared by the leaders of the revolutionary organizations. In attempting to explain the overthrow of the Arbenz regime, it has been argued that when the moment of truth arrived, the revolution simply did not have enough popular support; when the peasantry and the workers upon whom Arbenz had staked his political future were called upon to defend the revolution, they refused. Certainly there were some broad sectors of the peasantry, frightened by the unrest in the countryside and worried about perceived threats to their land, who were not prepared to defend the revolution. Entire communities that had grown increasingly angry about the application of the agrarian reform to municipal land were sympathetic to the Liberation. Nevertheless, much of rural Guatemala was prepared to rise up in defense of the revolution. The national offices of all the revolutionary organizations were flooded with declarations of support from their affiliates in the countryside; they were besieged by reports of discovered caches of arms. The revolutionary organizations invariably informed their members to turn the arms over to the military authorities, to place themselves at their disposal, and to await orders to defend the country if necessary.[48]

This faith that the military would act to defend the Arbenz administration was misplaced; the orders never came. The military responded as it did for a complex web of reasons. The U.S. campaign to demoralize the military had some effect. Officers were bribed, the isolation of the country from its neighbors in Central America disturbed military leaders, and the lack of equipment restricted them. The constant pressures placed on them by the very obvious preparations for the invasion, fully reported in the press for almost two years, and U.S. efforts to arm Guatemala's now-hostile neighbors contributed to plummeting morale among the forces, despite widespread attempts by the government and revolutionary organizations to bolster army confidence in the months before the Liberation.[49]

Despite these very serious concerns, the army was most disturbed about the influence of communists and the growing challenge to its position in rural Guatemala from peasant leagues and rural workers' unions. As early as August 1953, Colonel Enrique Peralta Azurdía reported to Ambassador Schoenfeld that the military high command was "closely watching the movements of communist leaders."[50] On 5 June 1954 the top military commanders met with Arbenz, purportedly to thank him for finally getting arms. However, they took advantage of the occasion to present him with a list of questions concerning his connections to the communists and their influence over him. Arbenz offered to answer the questions at a later meeting. After some delay, a meeting was held on 14 June with a much larger group of officers. Arbenz attempted to respond to their concerns and left the meeting feeling relatively confident that he had allayed their fears. He later commented that he recognized too late that the meeting was indeed an ultimatum. Others have argued that at the meeting the military officers gave Arbenz twenty-four hours to reply to their demands to oust the communists. The CIA reported that a mutiny was sure to occur if Arbenz continued to stall and did not respond effectively to the officers' concerns.[51]

In the midst of this pressure, the Liberation army entered Guatemala on 17 June 1954. The next day, bombing raids from bases in Nicaragua were launched. Exaggerated reports that these raids had almost completely destroyed the cities of Zacapa and Chiquimula circulated. The Guatemalan military, with its moribund air force, was unable to respond.[52]

Arbenz was relatively confident, despite the meeting earlier in the month, that the military would defend the government and that, as in 1949, a combination of armed civilians and the military would readily defeat the invasion. Arbenz asked Díaz to have the arms from the *Alfhem* distributed to worker and peasant militias, fully expecting the order to be obeyed. However, Díaz refused to follow the order. The top military officers had reached the end of their rope; they would not defend a government that, in their opinion, was supporting a dangerous radical force within the country. They certainly would not consent to arm that force. Finally, in the company of Colonel Carlos Sartí, president of the Superior Council of National

Defense, and Colonel Enrique Parinello, chief of staff, having ordered that the palace be surrounded by the military if they did not come out shortly, Díaz informed Arbenz that the army demanded his resignation and that he, Díaz, would take command of the country in his place.

Discouraged and disillusioned, Arbenz would not attempt to rule without the support of the military and agreed to turn over power to Díaz. A few hours later, on 27 June, in a radio address written by José Manuel Fortuny, he resigned his position, denouncing the UFCo and the United States. The revolution had effectively ended.[53]

THE LIBERATION

8

We have been victims of many threats
from the owner . . . and [we wish] to insure
we do not fall into the horror . . . presently
occurring of dislocating the peasants
through the means of one simple decree,
without taking into account the needs of
each peasant, and without taking into
account that we all have children for
whom we are responsible.

—Letter from 136 peasants of the aldea
Rejón 4 to Castillo Armas, 2 October 1955

When writing history, lost in footnotes and statistics, it is often easy to forget we are chronicling the lives of individuals. Unfortunately, for those of us who study Guatemala, the painful legacies of that history are everywhere apparent and make it almost impossible to ignore the human dimensions of the accounts we write. For those of us intent on explaining the roots of that pain, the ending of the revolution and the triumph of the Liberation are necessary, if depressing, subjects to explore.

Arbenz's resignation did not necessarily mean that forces opposing all progressive change in the countryside would come to power, nor did it necessarily mean that all or most of the gains of the revolution would be lost. To understand why these outcomes did indeed occur, it is important to examine closely the changes that the Liberation wrought in the first few years after Arbenz's resignation, changes in national politics and in the countryside.

The significance of Arbenz's resignation was not quickly understood in Guatemala. A *Parisien libére* reporter commented: "The population has not understood Arbenz's departure very well. Here his return is obviously hoped for, and present changes are seen as mere sleight-of-hand tricks required of [the] situation, an official pretext to wash [the] country of accusations of Communism made against him and to avoid continuing massacres of civilians. Guatemalans agree on at least one point: all are asking they be guaranteed maintenance of social conquests."[1] At first it appeared that what the reporter believed all Guatemalans hoped for might indeed occur. The military had not been defeated by the Liberation, nor was it clear that the officers had repudiated the revolution. In the first few days after Arbenz's resignation, Colonel Díaz declared the PGT to be illegal, but this action was accompanied by conciliatory remarks about the maintenance of worker and peasant rights. The agrarian reform was to be continued; only land taken illegally was to be returned, and the process of expropriation and distribution would be controlled more carefully. The PAR, the PRG, and the RN, although clearly reeling from the blows they had suffered, were still intact and called on their members to support Díaz.[2]

Perhaps of most importance, the military continued to combat the Liberation forces and, true to his promise to Arbenz, Díaz refused to consider a meeting with the leader of the Liberation forces, Colonel Carlos Castillo Armas. However, in attempting to arrange a cease-fire and stop the bombing, Díaz, Colonel Monzón, Defense Minister José Angel Sánchez, Colonel Parinello, and Colonel Sartí had been holding secret meetings with the

U.S. ambassador, John Peurifoy, William Krieg, and the two U.S. military attachés even before the resignation of Arbenz. Peurifoy clearly did not trust Díaz, and after Arbenz had been allowed to condemn the United States in his farewell address, Peurifoy pressured Díaz out of the junta, now headed by Monzón.[3]

Monzón also clearly disliked the idea of any discussion with Castillo Armas and any suggestion that the Liberation army be allowed official status. However, these few officers were caught up in a whirlwind of political intrigue; having taken the initial steps to abandon the revolution, they found it difficult not to embrace the reaction. Peurifoy continued to play musical chairs with military juntas. He was determined that Castillo Armas, who he felt could be trusted to be appropriately harsh with "communists," be manipulated into a dominant position in a new junta. He arranged for Monzón and Castillo Armas to attend meetings in El Salvador, where an accord might be reached between the Guatemalan army and the Liberation forces. Peurifoy and Castillo Armas's main adviser, Juan Córdova Cerna, were able to manipulate Castillo Armas into a position of authority in the final reincarnation of the junta, sharing power with Monzón. Castillo Armas was enticed into the final junta patched together in El Salvador by Peurifoy only after a promise of U.S. support for the presidency in "free and democratic elections" six months down the road.[4]

By 7 July, with Castillo Armas the dominant member of the junta and the Liberation army encamped in the Roosevelt Hospital, any hope that the revolution would survive was abandoned. Within a month, the PAR, the PRG, the RN, the CGTG, the CNCG, the SAMF, and the STEG — all of the most important unions and political organizations of the revolution — werc declared illegal. Nearly 700 people sought asylum at the Mexican and Argentinian embassies, awaiting safe-conduct out of the country. For some it was a painful reenactment; less than a decade earlier, they had huddled in the same embassies hoping for the overthrow of Ponce.[5]

The final important national opposition to Castillo Armas appeared in the form of a revolt by cadets in the Escuela Politécnica in early August. The cadets, angered by a speech during the Day of National Unity for the army and upset by attempts to integrate the Liberation forces into the army and the abuse they had suffered at the hands of the Liberationists, attacked the Liberation forces at the Roosevelt Hospital. The cadets forced the Liberation forces to leave the hospital and return to Zacapa but were eventually convinced to abandon the revolt. While Castillo Armas continued to face sporadic opposition from sectors of the army, by September 1954 it was clear that little stood in the way of a more permanent assumption of power on the part of Castillo Armas.[6] On 10 October, Castillo Armas was confirmed in the presidency by an oral public vote, gaining the approval of slightly less than 100 percent of those "voting." His followers dominated the new assembly.[7]

With his power now entrenched, Castillo Armas set out to try to reconstruct Guatemala. He espoused a position "neither to the right nor to the left, but upward," and it is clear that he did not go as far in reinstating the power and privilege of the dominant elite as many would have liked. He imposed a special "Liberation" tax that angered landowners and business leaders and began to feud with his former adviser and the most powerful representative of the business elite, Córdova Cerna.[8] There were also constant complaints that his government had not been as diligent as it could have been in identifying and arresting "communist" leaders still at liberty in Guatemala.[9]

The "Liberation" in the Countryside

While the Liberation forces may have been forced to exercise some restraint in the national capital and the larger departmental cities, in the countryside they struck back at peasants who had benefited from the revolution with a vengeance. Some revolutionary leaders might have still been enjoying their liberty in Guatemala City, but over 5,000 peasants filled "the jails to overflowing." Peasant organizers and activists and even simple beneficiaries of the agrarian reform fled their community, the region, or the country. Hundreds of peasants and rural organizers were killed in the first months after the Liberation. The true extent of the violence in the countryside following the overthrow of Arbenz will probably never be known. We can only catch some glimpses of it through anecdotal accounts from specific communities. Testimony in the early 1980s collected by Father Ricardo Falla from peasants in Tiquisate described the large number of bodies, victims of the Liberation, buried by a tractor in the finca Jocotén in 1954. An anthropologist working in San Juan Sacatepéquez in the 1970s recounted how news of the Panzos massacre prompted residents in the community to recall the repression in San Juan following Arbenz's overthrow. They talked about discovering bodies floating in the river for days after the Liberation.[10] By September 1954, even the second secretary of the U.S. embassy warned: "Their continued imprisonment of large numbers of campesinos and often indiscriminate arrests . . . [are] opening up the Guatemalan Government to charges from abroad of operating a police state."[11] This pervasive violence provided the canvas on which the Liberation's agrarian decrees were painted. Despite the moderate and conciliatory tone of the decrees, few peasants were able to hang on to land they had gained during the revolution.

The Liberation government issued two substantial agrarian decrees, numbers 31 and 559, in 1954 and 1956, respectively. Decree 31 declared that it was the new government's intention to increase agricultural productivity and to better the lot of the peasantry. It recognized that all Guatemalans "have the right to be given land, sufficient for the subsistence economy of the family, in private property and fully guaranteed." To guarantee this, the decree accepted the "legal" decisions made under the revolution's decree 900 and provided a series of protections for the beneficiaries of the law. Further expropriations under decree 900 were forbidden, and landlords could petition for the return of land taken "illegally" (that is, not according to the provisions of the law) under decree 900. When petitions for the return of land were received, agrarian officials were to interview peasants on the land and landlords before recommending action. Landlords had to submit proposals for the development of their property to the DGAA proving they were intent on efficient production that provided for the well-being of resident laborers. If beneficiaries of decree 900 were to be removed from the land, they were guaranteed the right to harvest crops they had planted and payment for any improvements they had made to the land.[12]

In 1956 the more complete decree 559 was issued. In some ways it was strikingly similar to the revolutionary Agrarian Reform Law. Its stated goals were to increase the "purchasing power" of the peasantry and agricultural productivity in general. The decree issued guidelines concerning what constituted efficient use of land and created a series of taxes on land not used efficiently. It established procedures for the expropriation of unused land that, if followed, would have constituted an attack on latifundia similar to that envisioned by Arbenz. Uncultivated land could be expropriated for the public good, to be paid for at either a mutually agreed upon price or a price set by two independent appraisers. The decree also declared that rents for agricultural land were not to exceed 6 percent of the value of the harvest, similar to the revolution's Laws of Forced Rental.[13]

The major difference between these two laws and decree 900 was the determination expressed in the Liberation's decrees to reduce tension in the countryside and to eliminate the power of the peasantry to determine the outcome of agrarian decisions. According to the decrees, the Agrarian Reform Law had "provoked a bitter class struggle in rural areas" and had "converted the Guatemalan peasantry into a political instrument of the government and restricted groups within the official political parties." Consequently, decree 31 declared that all agrarian officials "must be guided by the principle of finding the greatest possible conciliation and agreement among the diverse sectors that form the rural population." To insure that "conciliation" prevailed, the decree excluded peasant organizations from any direct participation in the agrarian agencies. All decisions were to be made by representatives of the DGAA, who were to be technocrats capable of "minuscule technical studies" that "justly and within a strict adherence to national reality will establish the basis for assuring the multiplication of private property, which will not only result in increased production but also will resolve the social problems of the peasant."[14]

Decree 559 expressed a similar philosophy. Individuals could solicit lots from purchased and expropriated land provided they owned no land elsewhere or had not received land under decree 900. However, the DGAA was to maintain rigid control over the process. Peasants could not initiate proceedings against estates; they could not organize to help defend their interests within the law; and they could not lobby agrarian officials in specific cases. They were to be passive recipients of private plots of land given out to unorganized individuals.[15]

Despite these restrictions, the agrarian decrees of the Liberation would have seemed to offer at least a measure of hope to those who had benefited from the Agrarian Reform Law and to those still hoping to get land. Agrarian officials and peasants had occasionally overstepped the bounds of the law in the application of decree 900, but overall there had been an attempt to apply the law legally. These "legal" decisions were to be respected by the new agrarian agencies, and by 1956, new avenues were opened for the most needy to apply for land. But, of course, the agrarian decrees of the Liberation were not implemented in a vacuum. The repressive atmosphere that prevailed in rural Guatemala after the overthrow of Arbenz insured that few peasants were able to take advantage of the theoretical protections offered through these two new laws. Their interests were most often ignored while agrarian officials worked with large landlords to insure the return of their land under whatever legal pretext they could manage. Nonetheless, the Liberation's fear of rural unrest and the provisions of the two decrees occasionally combined to allow some beneficiaries of decree 900, through determination and perseverance, to hang on to their plots.

In total, of 765,233 manzanas of land expropriated under the 1952 Agrarian Reform Law, 603,775 were returned. If the land taken from and returned to the United Fruit Company — in which somewhat different factors were at work — is excluded, 368,481 manzanas of the 529,939 taken were returned.[16] This is significantly less than the 96.6 percent figure that is usually cited as the amount of land returned under the Liberation, but it is still a significant percentage representing a massive transfer of land.[17] The level of fear and repression in rural Guatemala, which the Liberation government apparently felt was necessary to control rural society while returning these lands, is evident, if at times consciously buried, in the records of the DGAA following the overthrow of Arbenz.

Land was returned to owners using two legal pretexts: the initial expropriation had not been done legally or little "social damage" would be caused by the return of the land. Often the DGAA officials declared that the expropriation was illegal because for one reason or another the land had been used "effectively" before the expropriation. Liberation officials went out of their way to prove that even the most limited "use" of the land precluded expropriation. This was especially true in the case of cattle estates. Liberation officials usually accepted arguments that the existence of a few head of cattle represented efficient use. The revolutionary officials had been skeptical of these claims and usually demanded proof of substantial improvements to the property before accepting such assertions.[18]

In addition, decree 31 expressly declared that various fincas owned by the same proprietor could not be considered one property for the purposes of the Agrarian Reform Law. Revolutionary agrarian officials had used this tactic to expropriate land from landowners who had various properties scattered throughout the highlands, most of them below the two-caballería limit. With the new decree, such famous terratenientes and labor contractors as Casimiro Gutiérrez, who had had twenty-five of his seventy-three properties in El Quiché denounced during the revolution, got most of their land back.[19]

In a large number of cases, however, the new agrarian officials, try as they might, were unable to find legal fault with the decisions made under decree 900, despite their flexible guidelines. In these cases, they needed to produce more imaginative justification for the return of the land. Although there was nothing in either of the Liberation's agrarian decrees that explicitly approved the return of land taken under decree 900 solely because beneficiaries were not on the land, in practice land was frequently returned for this reason. On occasion, there were no beneficiaries on the land simply because it had not been parceled out before the Liberation. This was especially the case with land taken in the final spurt of expropriations beginning in May 1954 and land located in the less densely populated lowlands.[20]

More often, beneficiaries of decree 900, fearing the retribution of landlords and new government officials, had fled the land, region, or country. In the finca Las Bolas in San Marcos, the agrarian inspector reported that he could not interview the beneficiaries because "they all had fled to the Republic of Mexico two years ago when the Liberation movement triumphed." For the inspector, this proved that there "were now no agrarian problems on the finca" and that the expropriated land should be returned. Romualdo Arenas, in petitioning to have his land returned in Chimaltenango, was even more explicit. He declared, "The . . . invaders of my land abandoned their parcels and fled to avoid persecution for their activities in the PGT with the Liberation." He concluded that, since he was in effective control of all his land, it should be legally returned to him. The DGAA agreed on 28 February 1955.[21]

Of course, despite the radically changed relations in the countryside, many peasants who had fought desperately for land during the years of the revolution were not easily driven away. Peasants wishing to protest the reports of the agrarian officials, who almost always advised the return of the land, faced a daunting prospect. Initial inspections for the DGAA were carried out by local alcaldes; following the Liberation these positions were quickly dominated by adherents of the Liberation or paniaguados (flunkies) of the largest local landlords. In more advanced cases, peasants were required to give their statements in front of the departmental governors, all of whom were military officers and few of whom would have been sympathetic to beneficiaries of the revolution's laws. In these circumstances, it was an act of substantial courage for peasants to protest their expulsion from the land. In one case, for example, in Granados, Baja Verapaz, the new alcalde was the son of the owner of the finca Estación de García. His report, not surprisingly, assured the DGAA that all the beneficiaries of the Agrarian Reform Law who had land on the finca were in complete agreement with the return of the land to his mother. Similarly, the powerful Herrera brothers had little problem in getting their land returned. In one of their fincas in Escuintla, the agrarian inspector dutifully obtained statements from the requisite three beneficiaries. One reported that he had been a worker on the finca before the agrarian reform. Under decree 900 he had received twenty-five manzanas and Q174 from the National Agrarian Bank. In March 1955, he was forced from his new farm and given three manzanas of "useless, rocky" land elsewhere on the finca. Nonetheless, in his statement given before the agrarian officials and the new military governor of the department, he assured them that he had absolutely no objection to the treatment he had received and did not oppose the return of the land, his land in part, to the Herrera brothers.[22]

Even when peasants courageously protested the return of the land, they often faced insurmountable difficulties. Many times they were required to prove they were official beneficiaries and not invaders. With DAN records much less complete on beneficiaries than they were on expropriations, obtaining this proof often proved difficult. Finca owners branded almost all those who received land as invaders, especially if they had not been resident on the finca before the expropriation, and often their reports were accepted with little question. When agents for María Josefa Barrios petitioned to have her finca in Sacatepéquez returned, they told the DGAA there were no beneficiaries on the land. The DGAA immediately declared that it should be returned. Eight months later, however, fifty peasants on the finca wrote to the DGAA saying they had received land under decree 900 and were still farming the land. The owner responded with the charge that they were invaders with no legal right to the property. Although the records of the DAN were not complete and the case could not be proven conclusively, the land was returned to the original owner by June 1958.[23]

Similarly, when the owner of the finca Pueblo Nuevo in Escuintla petitioned to have his property returned, he argued that those peasants now farming his land were invaders. Moreover, they had occupied the whole finca, not just the two caballerías legally expropriated, and even months after the Liberation, they were still rebellious, menacing the manager of the finca and boasting that "no one was going to throw them off the land because it had been given to them by [Víctor Manuel] Gutiérrez." The peasants disagreed: they had never invaded the land but had waited for the allocation to be official before occupying their property; they put up a fence to separate the expropriated part of the finca from the rest; and they had never touched the land not affected. Even the agrarian inspector agreed with this version and recommended to the DGAA that they be allowed to keep the land since they were farming it responsibly. This testimony had little effect, however, and the land was returned to the original owner in December 1954.[24]

On a few occasions, landlords had to be somewhat more patient. In early decisions following the Liberation, the DGAA occasionally ordered fincas returned, except for land that was actually occupied by the beneficiaries. In the hostile climate of rural Guatemala after the Liberation, landowners were most often able to convince beneficiaries to leave fincas after a few seasons. Further petitions usually brought the return of all the land. When the owner of the finca Louisiana petitioned to have the three caballerías that had been expropriated from his finca returned, the beneficiaries protested. The DGAA hesitated and tried to work out an accord between the owner and the beneficiaries, apparently because it was concerned about reports of continued unrest caused by "the agitation of hidden leaders." By early 1956, however, the alcalde reported that all the beneficiaries had fled the finca after harvesting their crops; the rest of the land was returned later that year. Similarly, the owners of the finca Cerro Azul in San Miguel Uspantán petitioned to have the fourteen caballerías of their land that had been taken returned. At first, the DGAA only returned eight, saying that it could not take land away from beneficiaries who were legally on the land and farming it. Nonetheless, by September 1957, with fears of rural unrest less prominent, the DGAA had changed its mind and the remaining six caballerías were returned. The eighty-two peasants thrown off the finca were given vague promises about empty land in El Quiché.[25]

What accounts for the land not returned? Some land was not returned because the owners had been associated with the revolutionary government and were thus punished by the Liberation or were living in exile and unable to petition to have their land returned; this included many of the prominent officials in the Arbenz administration. When petitions were presented for the return of such land, the deliberations of the DGAA were interesting. Peasants on Guillermo Toriello's finca had been given eight caballerías during the revolution. Liberation officials were clearly in a sort of quandary in regard to his land. They could not conceivably give it back to Toriello, but they did not want to benefit the revolutionary peasants who had received the land. The DGAA left them in limbo, neither returning the land nor confirming their possession of it. Finally, in 1962, after years of petitioning, they were given title to the property.[26] Even Pedro Brol, the brother of Arbenz's minister of agriculture, was denied the return of four caballerías expropriated from his lands after his first petition. Only after a number of prominent people wrote to government officials explaining that Pedro and his brother had been estranged and that Pedro "always has been and still is completely anticommunist" was his land returned.[27]

The most significant reason for the DGAA not to reverse a decision of the DAN was the continued fear of peasant unrest. Most of the land not returned was retained because the beneficiaries of decree 900 were still on their plots and refused to be removed. The new agrarian officials, worried about rural unrest, repeatedly argued that "greater social damage" would occur if the decisions concerning some fincas were reversed. When Jenny Sandoval asked for the return of the twenty-three caballerías that had been taken from her, the DGAA refused and turned the land over to the parcelarios. The agrarian officials reported that "we are confronted with the problem that the workers of the finca are in possession of the whole property and they have established a rural population that would be almost impossible to dislocate." Similarly, the parcelarios on the finca Santo Domingo Los Ocotes in El Progreso were able to get title to their lots because they stuck tenaciously to the land, sent numerous protests to the governor, and were eventually able to prove that the property had been improperly taken from the neighboring community during the presidency of Ubico. In another example, the finca La Trinidad had lost 153 of its 173 caballerías under decree 900. By the time of the Liberation, parcelarios were farming about thirty caballerías. The DGAA wanted to return the land to the owner, but there was a threat of intense unrest on the finca. The parcelarios refused to move, to pay rent, or to work for the finca. The owner blamed the local municipal secretary, who was described as an "old communist and unconditional servant of Arévalo and Arbenz." Because of him, the owner claimed, the peasants, "in spite of having been notified by the DGAA that the expropriation was invalid, . . . persist in the idea that the land belongs to them." Eventually, the owner was forced to donate thirty caballerías to the parcelarios to gain peace.[28]

The peasants in La Trinidad were exceptions. Most beneficiaries of the agrarian reform were treated much more harshly. Despite the promises of the Liberation to "guarantee all Guatemalans land, sufficient for the subsistence economy of the family," it oversaw a massive transfer of land from peasants to large landowners that almost completely undid the agrarian reform of the revolution. Brought to power partly by the reaction of large landowners opposed to the revolution and obsessed with rooting out communist influence—a presence Liberation officials saw in every peasant protest—the Liberation was quick to respond to landowners' demands for the return of their property and was determined to disempower peasants throughout rural Guatemala. Most beneficiaries of the agrarian reform fled in the face of the repressive atmosphere that prevailed in rural Guatemala after 1954, abandoning their land and the gains of the revolution. The majority of those who stayed and fought were ultimately unsuccessful. As the "159 poor peasants" who had received land from the finca Monte María in Alotenango discovered when they asked for the assistance of

Castillo Armas, "believing that the Liberation movement came to liberate us from communism not so the rich and the terratenientes could throw us from our land," in most instances the Liberation proved it had come to do the latter.[29]

The Liberation's promises of bettering the lives of peasants and fostering social harmony in rural Guatemala were as hollow as the rest of its pronouncements. These promises fit the pattern; Guatemala was thrust back into, as Eduardo Galeano has described it, "a world where only rarely does the sound of words coincide with their meaning and where the vast majority of the people are condemned to the mute language of fear and solitude. Official language rants deliriously and its delirium is the system's normality."[30] In Liberation Guatemala, the government dissolved all the political parties and called it democracy, attacked workers and called it social justice, oversaw the killing of thousands because they had dreamed of a different Guatemala and called it peace, and forced tens of thousands of peasants and rural workers from the land they had so recently torn from the estates of landlords and called it agrarian reform. There was no "harmony" in rural Guatemala, only an uneasy quietude shrouded in fear, a quiet that would not last.

Evaluating the Revolution's Rural Policies

The rural policies of the two administrations of the revolution have been attacked from a variety of different perspectives. During the Arévalo administration, landlords, military officers, and much of the urban press warned that the government was fostering anarchy and lawlessness in the countryside. The specter of a peasant and/or Indian uprising was continually raised. The essential coffee harvest was constantly reported to be in jeopardy. On the other hand, the more determined reformers complained that the reforms of the Arévalo administration had barely dented the shield that landlords and the military had constructed to prevent any serious alteration in rural social relations.

The Arbenz administration was much more determined to alter economic and social relations in rural areas as a prerequisite to transforming Guatemala. Its policies in the countryside were more vehemently attacked and have since been more consistently criticized. According to his critics at the time, Arbenz was sowing class and racial dissension where none had existed before; he was disrupting Guatemala's natural economy and endangering the coffee harvest; he was disregarding the law and applying the agrarian reform in an arbitrary fashion; and, of course, he was paving the way for communist organizers to gain complete control over the countryside, a control that could never be pried away. On the other hand, rural activists and peasants clamoring for land attacked the government for moving too timidly in applying the agrarian reform and in challenging the position of landlords; thousands of peasants were discouraged when denunciations of land were rejected; organizers gave up the struggle when they could not goad the administration into a more dramatic confrontation with landlords; and revolutionary political parties fumed when more rewards were not forthcoming in response to their work in the countryside.

Following the overthrow of Arbenz, in the numerous postmortems that emanated from revolutionary politicians in exile, the self-congratulatory accounts of U.S. officials, the somewhat myopic accounts of anthropologists, the polite warnings issued by U.S. academics in the second half of the 1950s, and the strident denunciations of U.S. actions by later academics, the rural policies of the Arbenz administration were similarly criticized. According to these accounts, Arbenz's rural policies were bourgeois and timid and thus doomed to failure. They were condemned, somewhat contradictorily, as both chaotic and uncontrolled and dictatorial and undemocratic. They allegedly had led to the destruction of Indian communities, would have led to the permanent impoverishment of the peasantry, and had threatened to destroy democratic institutions. They were thought either too limited or too radical, or the goals were too limited while the means used to attain those goals were too radical. In these ways, according to the critics, through some fatal flaw in policy or in implementing policy, the rural program of the Arbenz administration contributed to the demise of the revolution.

Of course, many of the works that deal with the overthrow of the Arbenz government do not place any emphasis on these rural policies. For them, the drama of 1954 was a two-character play, featuring an imperialistic U.S. government and a brave, nationalistic administration seeking social justice against entrenched interests. According to such studies, Guatemala could be anywhere in Latin America, and the distinct and in many ways unique characteristics of rural Guatemala did not contribute to that drama. The various forces described in this work rarely even merit bit parts.

Contrarily, a closer analysis of the "revolution in the countryside" reveals a different scenario. The Arbenz administration's rural policies did not fail because of some fatal flaw in their creation or implementation that can be easily linked to the overthrow of the government. Nor was the Arbenz administration overthrown in a struggle of global dimensions that renders irrelevant the actions of Guatemalans and the contours of the rural landscape. The Arbenz administration was overthrown partly because its policies in rural Guatemala were working well, partly because those policies set in motion an expected reaction, partly because that reaction was more virulent than expected, but also because the complex and dense social relations that permeated rural Guatemala would not fit into the somewhat simplistic blueprint drawn up for them.

There were contradictions in the rural policies of both administrations. The politicians who darted around the edges of power during the Arévalo administration neither understood nor trusted rural Guatemala; like so many sand crabs too timid to leave their holes for long, they only occasionally ventured out into that threatening universe. Partly as a consequence, the Arévalo administration talked of justice, social change, and spiritual socialism, but it did little to alter the nature of social relations in the countryside. Inspired partly by the rhetoric of change, Mayan and Ladino peasants confronted local landowners, protested corrupt local politics, and struck against unfair wages during the harvest. Frightened of the unrest as well as the reaction of the military and urban middle class, the Arévalo administration allowed the military to stamp out the scattered brushfires of unrest that ignited across rural Guatemala.

To a great extent, Arbenz and the politicians who surrounded and advised him divested themselves of the most paralyzing aspects of that fear. They believed intensely that the revolution would forever be incomplete, and insecure, if it was not decisively extended to embrace the desires of the inhabitants of villages and towns throughout rural Guatemala. Those politicians who would have hesitated were forced to extend the revolution, and in some ways confront their fears, or lose any hope of political influence. Of course, for much of the urban middle class, including many of those involved in the revolutionary political parties, this was too much to ask. They could accept reforms as long as they and their colleagues from the University of San Carlos or the Escuela Politécnica controlled them, but they succumbed to their anxieties when they were forced to relinquish some of that control to peasant organizations in the countryside. This was especially true as Maya joined and, at least in some areas, began to dominate these organizations. This was too radical for many politicians, who abandoned the revolution in droves.

While the extension of the revolution into the countryside was felt in myriad ways, from the explosion of political activity in the municipios to the growth of peasant and rural worker organizations, it was the agrarian reform that formed the centerpiece of that expansion. From its inception, the agrarian reform was contradictory and confused. It talked of strengthening the "capitalist economy of the peasants" while it gave land in ownership to very few recipients; most of the land, in effect, became the patrimony of the state. It talked of destroying "feudalism" in the countryside while it attacked the economic position of estates clearly run on a capitalist basis. The enactment of the agrarian reform proved to be contradictory and confused, as well. The relatively simple articles of decree 900 lost their clarity as they were enveloped by the dense fog of the immensely complicated social relations of rural Guatemala. Class, ethnic, and community conflict rarely followed the simple bipolar lines espoused by those intent on implementing the reform. Political struggles, personal ambition, and extensive corruption among revolutionary politicians impeded the reform and embittered peasants and the middle class.

Still, the agrarian reform was "the most precious fruit of the revolution" and set in motion the process of implementing social and economic reform in the countryside. Despite its problems, within two years more than a million acres of land were taken from the hands of large landowners, much of it transferred to the control of poor peasants, both Mayan and Ladino. A few cooperatives were formed and functioned moderately well on the formerly moribund national fincas. Thousands of beneficiaries of the reform received small but crucial amounts of credit to begin the process of diversification and investment on their new holdings. Moreover, the measures adopted to indemnify landowners — agrarian bonds based on self-declared tax assessments — insured that along with the transfer of land a very real distribution of wealth occurred. While landowners complained vociferously about this system of payment, it was necessary in order to carry out the reform.

The amount of land affected by the Guatemalan agrarian reform of 1952–54 and the number of beneficiaries of the reform do not approach the numbers involved in reforms that took place in Mexico, Peru, and elsewhere in Latin America. In those countries, new patterns of domination emerged and new forms of oppression were instituted. It is possible that, had the Liberation not occurred, Guatemala would be no different. Still, perhaps the most important aspect of the revolution in the countryside — and the aspect that, if anything, justifies employing the term "revolution" — is the dramatic alteration the agrarian reform helped inspire in the relations of power in the countryside. If decree 900 sought moderate change, that change was to be implemented using radically new levels of mobilization in the countryside. The peasant league, the rural workers' unions, the CALs, the comunidades campesinas, and the comunidades indígenas were either new and powerful organizations or were used to transform existing institutions. They were, in some ways, extensions of national political institutions meant to perform functions of state building. However, precisely because national political power was so fragmented, because even those forces supporting the revolution were so divided, these organizations developed significant autonomy and, operating independently, pursued local goals. It was this independence that, if the Liberation had not intervened, possibly would have insured that the process of agrarian reform continue and the transformation of rural society in Guatemala deepen.

Perhaps ironically, it was this very independence that caused many of the problems that confronted the Arbenz administration in rural areas. Local organizations, invigorated and no longer fearing a repressive central government, used these new institutions and changed circumstances to engage in battles over local issues. This led to new outbreaks of conflict over enduring issues that made little sense to national politicians (such as the geographic limits to and nature of "community"), conflict that national politicians wished to ignore (such as ethnic conflict), or conflict that national politicians hoped to prevent (such as battles over land held in estates much smaller than those slated to be affected by decree 900). These conflicts led to intense levels of unrest in the countryside and helped insure that increasing numbers of rural people, even among those "classes" the Arbenz administration sought to favor, would oppose the government. Some of this conflict was an inevitable result of opposition to the extension of state power and the strengthening presence of state institutions in areas that had felt it only sporadically before, as the Arbenz administration used the implementation of decree 900 to increase dramatically its presence in rural Guatemala.

Many different sectors of Guatemalan society were alarmed by the changing relationships in rural Guatemala and the apparently uncontrollable levels of conflict that resulted. The urban middle class, traditionally paranoid about native unrest, became increasingly alarmed, especially as this traditional specter was joined by a not entirely unsubstantiated concern over communist influence in the government and the countryside. Large landowners, even those not large enough to fall within the parameters of decree 900, almost unanimously opposed the government and feared the increasing unrest. No sector of Guatemalan society was more alarmed than the military.

All of these elements of revolution in the countryside contributed to the overthrow of the Arbenz administration and the coming to power of the Liberation. They need to be understood before any explanation of the overthrow and the Liberation can be given. More importantly, however, the revolution in the countryside needs to be understood not simply to help explain the failure of the revolution but to help understand the nature of the countryside itself. The changes that occurred in rural Guatemala during the revolution illuminate the nature of rural society in Guatemala and also help to explain the continuing conflict there, a conflict that erupted with heightened violence and even more disastrous consequences more than twenty years after the Liberation's agrarian decrees bemoaned the "bitter class struggle in rural areas" purportedly inspired by decree 900.

The continuing conflict in rural Guatemala in the decades after the revolution demonstrates two things: that Arbenz was correct in describing the agrarian reform as the "most precious fruit of the revolution," without which, no matter the difficulties inherent in trying to implement it, no revolution would occur; and that the struggle for land and local empowerment did not begin with nor did it end with the revolution. In 1967, more than a decade after the end of the revolution, the former parcelarios of the finca Palmilla retook the land they had been granted by the revolution and denied by the Liberation. For them, clearly, the process of revolution and reaction described here was simply another stage in a long struggle for land that had lasted for centuries.[31]

Perhaps the final word about the revolution in the countryside should come from the godfather of the revolution, Juan José Arévalo Bermejo. It is suitably contradictory. In the summer of 1989, campesinos integrated into the Asociación Pro-tierra, led by Father Andrés Girón, invaded land owned by Mariano Arévalo, the brother of Juan. The peasants claimed the land had been taken from them illegally decades before and refused to leave despite threats from the army and two rulings from the courts. According to *Prensa libre*, the former president himself returned to Guatemala from his self-imposed exile to demand that President Vinicio Cerezo take steps to force the invaders from his brother's property. Their battle for land continues.[32]

NOTES

Abbreviations

The following abbreviations are used throughout the notes.

AMC   Archivos de Materiales Culturales, Instituto Indigenista Nacional, Guatemala City

CIA-RR   Central Intelligence Agency Research Reports, reel 5, Latin America, 1946–76

dec. ser.   decimal series

Guat. Doc. Guatemalan Documents, Manuscript Division, Library of Congress, Washington, D.C.

INTA   Records of the Departamento Agrario Nacional, Instituto Nacional de Transformación Agraria, Guatemala City

PAC   Public Archives of Canada, Ottawa, Canada

RG   Record Group

USNA-DS General Records of the Department of State, Record Group 59, U.S. National Archives, Washington, D.C.

Chapter 1

1. Cited in Valle Matheu, *La Verdad sobre el "caso de Guatemala,"* 25–26. Unless otherwise noted, all translations throughout are my own.

2. For more detailed discussions of these various trends, see MacLeod, *Spanish Central America*, esp. 136–40; Horacio de Jesús Cabezas, *Las Reducciones indígenas en Guatemala durante el siglo XVI* (Guatemala City: Editorial Universitaria, 1974), esp. 10–13, 56–58; Francisco de Solano, "Política de concentración de la población indígena: objetivos, procesos, problemas, resultados," *Revista de Indies* 36 (July 1976): 7–30; and Carmelo Sáenz de Santa María, "La Reducción a poblados en el siglo XVI en Guatemala," *Anuario de estudios americanos* 29 (1972): 187–228.

3. It should be noted that Carol Smith has argued that the designation of Ladinos, at least as a social group playing a specific role in society and distinct from Indians, is a creation of the late nineteenth century. See C. Smith, "Origins of the National Question," 72–95. While there is little doubt that racial tension was heightened during this period, there is also plenty of evidence that Ladinos, as a recognizable social group of mixed cultural and/or ethnic background, did not spring from nineteenth-century cultural and economic change. See, for example, Dr. A. Larrazábal, "Apuntamientos sobre la agricultura y comercio del reyno de Guatemala" (1810), cited in Carlos Meléndez, ed., *Textos fundamentales de la independencia centroamericana* (San José, Costa Rica: Editorial Universitaria, 1971), 74.

4. For further discussion of this period, see Ralph Lee Woodward, Jr., "Liberalismo, conservadurismo, y la actitud de los campesinos de la montaña hacia el gobierno de Guatemala, 1821–1850," *Anales de la Academia de Geografía e Historia de Guatemala* 56 (1982): 195–210, and "Social Revolution in Guatemala: The Carrera Revolt," in *Applied Enlightenment: Nineteenth Century Liberalism* (New Orleans: Tulane University, 1972), 43–70; H. M. Ingersoll, "The War of the Mountains" (Ph.D. diss., George Washington University, 1971); and Handy, *Gift of the Devil*, 35–56.

5. Carmack, "Spanish-Indian Relations," 215–53; Samayoa Coronado, *La Escuela Politécnica*, vol. 1; C. Smith, "Local History in Global Context," esp. 208–9. For further discussion, see Handy, *Gift of the Devil*, 61–73.

6. Aybar de Soto, *Dependency and Intervention*, 84; Mosk, "Coffee Economy of Guatemala, 1859–1918," esp. 13; Kepner and Soothill, *The Banana Empire*; Cardoza y Aragón, "Guatemala y el imperio bananero," esp. 19.

7. C. V. Erckert cited in Castellano Cambranes, *Aspectos del desarrollo económico y social de Guatemala*, 81.

8. Náñez Falcón, "Erwin Paul Dieseldorf," 303.

9. Cited in LaGuardia, *El Pensamiento liberal de Guatemala*, 221.

10. R. Burkitt, "Explorations in the Highlands of Western Guatemala," *Museum Journal of the University of Pennsylvania* 21 (1930): 58, cited in Lovell, "Surviving Conquest," 41.

11. Cited in Madigan, "Santiago Atitlán," 248.

12. Lincoln, "An Ethnological Study of the Ixil Indians," 74; Wagley, *Economics of a Guatemalan Village*, 30; Madigan, "Santiago Atitlán," 247. See also McCreery, "Debt Servitude in Rural Guatemala."

13. Cited in Higbee, "Agricultural Regions of Guatemala." See also McCreery, "Debt Servitude in Rural Guatemala," 748–49; Woodward, "Economic Development of Guatemala," 18; and King, *Cobán and the Verapaz*, 34, 38.

14. McCreery, "Coffee and Class," esp. 457. See also Herrick, *Desarrollo económico y político de Guatemala*, 232–38, and McCreery, "State Power," 96–115.

15. McCreery, " 'An Odious Feudalism' "; Carmack, "Spanish-Indian Relations," 242–43.

16. Lincoln, "An Ethnological Study of the Ixil Indians," 60–98. See also Warren, *Symbolism of Subordination*, 61, and Farrell, "Community Development," 47–49.

17. Wagley, *Economics of a Guatemalan Village*, 77; Bunzel, *Chichicastenango*, 9; Nash, "Impact of Mid-Nineteenth Century Economic Change," 170–83; Dessaint, "Effects of the Hacienda and Plantation Systems."

18. Cited in Kitchen, "Municipal Government in Guatemala," 48.

19. Falla, "Actitud de los indígenas de Guatemala"; Diós Rosales, "Notes on San Pedro La Laguna," 132–33; Watanabe, " 'We Who Are Here,' " 165–70; Carmack, "Spanish-Indian Relations," 242.

20. Lovell, "Surviving Conquest," 39.

21. It is not possible to list all of the anthropological studies done on Guatemalan communities during the 1930s and 1940s and the diversity they reflect. The most

important series are the surveys done by the Instituto Indigenista Nacional, collectively entitled Síntesis socio-económico de una comunidad indígena, located in the Archivos de Materiales Culturales of the Instituto Indigenista Nacional in Guatemala City, as well as the various anthropological reports and field notes available in the Microfilm Collection of Manuscripts on Middle American Cultural Anthropology, University of Chicago.

22. Bunzel, *Chichicastenango*, 12; *Censo general . . . 1893*, 16, 189; *Censo de la república de Guatemala, 1921*, 18; *Sexto censo de población, 1950*, xxxi–xxxii.

23. *Censo agropecuario, 1950*, 3:118.

24. Nash, "Impact of Mid-Nineteenth Century Economic Change," 174, 183.

25. For a fuller discussion, see Handy, " 'Anxiety and Dread,' " and C. Smith, "Origins of the National Question."

26. Seligson, *Agrarian Capitalism*, 23.

27. Karl Marx, *Capital* (New York: Monthly Review Press, 1967), 1:714, 765, 3:618, 886; V. I. Lenin, *Collected Works* (Moscow: Progress Books, 1960), 2:181, 4:174.

28. See, for example, William Roseberry, "Rent, Differentiation, and the Development of Capitalism among Peasants," *American Anthropologist* 78 (1976): 45–58; Bartra, *Campesinado y poder político en México*, 48–49; and Scott, *Moral Economy of the Peasant*, 27.

29. Luxemburg, *Accumulation of Capital*, 112.

30. Meillassoux, "From Reproduction to Production," 105.

31. P. Rey, *Les Alliances des classes*, esp. 72–92; Dupré and P. Rey, "Reflections."

32. de Janvry, *The Agrarian Question*, 106. See ibid., 122–23, and Bartra, *Estructura agraria y clases sociales*, 88–92, for the argument that the apparent vitality of peasant production in some regions is simply the result of an increased number of peasants due to the lack of alternative opportunities. Peasants therefore hang onto some of their land but are forced out of commodity production, becoming in effect a semi-proletariat. A similar argument is made for Guatemala in Flores Alvarado, *Proletarización del campesino de Guatemala*, and in Figueroa Ibarra, *El Proletariado rural*. It is an argument that others, perhaps most notably Kostas Vergopoulos, disagree with, arguing that the increase in the number of peasants is in reality the continuing reproduction of peasant production. See Vergopoulos, "El Capitalismo disforme."

33. C. Smith, "Exchange Systems," esp. 311, 342. See also C. Smith, "Does a Commodity Economy Enrich the Few?"

34. González Casanova, "Internal Colonialism"; Stavenhagen, *Social Classes*, 103; Wasserstrom, "Spaniards and Indians in Colonial Chiapas," esp. 92–93, and "Revolution in Guatemala," esp. 444–46.

35. Wolf, "Closed Corporate Peasant Communities."

36. Wolf, "Types of Latin American Peasantry," esp. 509. See also C. Smith, "Local History in Global Context," 195; F. Cancian, *Economics and Prestige in a Maya Community: The Religious Cargo System of Zinacantan* (Stanford: Stanford University Press, 1965), 139; and W. Smith, *Fiesta System*, 14.

37. I am grateful to the participants of a three-day discussion on "Highland Guatemala in Historical Perspective" held in Guelph and Elora, Ontario, in February 1988, organized by Kris Inwood and sponsored by the University of Guelph and the Social Science and Humanities Research Council of Canada. Particularly helpful were the comments of George Lovell, David McCreery, and John Watanabe. For further discussion, see Handy, "Corporate Community."

38. MacLeod, *Spanish Central America*, 327; Gramsci, *Selections from the Prison Notebooks*, 258–63.

39. C. Smith, "Exchange Systems," 342–43.

Chapter 2

1. Cited in *El Imparcial*, 2 July 1944, p. 5. Note that unless otherwise indicated newspapers are published in Guatemala City and references are to articles that begin on p. 1.

2. Jorge García Granados, Roberto Arzú, and Juan José Arévalo, "Manifesto del frente unido de partidos políticos y asociaciones cívicas, 15 Oct. 1944," reprinted in Arévalo Bermejo, *Escritos políticos*, 114–17; *El Imparcial*, 11, 31 July, 1, 2 Aug., 27, 28 Sept. 1944; *Diario de Centroamérica*, 14 Nov. 1944; Ruiz Franco, *Hambre y miseria*, esp. 51; Nájera Farfán, *Los Estafadores*, 40–41. For a fuller discussion, see Handy, "Revolution and Reaction," 79–88.

3. Nájera Farfán, *Los Estafadores*, 40–41, 50–53; *El Imparcial*, 2, 19, 28, 31 Oct. 1944; William C. Afford, Jr., U.S. chargé, to secretary of state, 17 Oct. 1944, USNA-DS, dec. ser. 714.

4. "Palabras leídas por radio para todo el país el 23 de octubre de 1944," in Arévalo Bermejo, *Escritos políticos*, 126.

5. Asamblea Constituyente, *Diario de sesiones*, 464–65, 472; Robert Woodward, deputy chief of mission of the U.S. embassy, to Department of State, 15 June 1945, USNA-DS, dec. ser. 714.

6. Asamblea Constituyente, *Diario de sesiones*, 117, 125, 127; *El Imparcial*, 19, 30 Jan., 2, 3, 6, 7 Feb. 1945. Ley electoral, decree 255, is reprinted in *Alerta!*, 31 Aug. 1946, pp. 494–506, 30 Sept. 1946, pp. 93–95, 20 Oct. 1946, pp. 171–75. For a further discussion of the various debates, see Marroquín Rojas, *Crónicas de la constituyente del 45*, and Asamblea Constituyente, *Comisión de los quince encargada*.

7. Arévalo Bermejo, "Conservadores, liberales, y socialistas," in *Escritos políticos*, 147–49. See also *El Imparcial*, 30 Oct. 1944, for a discussion of the reception of this idea.

8. Arévalo Bermejo, "Al asumir la presidencia," in *Discursos en la presidencia*, 15, 24.

9. "Principios de la acción económica del estado," *Revista de economía* 2 (Jan.–Mar. 1950): 7–10.

10. *El Imparcial*, 24, 26 Aug. 1946; *Diario de Centroamérica*, 21, 28 Oct. 1949. See also *Informe de las labores del organismo ejecutivo en el ramo de agricultura: durante*

el año administrativa de 1945, presentado al congreso de la república en su primer periodo de sesiones ordinarias de 1946 (Guatemala City: Tipografía Nacional, 1951).

11. *Discursos pronunciados*, 17. See also Carlos Leonidas Acevado, "El Instituto de Fomento de la Producción y la transformación económica de Guatemala," in Ordóñez Arguello, *Transformación económica*, 88–92; "Informe preliminar de realizaciones del INFOP, 1949," *Revista de economía* 2 (Jan.–Mar. 1950): 83–122; and J. H. Adler et al., *Public Finance and Economic Development in Guatemala* (Stanford: Stanford University Press, 1952), 17.

12. "El Cooperativismo en marcha hacia la liberación económico-social de los trabajadores del país," in Ordóñez Arguello, *Transformación económica*, 95–107, esp. 99; Raul Sierra Franco, "Las Cooperativas agrícolas," in *El Triángulo de Escuintla*, 259–66; *El Imparcial*, 15 Aug., 10 Dec. 1945; Blanca Miriam Matos Hermosilla, "Estudio del cooperativismo y su porvenir para Guatemala," *El Mes económico y financiero*, 31 Aug. 1948, pp. 7–8. See also five editorials on cooperatives by Gregorio Eraza Villeda in *El Imparcial*, 28 May–8 June 1945.

13. Bulmer-Thomas, *Political Economy of Central America*, 316.

14. "Discurso del ministro de educación pública, Manuel Galich," *Universidad de San Carlos* 1 (1945): 75–85; Salvador R. Merlos, "El Analfabetismo: dolencia social, se origina en un problema de naturaleza escolar," *Universidad de San Carlos* 3 (1946): 58–65; *El Imparcial*, 2, 3, 10 Mar. 1945, 11 Jan. 1946, 7 May 1948.

15. Barahona and Dittel, *Bases de la seguridad social*; Suslow, "Social Security in Guatemala"; Rubén Homero López Mijangos, "Introducción al estudio de la seguridad social de Guatemala" (Thesis, Universidad de San Carlos, 1966). See also Arévalo Bermejo, *Discursos en la presidencia*, 37; *Informe del ciudadano presidente de la república, doctor Juan José Arévalo* (1951), 10; and *Informe del ciudadano presidente de la república, doctor Juan José Arévalo* (1950), 196–97.

16. *El Imparcial*, 10 June, 8 July 1948, 6, 14 Oct. 1950; *Diario de Centroamérica*, 23 Oct. 1950; "Informe de la junta monetaria al gobierno de la república sobre aspectos de la situación monetaria del país," *El Mes económico y financiero*, 31 Oct. 1947, pp. 1–2; "U.S. Annual Economic Report, 1950," p. 1, USNA-DS, dec. ser. 714. Prices for thirteen basic agricultural products had risen from a base of 100 in 1937 to 247.7 in 1949. "Sección de estadística," *El Mes económico y financiero*, Feb. 1950, pp. 25–28.

17. Ernest V. Siracusa, third secretary of the U.S. embassy, to Department of State, 1 Feb. 1949, USNA-DS, dec. ser. 714. See also *El Imparcial*, 26, 31 Jan. 1945, and Milton K. Wells to Department of State, 31 Oct. 1949, USNA-DS, dec. ser. 714. See Mario López Larrave, *Breve historia del movimiento sindical guatemalteco* (Guatemala City: Editorial Universitaria, 1979), esp. 13–24; Bishop, "Guatemalan Labor Movement"; and Bush, "Organized Labor in Guatemala," for background on labor during the revolution.

18. William A. Hodgman, commercial attaché in Guatemala, to Department of State, 16 Oct. 1946, USNA-DS, dec. ser. 714. See also *El Imparcial*, 27 Mar. 1945, 15, 16, 23, 25 Oct. 1946.

19. STEG bulletin, 3 Sept., 8 Dec. 1946, 11 June 1947, Guat. Doc., reel 4.

20. For the various conflicts between the two organizations, see Ruiz Franco, *Hambre y miseria*, 71, 139–41, and *El Imparcial*, 4, 8 June, 5, 6, 9 Nov. 1945, 8, 9, 28 Jan., 12 Nov. 1946.

21. *Código de trabajo* (1947); Arévalo Bermejo, "Al entregar el código de trabajo," in *Discursos en la presidencia*, 207. On the 1948 revisions, see *El Imparcial*, 17, 28 June 1948, and José Angel Recinos, "Nuestro código de trabajo," *El Mes económico y financiero*, Nov.–Dec. 1948, pp. 7, 18.

22. John W. Fishburn to Assistant Secretary of State Edward Miller, 19 Apr. 1950, in U.S. Department of State, *Foreign Relations of the United States, 1950*, 3:880–84; memorandum from Nitze, Office of International Trade Policy, to the Office of Middle American Affairs, 21 July 1947, USNA-DS, dec. ser. 714; Edward Clark to Wells, 6 June 1950, in U.S. Department of State, *Foreign Relations of the United States, 1950*, 2:903; memorandum of conversation between Spruile Braden, assistant secretary of state, and Samuel Zemurray, Mr. Montgomery, and R. LaFollete, Jr., of UFCo, 23 May 1947, USNA-DS, dec. ser. 714.

23. For labor complaints, see *El Imparcial*, 10 July 1947, and interview with Pinto Usaga and Víctor Manuel Gutiérrez by A. B. Magill, in *Octubre*, 11 July 1951.

24. Arévalo Bermejo, "El Presidente electo al pueblo de Guatemala leido por radio, 15 de febrero de 1945," in *Escritos políticos*, 179.

25. See, for example, the coverage of battles between José Manuel Fortuny and Jorge Toriello in *El Imparcial*, 2, 4 June 1945. For periodic calls for unity, see ibid., 9 Feb., 6, 30 Aug. 1945.

26. Ibid., 4, 5, 8, 10 Jan. 1945, 10 July 1946, 1 Feb., 31 May 1947. See also "Copia de actas de PAR," n.d., Guat. Doc., box 7, and "Carta abierta" from the FPL executive to the FSG, 7 Jan. 1948, Guat. Doc., box 6.

27. *El Imparcial*, 6 June 1945.

28. Ibid., 27 Jan., 19, 20 July 1948.

29. Cited in *Diario de Centroamérica*, 19 Feb. 1945. See also Arévalo Bermejo, "Palabras al pueblo," in *Discursos en la presidencia*, 47–48.

30. See PAR executive to Arévalo, 26 May 1948, and RN executive to Arévalo, 28 May 1948, both in Guat. Doc., box 6, and Fortuny to Eliseo Martínez Zelada, Guatemalan ambassador to Mexico, 15 July 1948, Guat. Doc., box 7.

31. AGA bulletin reprinted in *El Imparcial*, 2, 26, 27, 28 Jan., 12 Mar. 1948. See also the open letters from the AGA: "Señor presidente constitucional de la república," ibid., 21 Feb. 1950, p. 8; "Piden el veto de las reformas al código de trabajo," ibid., 10 July 1948, p. 8; "Actúan como guatemaltecos nuestros legisladores," ibid., 26 June 1948, p. 8; and "No hacer obra es mejor que hacerla mala," ibid., 19 June 1948, p. 8.

32. Arévalo Bermejo, "El Presidente electo al pueblo," in *Escritos políticos*, 179; *El Imparcial*, 7 Sept. 1945.

33. For a fuller discussion, see Handy, "Guatemalan Revolution and Civil Rights."

34. *El Imparcial*, 26 May 1948. See also Cáceres Lehnhoff, "Revolutionarios?

reaccionarios?," ibid., 8 July 1946, and advertisement from RN executive, "Tras la careta de la UNE aparacen las orejas reaccionarios," ibid., 2 July 1948, p. 10.

35. Advertisement by the Liga Demócratica de Guatemala contra el Comunismo, ibid., 19 June 1948, p. 8; "Alerta Guatemala," ibid., 19 Aug. 1948, p. 12; "Patria y libertad," ibid., 31 July 1948, p. 8; "Comunismo y democracia," ibid., 17 July 1948, p. 3. De Courcy's claims are in ibid., 14, 18 Jan. 1950.

36. See, for example, the minutes of the round table discussion of the PAR national executive, Aug. 1948, Guat. Doc., box 6.

37. See the editorial by Clemente Marroquín Rojas in *La Hora* cited in chargé to Department of State, 11 Dec. 1946, in U.S. Department of State, *Foreign Relations of the United States, 1946*, 11:893. Relations were especially tense while Alfonso Bauer Paiz was minister of economy. Bauer Paiz published two controversial books. The first, *La Organización obrera* (1947), prompted complaints from both U.S. and native companies that he was too closely connected to the labor unions to act impartially as minister. The second, *La Frutera ante la ley* (1949), appeared at the time of a bitter dispute between the UFCo and dock workers in Puerto Barrios. The company suspended sailing from the port in what was considered to be an attempt to hold the country at ransom. Arévalo eventually declared the company a public utility and ordered both sides to arbitration. The company saw this declaration as a prelude to expropriation. Heightened by the abrasive personalities of Bauer Paiz and U.S. ambassador William Patterson, conflict surrounding this strike seems to have marked a turning point in relations between the two countries. See Patterson to Department of State, 11 Dec. 1948, 31 Jan., 23, 26 Feb. 1949, and Air Force attaché to Department of State, 5 Aug. 1949, all in USNA-DS, dec. ser. 714, 814, and joint weeka series. See also Bauer Paiz, "El Gobierno de Guatemala y el conflicto de la United Fruit Company, respuesta al senador Lodge y Cia, discurso ante el congreso de la república," reprinted in *El Mes económico y financiero*, Feb.–Mar. 1949, pp. 1–2.

38. Víctor Manuel Gutiérrez, secretary of organization of the Comité Nacional de Unidad Sindical, and Pinto Usaga, secretary-general of the Comité Nacional de Unidad Sindical, to the defense minister, the chief of the armed forces, and members of the Superior Council of National Defense, 16 Aug. 1949, and Colonel Carlos Paz Tejada, the new chief of the armed forces, to the FSG, 26 June 1950, both in Guat. Doc., box 1.

39. *El Imparcial*, 29, 31 May, 1 June 1950; *Octubre*, 21 June 1950, esp. the opening editorial, "Por un gran partido comunista"; petition to Arévalo from the CTG demanding action against Monzón, n.d., Guat. Doc., box 7; telegram from Arévalo to Fortuny, 20 Sept. 1950, Guat. Doc., box 8; *El Imparcial*, 9, 30 Sept. 1950; Sierra Roldán, *Diálogos con el coronel Monzón*, 30.

40. For further discussion of the presidential campaign, see Handy, "Revolution and Reaction," 140–50. For official results of the election, see *El Imparcial*, 6 Dec. 1950.

41. *El Imparcial*, 8 Feb., 19 July 1950; CIA report, 27 July 1950, pp. 45–46, CIA-RR; Ambassador Patterson to Department of State, 10 Aug. 1949, in U.S. Department of State, *Foreign Relations of the United States, 1949*, 2:661.

42. Ydígoras cited in *La Hora*, 25 June 1950. For assessments of García Granados's

campaign, see Edward Fisher to Department of State, 12, 20 Sept. 1950, USNA-DS, dec. ser. 714; CIA report, 27 July 1950, p. 5, CIA-RR; Silvert, *A Study in Government*, 14–15; and *El Imparcial*, 21, 27 June, 4 July 1950. On Ydígoras's campaign, see ibid., 2 Feb. 1950, p. 12, 16 Mar. 1950, 20 Mar. 1950, p. 12, 22 Apr. 1950, pp. 6–7.

43. Fisher to Department of State, 17 July 1950, USNA-DS, dec. ser. 714; *El Imparcial*, 11 Oct. 1950.

44. *El Imparcial*, 6 Dec. 1950.

45. Wells to Department of State, 19 Mar. 1951, USNA-DS, dec. ser. 714. For comments on Arbenz's speeches and for the hope that he would turn his back on labor, see Fisher to Department of State, 2 June, 14 Oct. 1950, USNA-DS, dec. ser. 714, and CIA report, 27 July 1950, pp. 45–46, CIA-RR.

46. *Discursos del doctor Juan José Arévalo y del teniente coronel Jacobo Arbenz Guzmán*, 25–26, 29; Wells to Department of State, 19 Mar. 1951, USNA-DS, dec. ser. 714.

47. *Exposición del presidente*, esp. 3–10; *Diario de Centroamérica*, 3 May 1951, pp. 1, 2, 8.

48. International Bank for Reconstruction and Development, *Economic Development of Guatemala*, esp. 22–88; *Diario de Centroamérica*, 12 Nov. 1951, pp. 3, 7. For the embassy's very critical reception of this report, see U.S. ambassador Rudolph Schoenfeld to Department of State, 13 Mar. 1952, USNA-DS, dec. ser. 714.

49. *Diario de Centroamérica*, 14 June, 3 Aug. 1951; *Noticiero Atlántico*, 1 July 1952, in Guat. Doc., reel 2; Schoenfeld to Department of State, 9 July 1953, USNA-DS, dec. ser. 714; *Diario de Centroamérica*, 26 Sept. 1951.

50. Cited in *El Imparcial*, 20 Mar. 1951.

51. Ibid., 12, 19 Jan., 6, 7 Nov., 1 Dec. 1951; *Diario de Centroamérica*, 30, 31 May 1951; Schoenfeld to Department of State, 19 Nov. 1951, USNA-DS, dec. ser. 714; Wardlaw to Department of State, 8 June 1951, USNA-DS, dec. ser. 814; "Whither Guatemala," Albert Depocas, Canadian trade commissioner, to Trade Commissioner Service, 4 June 1951, RG 20, PAC.

52. "Chronology of Events, 1952," William Krieg, deputy chief of mission of the U.S. embassy, to Department of State, 18 Dec. 1953, USNA-DS, dec. ser. 714. Quote is from *El Imparcial*, 3, 4 May 1952.

53. Depocas to Trade Commissioner Service, 16 July 1951, RG 20, PAC. For a good if slightly exaggerated discussion of this tendency, see Krieg to Department of State, 30 Mar. 1954, USNA-DS, dec. ser. 714.

54. *Tribuna popular*, 21, 24 Mar. 1954.

55. *Octubre*, 23 May 1951; interview with Fortuny, in *La Hora dominical*, 1 July 1951; interview with Víctor Manuel Gutiérrez, in ibid., 8 July 1951; "Bases fundamentales del programa del Partido Comunista de Guatemala," Nov. 1951, Guat. Doc., box 7.

56. *Octubre*, 21 June 1950, 23 May 1951.

57. Letter from Charnaud reprinted in *Diario de Centroamérica*, 17 May 1951; Leonardo Castillo Flores and other CNCG officials to R. Alvarado Fuentes, secretary-general of the PAR, 19 May 1951, Guat. Doc., reel 50.

58. See *Estatutos del Partido Socialista* (Guatemala City, 1952), Guat. Doc., box 8, and *Diario de Centroamérica*, 10 Sept. 1951, for members of the party executive. For affiliates changing loyalties, see Fernando Castillo Rivas to Castillo Flores, 16 Nov. 1951, Guat. Doc., reel 50; Castillo Flores to Florentin López Hernández, secretary-general of the unión campesina, Quiriguá, 10 Sept. 1951, Guat. Doc., reel 52; and Filiberto Cárcama, secretary-general of the Socialist Party in San Pedro Pinula, to Castillo Flores, 6 July 1952, Guat. Doc., reel 50.

59. Quote is from "Manifesto del Partido Integridad Nacional al pueblo," 31 July 1951, Guat. Doc., box 7. See also *Diario de Centroamérica*, 6, 22, 23 July 1951.

60. *Diario de Centroamérica*, 28 July 1951; *Octubre*, 7 Feb., 20 Mar. 1952.

61. *El Imparcial*, 3 July 1952; *Diario de Centroamérica*, 3 July 1952; Schoenfeld to Department of State, 25 June, 2 July 1952, USNA-DS, dec. ser. 714; secretary of interior of the RN to the PRG, 20 June 1952, Guat. Doc., box 9.

62. For the APRISTA charge, see Schoenfeld to Department of State, 31 July 1952, USNA-DS, dec. ser. 714. See also Alfonso Rodrigo Trangay, secretary-general of the Socialist Party in Coatepeque, to Juan José Tejada Barrientos, secretary of organization of the party, 22 July 1952, Guat. Doc., box 9.

63. *El Imparcial*, 15, 26 July 1952; *Diario de Centroamérica*, 22 July 1952, p. 2, 25 July 1952, p. 2, 26 July, 1 Oct. 1952; Schoenfeld to Department of State, 4 Aug. 1952, USNA-DS, dec. ser. 714.

64. *Diario de Centroamérica*, 24 July, 14 Aug. 1952. For the estimate of PAR strength, see "Report on the Meeting of the National Democratic Front," 18 May 1954, Marco Antonio Villamar to PRG executive, Guat. Doc., box 8.

65. Silvert, *A Study in Government*, 42; Krieg to Department of State, 26 Mar. 1954, USNA-DS, dec. ser. 714; *Diario de Centroamérica*, 1 Sept. 1953.

66. Silvert, *A Study in Government*, 43. In 1952, after elections for congressional posts were held, congress found itself in a legal predicament. The president and vice-president of congress were supposed to take over the president's position in the event of his being unable to continue to perform his duties. But both were under thirty-five and thus forbidden by the constitution to do so. In the event of Arbenz's incapacity, congress would have had to turn to the second vice-president to find someone old enough. Krieg to Department of State, 18 Dec. 1953, USNA-DS, dec. ser. 714.

67. For a further discussion of the growing importance of Gutiérrez and Pellecer and the accompanying reaction, see Handy, "Revolution and Reaction," 186–90; "Organización del Partido Comunista de Guatemala," Guat. Doc., box 8; and Pellecer, *Renuncia al comunismo*, esp. 11, 85–86.

Chapter 3

1. Cited in Frankel, "Political Development in Guatemala," 12.

2. Asturias, *El Problema social del indio*, 72, 101–13.

3. The most famous "Indian" novels of the period are Asturias's *Hombres de maíz* (1949) and Mario Monteforte Toledo's *Anaité* (1948), *Entre la piedra y la cruz* (1948), and *Donde acaban los caminos* (1953). Although it should be noted that the first two

novels by Monteforte dealt much more concretely with Indian social and economic problems, they all to a certain extent suggest that Indian superstition and ignorance made a major contribution to the current economic problems. For a further discussion, see Casey, "Indigenismo."

4. *El Imparcial*, 13 July, 4 Aug. 1944, 18 Aug., 27 Sept. 1945; *Constitución, 1945*, arts. 83, 137, par. 15.

5. Girón Cerna, "La Nueva paz del indio," esp. 69, 72.

6. Goubaud Carrera, "El Grupo étnico-indígena," esp. 29.

7. Goubaud cited in A. Marroquín, "Panorama del indigenismo," esp. 302. The studies done by the institute are collectively entitled Síntesis socio-económico de una comunidad indígena and are located in the AMC.

8. *Diario de Centroamérica*, 28 June 1945; *El Imparcial*, 6 July 1945; "Incorporación indígena," *Boletín del Instituto Indigenista Nacional* I (Oct. 1945): unpaginated; Goubaud Carrera, "La Nueva escuela rural."

9. Arévalo quote is from "Al asumir la presidencia," 1 Mar. 1945, in *Discursos en la presidencia*, 16–17. See also "Lo que son las misiones culturales," *Revista de la Guardia Civil* 2 (30 Nov. 1946): 230–31, and *Diario de Centroamérica*, 13, 15 Nov. 1947.

10. Ley de municipalidades, decree 226, reprinted in *Revista de la Guardia Civil* I (16 June 1946): 331–35, I (15 Aug. 1946): 413–21, and *Constitución, 1945*, arts. 201–5. On the debate over how much autonomy the municipal governments should have, see García Bauer, *Nuestra revolución legislativa*, 61–63, and *El Imparcial*, 8, 9 Jan., 5 Mar. 1945. Arévalo vetoed the first Municipal Law passed by congress, declaring that it did not give municipalities enough autonomy. *El Imparcial*, 7 Feb., 9 Mar. 1946.

11. *Constitución, 1945*, arts. 55, 58, par. 2, and 59.

12. Enclosure number 1 to dispatch, U.S. embassy to Department of State, 1 May 1945, USNA-DS, dec. ser. 814. See also International Bank for Reconstruction and Development, *Economic Development of Guatemala*, 9.

13. Antonio Goubaud Carrera, "Indian Adjustments to Modern National Culture," in *Acculturation in the Americas*, ed. Tax, 247.

14. Carmack, *Historia social de los Quichés*, 264–68; McDowell, "Political and Religious Change," 3; McCreery, "Debt Servitude in Rural Guatemala," 756; Náñez Falcón, "Erwin Paul Dieseldorf," 322–23; Lincoln, "An Ethnological Study of the Ixil Indians," 69; Goubaud, Rosales, and Tax, "Reconnaissance of Northern Guatemala," 92.

15. Tax, "Notes on Santo Tomás Chichicastenango," 12; Redfield, "Culture Contact without Conflict"; Diós Rosales, "Notes on Aguacatán," 32.

16. *El Imparcial*, 24 Oct. 1944.

17. *Sexto censo de población, 1950*, 102–228; *Censo agropecuario, 1950*, 1:28, 3:131; Síntesis socio-económico de una comunidad indígena, Patzicía, Chimaltenango, 1953, AMC.

18. *El Imparcial*, 24 Oct., 30 Nov. 1944.

19. See Richard Adams's excellent account of the various interpretations of the Patzicía massacre, "The Patzicía Massacre of 1944."

20. J. Schlesinger, *Revolución comunista*, 6.

21. *Sexto censo de población, 1950*, 101; *Censo agropecuario, 1950*, 3:138.

22. *El Imparcial*, 11 May 1945.

23. Quotes are from ibid., 1 June 1948. For CTG comments, see ibid., 6 May 1948.

24. On San Andrés Itzapa, see ibid., 30 Nov. 1944; on Olopa, see ibid., 24 Sept. 1945; on Montúfar, see ibid., 25 Feb. 1947; and on Camotán and Villa Canales, see Hodgman to Department of State, 25 Jan. 1946, USNA-DS, dec. ser. 714.

25. Castillo Flores to secretary-general of the unión campesina, Parramos, Chimaltenango, 13 Dec. 1951, Guat. Doc., reel 52. There were 314 municipios in 1947; by 1950, the number had increased to 318. *El Imparcial*, 18 Jan. 1950.

26. Ordóñez Paniagua, secretary-general of the RN, to José Manuel Fortuny, secretary-general of the PAR, 30 Aug. 1948, Guat. Doc., box 6; *El Imparcial*, 5, 10 July 1948.

27. *Censo general . . . 1893*, 101, 112; *Sexto censo de población, 1950*, 99, 224; *Censo agropecuario, 1950*, 3:136.

28. *El Imparcial*, 2, 5–8, 16, 29 Jan., 3, 4 Feb. 1948.

29. Wells to Department of State, 14 Feb. 1951, USNA-DS, dec. ser. 814; CIA report, 27 July 1950, p. 21, CIA-RR. Cindy Forester, working with judicial records in San Marcos, has recorded a much more detailed account of this incident in " 'No Somos Mozos — We're Nobody's Boys.' " Her account, although somewhat different, draws a picture of even greater unrest accompanying labor organization in San Marcos.

30. *El Imparcial*, 15 Jan. 1948.

31. *Sexto censo de población, 1950*, 104; *Censo agropecuario, 1950*, 3:141; letters to the editor from Governor Javiera Coronada and from a resident of the community, *El Imparcial*, 10 Jan. 1948; ibid., 12 Jan. 1948.

32. *El Imparcial*, 10, 13, 21 Jan. 1948.

33. Ibid., 10 Jan., 8 Feb. 1948.

34. Ibid., 2, 10 Jan. 1950. For the strike in Coatepeque, see ibid., 17, 18 Jan., 3, 11 Feb. 1950.

35. Ibid., 5 Apr., 4, 7, 8 Sept. 1951; *Octubre*, 6 Sept. 1951; memorandum of conversation with Margaret Dressler and George Shaw, chargé, U.S. embassy in San Salvador, to Department of State, 17 Sept. 1951, USNA-DS, dec. ser. 714; Margaret Dressler, interview with author, Antigua, 22, 23 Feb. 1983.

36. On PRG-PAR conflicts, see telegrams from the Coatepeque affiliate to secretary-general of the PAR, 14, 20 Dec. 1953, Guat. Doc., box 1; telegram from secretary-general of the unión campesina, Esquipulas, to Castillo Flores, 11 Feb. 1954, Guat. Doc., reel 52; and political commission of the PRG to members of the Comité de Dirección de los Partidos Revolucionarios de Elecciones, 22 Dec. 1952, Guat. Doc., box 9.

37. For the embassy's assessment, see Wells to Department of State, 18 Jan. 1950, USNA-DS, dec. ser. 714.

38. Cited in *El Imparcial*, 2, 18 June, 10 July 1945.

39. *Diario de Centroamérica*, 29 Sept. 1945.

40. *El Imparcial*, 2, 5 Oct. 1945; Woodward to Department of State, 19 Oct. 1945, USNA-DS, dec. ser. 814.

41. *El Imparcial*, 24, 28 Jan., 5 Feb. 1946. The bank report is in *Nuestro diario*, 15 Jan. 1946, and Hodgman to Department of State, 25 Jan. 1946, USNA-DS, dec. ser. 814.

42. *Diario de Centroamérica*, 5 Feb. 1946; *Nuestro diario*, 7 Feb. 1946; Norman Stines, third secretary of the U.S. embassy, to Department of State, 5 Feb. 1946, USNA-DS, dec. ser. 814.

43. Quote is from Norman Stines to Department of State, 9 Dec. 1946. See also *El Imparcial*, 2 Aug. 1946.

44. Norman Stines to Department of State, 27 Jan. 1947, USNA-DS, dec. ser. 814; *El Imparcial*, 2, 3, 4 Jan. 1947. The estimate of the cost of living for workers comes from workers' testimonies at the conference of workers, government, and business sponsored by Arévalo. *El Triángulo de Escuintla*, 125–26.

45. *El Imparcial*, 14 Jan., 7, 10 Apr. 1947; Norman Stines to Department of State, 2 Jan. 1947, USNA-DS, dec. ser. 814.

46. Memorandum of conversation between García Granados and Spruile Braden, 29 May 1947, USNA-DS, dec. ser. 714.

47. Cited in *El Imparcial*, 5 Oct. 1946.

48. For the text of the circular, see Andrew Donovan, first secretary of the U.S. embassy, to Department of State, 8 July 1947, USNA-DS, dec. ser. 814; Fortuny cited in *Nuestro diario*, 5 July 1947; Marroquín Rojas cited in *La Hora*, 8 July 1947.

49. Andrew Donovan to Department of State, 12 Aug. 1947, USNA-DS, dec. ser. 814.

50. For Retalhuleu, see *El Imparcial*, 5 Aug. 1947. The AGA quote is from ibid., 20 May 1948.

51. Report of José Domingo Seguro, labor inspector, zone 4, 31 Jan. 1953, Guat. Doc., reel 4. His account of the finca owner in Quezaltenango is in his 1 Nov. 1952 report, Guat. Doc., reel 3; see also his reports for Sept. and Oct. 1952, both in ibid.

52. *El Imparcial*, 17 Mar. 1950, 25 Oct., 20 Nov. 1951.

53. "Situación de la escuela guatemalteca y su orientación," unsigned document prepared for the Day of the Teacher celebration, 25 June 1954, Guat. Doc., reel 47.

54. On the government taking control of the fincas during the presidency of Ubico after the United States exerted pressure, see CIA report, 27 July 1950, p. 21, CIA-RR. Ponce introduced a bill to expropriate the fincas during his short term in office, but the bill was not recognized by the revolutionary government. See *Diario de Centro-américa*, 12 July 1944; Boaz Long, U.S. ambassador to Guatemala, to Department of State, 14 July, 14 Nov. 1944, USNA-DS, dec. ser. 714; and Hodgman to Department of State, 30 Oct. 1945, USNA-DS, dec. ser. 814. Data on the fincas comes from *Diario de Centroamérica*, 27 Sept. 1951. See also ibid., 7, 11 May 1948, 28 Nov. 1951, and *Octubre*, 15 Nov. 1951.

55. *El Imparcial*, 17 July 1945, 18 Aug. 1948; *Diario de Centroamérica*, 7 Aug. 1950; Raúl Salazar, agricultural expert, finca San Luis Malacatán, to secretary-general

of the CGTG, [July 1952], Guat. Doc., reel 2; sindicato, finca San Julián, to chief of the Commission to Liquidate the National Fincas, 21 Jan. 1953, Guat. Doc., reel 4; D. Ballantine, second secretary of the U.S. embassy, to Department of State, 19 June 1951, and Robert Wilson to Robert Woodward, 3 Dec. 1947, both in USNA-DS, dec. ser. 814.

56. *El Imparcial*, 1, 6 July 1948. For further complaints, see ibid., 22, 23, 24 Jan. 1948; workers at the finca San Francisco Miramar, Quezaltenango, to director of the national fincas, 23 July 1952, Guat. Doc., reel 2; and *Octubre*, 7 Feb. 1951. There were constant complaints about the dues; for example, see Jesús Jumique, secretary-general of the sindicato, national finca El Potosí, Chimaltenango, to Gutiérrez, 5 Mar. 1953, Guat. Doc., reel 4, and Dipnisio Rivera, finca Venezuela, San Marcos, to secretary-general of the CGTG, 9 June 1952, Guat. Doc., reel 2.

57. *Octubre*, 13 Dec. 1951.

58. Ibid., 3 Jan. 1951.

59. Ibid., 23 May, 6 June, 24 July, 6 Sept. 1951. For reports of the commission and Arbenz's intervention, see *Diario de Centroamérica*, 22 Aug., 4, 18, 19, 25 Sept. 1951, and *Octubre*, 13 Dec. 1951. For the extension of the campaign to private fincas, see *Octubre*, 17 Jan. 1952, 25 Feb. 1953, and petition to the manager of the finca La Libertad from the sindicato of the finca, 18 Sept. 1952, Guat. Doc., reel 3.

60. *El Imparcial*, 16 Aug. 1948; Norman Stines to Department of State, 1 Nov. 1946, USNA-DS, dec. ser. 814.

61. "Los Trabajadores de la educación ante las grandes tareas de movimiento obrero y campesino," STEG bulletin, number 10, 3 Feb. 1947, p. 2, Guat. Doc., reel 44.

62. Rita Morelos, Río Grande Abajo, Sansare, El Progreso, to Leonardo Castillo Flores, 13 Mar. 1954, Guat. Doc., reel 51; vecinos of Woshoro (Guishoro), Jalapa, to the teacher, 11 Feb. 1953, and Rafael Tischler, secretary-general of the STEG, to Marta de Torres, third secretary of the Department of Labor, 12 May 1954, both in Guat. Doc., reel 47.

63. Cited in *Octubre*, 19 July 1950.

64. Julian Flores Reyes, unión campesina, Estancia de la Virgen, San Martín Jilotepeque, to Castillo Flores, 5 June 1952, and Castillo Flores's reply, 13 June 1952, both in Guat. Doc., reel 46.

65. *Octubre*, 21 June 1950. See also Gutiérrez to Amor Velasco, former CTG member and now secretary of organization of the CNCG, reprinted in *El Imparcial*, 31 May 1950; "Resolutions of the Ninth General Assembly of CTG," 9, 10 Sept. 1950, Guat. Doc., reel 3.

66. For appeals for cooperation, see *El Imparcial*, 3, 5 June 1950; resolutions of the first congress of the CNCG, 2 Feb. 1951, reprinted in *Diario de Centroamérica*, 3 Feb. 1951. For conflict between the CNCG and the CTG, see Gutiérrez to Castillo Flores, 9 Sept. 1952, Guat. Doc., reel 3; Sebastian Aspuac, secretary of organization, sindicato, national finca Sofia, Yepocapa, Chimaltenango, to the CGTG, 17 Sept. 1952, and Gutiérrez's reply, 22 Sept. 1952, both in Guat. Doc., reel 3.

67. *Diario de Centroamérica*, 22 Feb. 1950; *El Imparcial*, 30 May 1950. For a list of

individual unions recognized, see *Informe del ciudadano presidente de la república, doctor Juan José Arévalo* (1950), 290–94.

68. For the first conference, see *Diario de Centroamérica*, 3 Feb. 1951. For estimates of strength, see Schoenfeld to Department of State, 21 Aug. 1952, USNA-DS, dec. ser. 714; public letter from Clodoveo Torres Moss, secretary of propaganda of the CNCG, 9 Oct. 1952, Guat. Doc., reel 50; and *Tribuna popular*, 2 Feb. 1954, p. 3. See also Murphy, "Stunted Growth of Guatemalan Peasant Movements," 448, and Pearson, "Confederación Nacional Campesina de Guatemala," 41. Correspondence relating to slightly more than 800 unions is included in the Guatemalan Documents.

69. Kenedon Steins, political officer at the U.S. embassy, to Department of State, 2 June 1950, USNA-DS, dec. ser. 814; resolutions of the first conference of the CNCG, 2 Feb. 1951, reprinted in *Diario de Centroamérica*, 3 Feb. 1951.

70. Alejandro Silva Falla to Castillo Flores, 2 Feb. 1952, Guat. Doc., box 10. Silva Falla was later forced out of the CNCG. Amor Velasco, the second most powerful member of the CNCG, left it in 1952 over political differences heightened by conflict between him and Castillo Flores. See secretary-general of the unión campesina, Tojcheche, San Marcos, to Castillo Flores, 9 Dec. 1952, Guat. Doc., reel 51, and *El Imparcial*, 3 Sept. 1952.

71. Castillo Flores to minister of public works, 9 June 1953, Guat. Doc., box 10; unión campesina, national finca San Francisco Miramar, to administrator of the finca, Dec. 1952, Guat. Doc., reel 4; Castillo Flores to minister of health, 5 Jan. 1952, Guat. Doc., reel 50; municipal government of San Agustín, El Progreso, to Castillo Flores, 10 June 1954, Guat. Doc., box 10; secretary of the CAL, Nenton, Huehuetenango, to Castillo Flores, 29 Mar. 1954, and Castillo Flores's reply, 6 Apr. 1954, both in Guat. Doc., reel 52; chief of the Guardia Civil, Jalapa, to Castillo Flores, 1 Jan., 17 Feb., 19 Mar. 1954, Castillo Flores's replies, 9 Jan., 12, 23 Mar. 1954, and governor of Chiquimula to Castillo Flores, thanking him for getting tires for his jeep, 10 Mar. 1954, all in Guat. Doc., box 10.

72. Carlos Titu, "De la vida de los pueblos: la pesadilla de los alcaldes," *El Imparcial*, 9 June 1948.

Chapter 4

1. *Informe del ciudadano presidente de la república, coronel Jacobo Arbenz Guzmán* (1953), 6.

2. For fuller discussions, see Handy, *Gift of the Devil*, 35–77, 98; Méndez Montenegro, "444 años de legislación agraria"; Skinner-Klée, *Legislación indigenista*; and Partido Revolucionario Obrero de Guatemala, *Recopiliación de leyes agrarias*.

3. The resolution of the Vanguardia Nacional is reprinted in *El Imparcial*, 18 Feb. 1945; Asamblea Constituyente, *Diario de sesiones*, 740–48.

4. Silvert, *A Study in Government*, 13–14. The constitution is reprinted in ibid., 207–39.

5. *El Imparcial*, 15 Nov. 1945.

6. *Excelsior*, 23 Mar. 1945, reprinted in *El Imparcial*, 14 Apr. 1945.

7. Cited in Pitti, "General Jorge Ubico," 226.

8. *Diario de Centroamérica*, 13 Aug. 1945; *El Imparcial*, 13 Feb. 1948.

9. *El Imparcial*, 8 Sept. 1952.

10. Ibid., 4 Oct. 1946, 4 June 1948; *Informaciones nacionales*, 1 June 1946, p. 11, 1 July 1946, p. 5; *Diario de Centroamérica*, 9 July 1945, 30 Apr. 1948. See also the Cáratula para expediente for the national finca Rejón de Osuna, which was parceled out to workers on 27 Oct. 1948, National Fincas, INTA.

11. Reina, "Chinautla," 544; Clodoveo Torres Moss, "Los Alcaldes y gobernadores frente al decreto 853," 17 Apr. 1952, Guat. Doc., reel 50; *Octubre*, 13 Sept. 1950, 31 Jan. 1952; memorandum to Arbenz from Leonardo Castillo Flores, 16 May 1951, Guat. Doc., box 10.

12. Roberto Quintano, "Cambio de ministro de economía y trabajo," *El Mes económico y financiero*, 31 Jan. 1947, p. 2; Felix Osequeda, "Sistemas de explotación de la tierra en Guatemala," ibid., 31 May 1947, p. 1; Manuel Villacorta Escobar, "Investigación para la economía agrícola," ibid., Nov. 1950, pp. 1, 3, and "Necesidad de un reajuste en el tamaño económico de la explotación agrícola," ibid., Jan. 1950, pp. 1, 18–19; PAR, "Declaraciones de los principios y bases fundamentales del programa político del PAR aprobados en sesión plenaria de la convención nacional celebrada el 18 de noviembre de 1946," Guat. Doc., box 1.

13. Norman Stines to Department of State, 1 Nov. 1946, USNA-DS, dec. ser. 814.

14. *El Imparcial*, 21 June 1945, 26 Aug. 1947, 3 May 1948; *Diario de Centroamérica*, 3 Oct. 1949, 21 May 1951.

15. Antonio Cerezo Ruiz, "Necesidad de procurar el desarrollo de regiones no explotados mediante la aplicación de medidas prácticas," in *El Triángulo de Escuintla*, 238–43; interview with Dr. Manuel F. Chavarría, president of the technical council of the Ministry of Agriculture, in *El Imparcial*, 9 May 1947.

16. Monteforte Toledo, *Guatemala*, 434; International Bank for Reconstruction and Development, *Economic Development of Guatemala*, 10, 26–35.

17. *Censo agropecuario, 1950*, 1:17–34. For examples of preliminary reports, see *Mensaje quincenal de estadística* 28 (15 Dec. 1951).

18. For a background on the census, see "Presentación," in *Censo agropecuario, 1950*, 1:introduction; U.S. Department of State, "La Reforma agraria: el reto mundial," translated by Officina de Información Exterior del Ministerio de Relaciones Exteriores, n.d., Guat. Doc., box 3.

19. *El Imparcial*, 10, 28 May, 14 June 1947; *Acción social cristiana*, 19 July 1945, p. 3.

20. *El Imparcial*, 27 May, 6 June 1947.

21. Ibid., 20 Feb. 1950; *Nuestro diario*, 2 June 1950.

22. Most of Arbenz's speeches are reprinted in correspondence in the USNA-DS; for example, see Fisher to Department of State, 9 June, 11 July 1950. See also *Discursos del doctor Juan José Arévalo y del teniente coronel Jacobo Arbenz Guzmán*, 26–27.

23. Partido Revolucionario Obrero de Guatemala, *Recopiliación de leyes agrarias*; *El Libertador*, 30 June 1951, cited in Sloan, "Electoral Game in Guatemala," 33–34.

24. *Octubre*, 6 Sept. 1950, 25 Oct. 1951, 10, 24 Jan. 1952.

25. Submissions to the CNCG preparatory commission for the first national congress, n.d., Guat. Doc., box 10; *Diario de Centroamérica*, 30 Dec. 1950, 5 Feb., 16 May 1951; *Octubre*, 15 May 1952. See also Gleijesis, "Agrarian Reform of Arbenz."

26. The six proposals were presented by the Comité Nacional de Unidad Sindical, the AGA, Clemente Marroquín Rojas, the Agrarian Studies Commission, Arbenz, and Gutiérrez and Humberto Ortiz. Three were reprinted in Ordóñez Arguello, *Transformación económica*, 156–66. See also "Translation of Agrarian Reform Project of Law of Agrarian Reform Submitted by the President to Congress, May 10, 1952," in "Guatemala: Political and Economic Conditions," vol. 1, RG 20, PAC. See *Diario de Centroamérica*, 6 Apr. 1951, for the proposal by Gutiérrez and Humberto Ortiz. For criticisms of the way the law was prepared, see Sierra Roldán, *Diálogos con el coronel Monzón*, 63–65; Monteforte Toledo, "La Reforma agraria en Guatemala"; memorandum of conversation between García Bauer and William Krieg, 28 July 1952, USNA-DS, dec. ser. 714; and Acosta L. and Acosta L., "La Reforma agraria en Guatemala." See also Gleijesis, *Shattered Hope*, 145.

27. *Octubre*, 5, 12 June 1952; Castillo Flores to the CGTG, 24, 26 May 1952, and reply from secretary-general of the CGTG, 26 May 1952, all in Guat. Doc., reel 14. For the pressures on Brol, see Schoenfeld to Department of State, 10 June 1952, USNA-DS, dec. ser. 714. Quote is from *El Imparcial*, 9 May 1952.

28. *Octubre*, 22 May 1952. See also "Declaración de la CGTG en torno al proyecto de la ley de reforma agraria," 22 May 1952, Guat. Doc., reel 12.

29. *Crítica al proyecto de ley agraria*.

30. *Ley de reforma agraria, decreto 900*.

31. *Informe del ciudadano presidente de la república, coronel Jacobo Arbenz Guzmán* (1953), 9–10.

32. *El Imparcial*, 15 July, 1 Aug. 1952; Clodoveo Torres Moss, peasant league representative to the CAN, to secretary-general of the unión campesina, San Vicente Pacaya, Escuintla, 14 Oct. 1952, in Guat. Doc., reel 51. For accounts of the first land being given out from private fincas, see *Diario de Centroamérica*, 7 Aug. 1952. For the first expropriation, see Carátula para expediente against Samuel Padilla, Private Fincas, Suchitepéquez, INTA.

33. *Tribuna popular*, 8 Oct. 1953, p. 3; Krieg to Department of State, 23 Oct. 1953, and Schoenfeld to Department of State, 19 July 1953, both in USNA-DS, dec. ser. 814. For reports of bonds, see *Diario de Centroamérica*, 2 Oct. 1953, and *Tribuna popular*, 1 May 1954, p. 10.

34. This total comes from the Carátulas para expedientes, Private Fincas, INTA. See also *Censo agropecuario, 1950*, 1:19.

35. *Tribuna popular*, 1 May 1954, p. 10. See also Paredes Moreira, *Reforma agraria*, 121. These figures do not include land taken illegally or municipal land distributed. The percentage is determined by dividing the number of beneficiaries under the law by the number of economically active people in rural areas between the ages of fifteen and seventy who did not already own or operate land over ten manzanas or who did not have guaranteed access to communal land. *Sexto censo de población,*

1950, lvii, lxi; *Censo agropecuario, 1950*, 1:19; *Mensaje quincenal de estadística*, 30 Feb. 1952.

36. *Diario de Centroamérica*, 3, 9 July 1953. For accounts of property taken from government officials, see Krieg to Department of State, 23 Nov. 1953, USNA-DS, dec. ser. 814; *El Imparcial*, 3 Jan. 1953; and Carátulas para expedientes, Private Fincas, Escuintla and Suchitepéquez, INTA. On Dieseldorf, see *Tribuna popular*, 20 Nov. 1953, p. 2, and Carátulas para expedientes, Private Fincas, Alta Verapaz, INTA, for expropriation of his finca Raxpec.

37. Paredes Moreira, *Reforma agraria*, 61; *Diario de Centroamérica*, 29 July, 3, 5 Aug., 2 Sept. 1953; Bulmer-Thomas, *Political Economy of Central America*, 314–19. See also "Economic and Financial Review," 1952–54, USNA-DS, dec. ser. 714.

38. Report of Mario Antonio Blanco, the agrarian inspector, in *Tribuna popular*, 11 Oct. 1953, p. 3; *Diario de Centroamérica*, 3 Dec. 1953. Quotes are from *Tribuna popular*, 22 Nov. 1953, pp. 8, 10, 8 June 1954.

39. Report of Castro Condé of the INFOP, in *Tribuna popular*, 6 Dec. 1953, pp. 3, 5. The agricultural plan is in ibid., 8 Jan. 1954, p. 8.

40. One example of a particularly jubilant distribution of land occurred in the national finca Concepción in Escuintla. The first rural workers' union in Guatemala had been formed there by Carlos Manuel Pellecer in 1944, and the workers on the finca had been in the forefront of the struggle for the right to organize and to strike and for a minimun wage. Almost ten years after the union was formed, in August 1953, the land in the finca was given to the workers. Pellecer received a rousing ovation from the workers, and the *Tribuna popular* called the "emotion and jubilation" of the occasion "indescribable" (23 Aug. 1953).

41. *Tribuna popular*, 23 Sept. 1953.

42. Telegram from Mario Sosa N., inspector-general of the DAN, to Walter Lemus, secretary of conflicts of the CNCG, 26 May 1954, Guat. Doc., reel 50.

43. Much of the records of the CNCG and the CGTG consists of such petitions for assistance and the responses to them. For examples, see Castillo Flores to secretary-general of the unión campesina, El Pinil, Monjas, Jalapa, 2 Sept. 1952, and circular from Castillo Flores to all uniones campesinas, 4 July 1952, both in Guat. Doc., box 10; and unión campesina, Panimaquip, Totonicapán, to Castillo Flores, 1 June 1954, and Castillo Flores to the National Agrarian Bank in response, 8 June 1954, both in Guat. Doc., reel 52. For an example of one of Castillo Flores's pep talks to workers, see his letter to Daniel Vanegas, 6 June 1952, Guat. Doc., box 10. For examples of the work of the CGTG, see sindicato of a shoe factory, Cobán, to Víctor Manuel Gutiérrez, 20 July 1952, and the reply, 25 July 1952, both in Guat. Doc., reel 2, concerning the application of the law. See also secretary-general of the sindicato, San Antonio Petacalpa, San Marcos, to Gutiérrez, 27 June 1952, Guat. Doc., reel 2, asking for an explanation of *usufructo vitalicio*.

44. The records of the DAN, located in the Archivos Generales of the Instituto Nacional de Transformación Agraria, contain all of the rulings by the various agrarian agencies and the appeals filed before them.

45. See, for example, the expropriation against Federico Rosengarten's finca, Santo Tomás, which was rejected because his property was an efficient *té de limón* farm, or that against José María Valladeres's finca in San Miguel Ixcanal, which was turned down because the property hosted 300 head of cattle, in Private Fincas, INTA.

46. See the expropriation proceedings against María Teresa Larraondo's finca in Palín, Escuintla, in Private Fincas, INTA.

47. Eduardo Sosa, inspector for the DAN, to Pinto, 28 May 1954, in the expropriation proceedings against the property, Private Fincas, Jalapa, INTA.

48. Report from the agricultural expert to the director-general of agrarian affairs, 17 Oct. 1956, and Miguel Pérez and Juan Antonio Cruz to the director-general, complaining about the way Mejía had gained possession of the land, 4 Jan. 1956, in the file concerning Mejía's finca, Private Fincas, El Progreso, INTA.

49. See, for example, the expropriations against the finca Alto Egipto, owned by Julio del Calderón, and against the finca El Rosario, owned by Herlinda Portillo, in Private Fincas, Sololá, INTA.

50. Eusebio Alvarez Mejía, Pachoj, El Quiché, to the chief of the DAN, 4 May 1954, in the proceedings against Gutiérrez's property in the municipio of Santa Cruz del Quiché, Private Fincas, INTA.

51. *El Imparcial*, 5 June 1952.

52. See the file concerning his property in Private Fincas, San Pedro Sacatepéquez, INTA; *El Imparcial*, 20 Jan. 1952.

53. In Guat. Doc., box 3, there is a folder of such telegrams. The Gutiérrez quote is from *Octubre*, 12 Feb. 1953.

54. Schoenfeld to Department of State, 10, 13 Feb. 1953, USNA-DS, dec. ser. 714; *El Imparcial*, 31 Jan. 1953.

55. *Octubre*, 12 Feb. 1953.

56. Quote is from *Tribuna popular*, 5 Jan. 1954, p. 8. For accounts of attacks on peasant leaders, see telegram from Alfredo Tki Cucul of the CAL, Carchá, Alta Verapaz, to Castillo Flores, 30 Oct. 1953, and telegram from secretary-general of the unión campesina, Santa Ana Huista, Huehuetenango, to Castillo Flores, 7 Nov. 1952, both in Guat. Doc., box 10; and the CAL, finca Las Delicias, Villa Canales, to the workers' federation, 26 Oct. 1952, and local sindicato, finca Morelia, Santa Sofia, Escuintla, to the federation, 9 Sept. 1952, both in Guat. Doc., reel 3. On the formation of self-defense committees, see the CAL, finca Alapa, La Reforma, San Marcos, to the workers' federation, 29 June 1952, Guat. Doc., reel 3.

57. *Sexto censo de población, 1950*, 99; *Censo agropecuario, 1950*, 1:30, 50, 74, 3:135.

58. *Octubre*, 3, 5, 17 July 1952; file on the expropriation of the finca Potrero Grande, San Andrés Semetabaj, Sololá, INTA.

59. Esther Rubio de Melgar, secretary of women's affairs of the PAR, to Martínez, 11 May 1954, Guat. Doc., reel 19. See also Max Salazar of the CGTG to the governor of Escuintla, 18 May 1954, and Salazar to the president of the CAL, finca Santiago, Tiquisate, 27 Apr. 1952, Guat. Doc., reel 2.

60. Schoenfeld to Department of State, 2 July 1952, USNA-DS, dec. ser. 714. See also *El Imparcial*, 1 July 1952.

61. *Diario de Centroamérica*, 1 July 1952. See "Carta abierta de Alfonso Martínez al Partido Acción Revolucionaria," in *Tribuna popular*, 20 Mar. 1954, p. 2, for background on Martínez's career. For a discussion of his career in the Escuela Politécnica, see *Diario de Centroamérica*, 28 Feb. 1944, on the occasion of his winning the García Granados prize.

62. *Octubre*, 3 July 1952. For Pellecer turning down the post, see Gutiérrez to Arbenz, 20 June 1952, Guat. Doc., reel 2, and Arbenz to Gutiérrez, 1 July 1952, Guat. Doc., reel 3.

63. On invasions, see Krieg to Department of State, 14 May 1954, USNA-DS, dec. ser. 814; Swiss consul to minister of external relations, 4 Mar. 1953, Guat. Doc., box 10; *El Imparcial*, 22, 23, 24, 26 Jan. 1953; and the file on the expropriation of the finca Loma de Lashin, Mixco, Guatemala, Private Fincas, INTA. On Arbenz's hopes for avoiding conflict, see his interview for the Mexican newspaper *Voz*, reprinted in *Diario de Centroamérica*, 16 Jan. 1951, p. 7. See also Cehelsky, "Habla Arbenz," 120–21, and the report from Mario Sosa, the inspector-general of the DAN, in *Tribuna popular*, 9 Jan. 1954, p. 8. For rumors about an invasion of Arbenz's property, see ibid., 15 Jan. 1954.

64. For a discussion of the treatment of ethnic relations, see Handy, " 'A Sea of Indians,' " and Adams, "Ethnic Images and Strategies."

65. "Arbenz Gives Guatemala back to the Indians," Depocas to Trade Commission, 22 May 1952, in "Political and Economic Conditions," vol. 1, RG 20, PAC; *El Imparcial*, 29 Jan. 1953; State Department office memorandum, Siracusa to Clark, 20 May 1952, USNA-DS, dec. ser. 714; *Tribuna popular*, 11 Sept. 1953, p. 5, 15 Sept. 1953, pp. 2, 5.

66. See testimony of Florencio Bamac Gómez to the director-general of agrarian affairs, 17 May 1955, and testimony of María Nieves Leal to the director-general, 20 Aug. 1954, both in the file on the finca Candelaría, San Marcos, Private Fincas, INTA.

67. See the campaign in *Octubre* and *Tribuna popular* in 1953 and 1954, esp. *Octubre*, 2, 9 Jan. 1953, and *Tribuna popular*, 11 Sept., 5, 9, 11, 29, 30 Dec. 1953, 7 Jan. 1954.

68. For complaints about inaction, see petition from the CAL and the unión campesina, finca El Guapinol, Malacatán, San Marcos, to the DAN, 31 May 1954, Guat. Doc., reel 51; secretary-general of the national finca El Belén to Gutiérrez, 17 Jan. 1953, Guat. Doc., reel 4; Juan Miranda, president of the CAL, finca El Pilar, to Gutiérrez, 2 June 1954, Guat. Doc., reel 9; petitions from Max Salazar of the CGTG to the inspector-general of the DAN, 7 May 1954, Guat. Doc., reel 13; secretary-general of the unión campesina, Cháyen, San Rafael Pie de la Cuesta, San Marcos, to Castillo Flores, 20 Mar. 1954, and CNCG representative to the CAD, Guatemala, to the CNCG, 14 Aug. 1952, both in Guat. Doc., reel 51; and telegram from the unión campesina, Totonicapán, to Castillo Flores, 1 June 1954, Guat. Doc., reel 52. For warnings about demoralization, see secretary-general of the federación campesina, Pueblo Nuevo, Tiquisate, Escuintla, to Castillo Flores, 21 Jan. 1954, Guat. Doc., reel 51.

69. Fortuny, *Por un frente único de masas*. See also Manuel Pinto Usaga to Fortuny, 30 July 1952, Guat. Doc., box 8, and Pellecer Duran, *Renuncia al comunismo*, 105.

70. For example, see Gutiérrez to Pedro Gilbert Pérez, finca Rosario Vista Hermosa, Escuintla, 21 June 1952, Guat. Doc., reel 2.

71. See telegram from the president of the CAL, Escuintla, to Castillo Flores, 5 Oct. 1953, Guat. Doc., reel 50, and telegram from secretary-general of the federación campesina, Suchitepéquez, to the CGTG, 28 Jan. 1953, and telegram from secretary of the campesinado of the sindicato, finca Buena Vista, to the CGTG, 8 Jan. 1953, both in Guat. Doc., reel 4.

72. For a good example of such independence, see unión campesina, El Rodeo, Sansarate, El Progreso, to Castillo Flores, 24 Oct. 1952, Guat. Doc., reel 51, demanding that a local CNCG organizer who was well liked be returned.

73. *El Imparcial*, 23, 29 Jan. 1953; Krieg to Department of State, 22 Jan., 1 Mar. 1954, USNA-DS, dec. ser. 814.

74. *La Hora*, 23 Feb. 1954.

75. See, for example, Arbenz's May Day speech of that year, during which he repeated the phrase, reprinted in *Octubre*, 7 May 1953, and María Arbenz's speech to the first conference of the Alianza Femenina of Guatemala, 26–28 Nov. 1953, in Guat. Doc., box 6.

76. *Informe del ciudadano presidente de la república, coronel Jacobo Arbenz Guzmán* (1954), 2.

77. Krieg to Department of State, 9 Apr. 1954, USNA-DS, dec. ser. 714; Martínez to secretary-general of the CGTG, 9 June 1954, Guat. Doc., reel 9.

Chapter 5

1. *Informe del ciudadano presidente de la república, coronel Jacobo Arbenz Guzmán* (1953), 11.

2. Eduardo Rosales, deputy alcalde, Monjas, Jalapa, to Castillo Flores, 3 Mar. 1954, Guat. Doc., box 10; Simon Morales, secretary-general of the unión campesina, to Castillo Flores, 24 Apr. 1952, and Vanegas to Castillo Flores, 9 July 1952, both in Guat. Doc., reel 51.

3. Héctor Lemus, alcalde, San Miguel Tucurú, to Castillo Flores, 8 Feb. 1954, Guat. Doc., reel 52.

4. *Tribuna popular*, 28, 29 Aug. 1953; Schoenfeld to Department of State, 4 Sept. 1953, USNA-DS, dec. ser. 814.

5. Nash, *Machine Age Maya*, 30–33, 87–96, 130–35; McDowell, "Political and Religious Change," 2, 280–81.

6. A. Silva Falla to governor of Chimaltenango, 31 Mar., 7, 20 Aug. 1952, Castillo Flores to deputy chief of the Guardia Civil, San Martín Jilotepeque, and Genaro Julian Reyes, 19 June 1952, and Castillo Flores to minister of gobernación, 15 Nov. 1952, all in Guat. Doc., box 10.

7. Act number 5, unión campesina, La Democracia, Huehuetenango, 3 Nov. 1952, Guat. Doc., reel 3.

8. Torres Moss, "Los Alcaldes y gobernadores frente el decreto 853," 17 Apr. 1952, Guat. Doc., box 10.

9. See *El Imparcial*, 6 July 1951, for mention of the apolitical nature of the organization. On links between the CNCG and the Socialists, see Fernando Castillo Rivas to Castillo Flores, 16 Nov. 1951, and Filiberto Cárcomo N., San Pedro Pinula, to Castillo Flores, 6 July 1952, both in Guat. Doc., reel 52; *El Imparcial*, 25 July 1952; and "Act of Formation of the Socialist Party in San Pedro Pinula," 22 July 1952, Guat. Doc., reel 52. For examples of opposition to this link, see Doroteo Villanueva to Castillo Flores, 23 Jan. 1952, Guat. Doc., reel 50, and *Octubre*, 29 Nov. 1951.

10. *El Imparcial*, 16 Aug. 1952.

11. Torres Moss to Felipe González, secretary of records, unión campesina, aldea of La Pastoria, Santa Rosa, 2 Sept. 1952, Guat. Doc., reel 52.

12. Castillo Flores to German Cajuac, El Cacao, San Jerónimo, 15 Nov. 1952, Guat. Doc., reel 51.

13. Castillo Flores and Otilio Marroquín Ruano, secretary of organization of the CNCG, to Edmundo Paíz, secretary-general of the unión campesina, San Pedro Ayumpac, Guatemala, 14 June 1954, Guat. Doc., reel 50; Teodoro Trinidad, secretary-general of the unión campesina, Quezaltepeque, to Castillo Flores, 6 June 1954, Guat. Doc., reel 51; Custodio de Jesús Mancháme, president of the CAL, Morales, Izabal, to Castillo Flores, 7 Mar. 1954, Guat. Doc., box 10.

14. Vanegas to Castillo Flores, 30 June, 9 July 1952, and statement of the CNCG executive, 12 June 1953, in response to Vanegas's denunciation in *La Hora*, both in Guat. Doc., reel 50.

15. Castillo Flores to secretary-general of the unión campesina, Tuisincé, Tejutla, San Marcos, 18 Oct. 1952, Guat. Doc., reel 51.

16. See unión campesina, Tuilelon, Comitancillo, San Marcos, to Castillo Flores, 17 Sept. 1952, and Castillo Flores's reply, 24 Sept. 1952, both in Guat. Doc., reel 51. The national pattern is discerned from letters and complaints in the records of the CNCG, Guat. Doc., reels 50–52, and of the various political parties, Guat. Doc., reels 18–21. See also "Report on the Meeting of the National Democratic Front," Marco Antonio Villamar to PRG executive, 18 May 1954, Guat. Doc., box 8.

17. See "Delegación de las comunidades y uniones campesinas de El Naranjo, Cubulco, Saltán Granados, Las Dantas Granados, Cotón Granados," 19 Feb. 1954, Guat. Doc., box 10, rejecting the CNCG representative to the CAD and suggesting someone else.

18. Tiburcia Castañeda to Castillo Flores, 7 July 1953, and Castillo Flores to PAR executive, 15 July 1953, both in Guat. Doc., reel 50.

19. Secretary-general of the local PRG affiliate, Chichicastenango, to Castillo Flores, 27 May 1954, and Castillo Flores to PRG executive, 7 June 1954, both in Guat. Doc., box 10.

20. Castillo Flores to Alionso Monroy Juárez, governor of Zacapa, 14 Oct. 1952, Guat. Doc., box 10.

21. Secretary-general of the unión campesina, El Quetzal, to Castillo Flores, 23 May 1953, and Castillo Flores's reply, 27 May 1953, both in Guat. Doc., reel 51. Castillo

Flores's reply was not very sympathetic as Bautista was an important member of both the PAR and the CNCG.

22. Memorandum from Eduardo Pineda to Angel Paiz Mejía, secretary of agrarian affairs of the PRG, 5 Feb. 1954, Guat. Doc., reel 21.

23. "Boletín para la prensa y radio, PRG," n.d., Guat. Doc., reel 21. See also *El Imparcial*, 4 Sept. 1952.

24. Quote is from Humberto Lewin Dueñas, secretary-general of the PAR, Quezaltenango, to PAR national executive, 10 Dec. 1953, Guat. Doc., box 6. See also *Tribuna popular*, 8 May 1954, p. 3, and members of the unión campesina, Las Guages, Escuintla, to Frente Democrático, 18 Mar. 1954, Guat. Doc., reel 51.

25. Castillo Flores, cited in *Tribuna popular*, 8 Jan. 1954, p. 3. See also *Octubre*, 24 Jan., 21 Feb. 1951; Gutiérrez to Castillo Flores, 19 Aug. 1952, Guat. Doc., box 10; and Carlos Chancez, secretary of organization of the federación regional campesina, Coatepeque, to Gutiérrez, 5 Sept. 1952, Guat. Doc., reel 3.

26. Galvino Luis Jacobo to Gutiérrez, 2 Oct. 1952, Guat. Doc., reel 3. See also Saturnino Bajxac Cajti, secretary-general of the sindicato, finca Catalán, San Martín Jilotepeque, to Gutiérrez, 25 Oct. 1952, Guat. Doc., reel 3; Castillo Flores to Juan Godino, secretary-general of the unión campesina, Parramos, Chimaltenango, 31 Jan. 1952, Guat. Doc., reel 52; *Octubre*, 27 Sept. 1951; *Tribuna popular*, 19 Aug. 1953, p. 2; Clodoveo Torres Moss to editor of *Tribuna popular*, 23 Oct. 1953, Guat. Doc., reel 3; Roberto Montenegro, editor of *Tierra nuestra*, the paper of the CNCG, to Castillo Flores, 1 Sept. 1952, Guat. Doc., box 10; and Gutiérrez to Castillo Flores, 1 Sept. 1952, Guat. Doc., reel 50, asking him to stop setting up unions where sindicatos already exist.

27. Gutiérrez to Castillo Flores, and Castillo Flores's reply, both on 7 Sept. 1953, Guat. Doc., box 7; Castillo Flores to Gutiérrez, 29 July 1952, Guat. Doc., reel 2.

28. Carlos A. Pérez, national finca San Julián Suchitepéquez, to Gutiérrez, 25 June 1952, Guat. Doc., reel 2; secretary-general of the sindicato, finca Santa Elisa, national finca San Francisco Miramar, 13 July 1952, Guat. Doc., reel 3; Filiberto Pérez to Gutiérrez, 26 June 1952, and M. Espinosa to Pérez, 30 June 1952, Guat. Doc., reel 2. See *Tribuna popular*, 23 Sept. 1953, p. 2, 23 Jan. 1954, p. 2, for reports on troubles at the fincas Concepción and San Francisco Miramar, respectively. For workers refusing to join cooperatives or changing their minds about cooperatives, see "Actas del sindicato, finca nacional Concepción," 21 Aug. 1952, and the CAL, finca El Porvenir, San Pablo, San Marcos, to chief of the DAN, 30 Aug. 1952, both in Guat. Doc., reel 3.

29. For calls for unity, see Torres Moss to Simón Morales, 21 Apr. 1953, Guat. Doc., reel 50; Ernesto Marroquín Wyss to Gutiérrez, [Nov. 1952], and Gutiérrez's response, 13 Nov. 1952, both in Guat. Doc., reel 3; and Fortuny, *Por un frente único de masas*. On the joint commissions, see Castillo Flores to Angel María Sarazua, San Martín Jilotepeque, 22 Mar. 1954, Guat. Doc., reel 52; Castillo Flores to Alfonso Martínez Estéves, 9 June 1954, Guat. Doc., box 10; and Martínez to Gutiérrez, 9 June 1954, Guat. Doc., reel 3.

30. Report of Rubén Castellanos Fuentes, agrarian inspector, 7 Aug. 1953, and Simón Pérez, member of the CAL, El Naranjo, n.d., Guat. Doc., reel 2. See also the file on the finca in Private Fincas, San Marcos, INTA.

31. See the file on the private finca Rabinala y anexos, Cubulco, Baja Verapaz, INTA, esp. petition to the CAN, 18 Nov. 1953, and declaration by the CAN, 4 Feb. 1954.

32. *Octubre*, 28 Feb. 1952.

33. Arnulfo García Juárez, secretary-general of the unión campesina, to Castillo Flores, 10 May 1954, Guat. Doc., box 10.

34. *Tribuna popular*, 11 Sept. 1953, p. 2. See also the file on the finca in Private Fincas, San Juan Sacatepéquez, INTA, esp. denunciation from the comunidad agraria campesina, 15 Dec. 1952.

35. José Domingo Seguro, labor inspector, Retalhuleu, to Gutiérrez, n.d., Guat. Doc., box 1.

36. Absalom Maldonado, alcalde municipal, Cuilco, Huehuetenango, to Castillo Flores, 17 Apr. 1953, and Castillo Flores's reply, 25 Apr. 1953, both in Guat. Doc., reel 52.

37. See the file on the finca Santa Rosa Caníbal, Private Fincas, Huehuetenango, INTA, esp. letter from workers on the finca to the DAN, 13 Sept. 1952, the three denunciations, and the report of the secretary to the department's agrarian commission, 21 July 1955.

38. Private Fincas, Chimaltenango, INTA, esp. denunciation, 27 Aug. 1952.

39. Virgilio Escobar, secretary-general of the unión campesina, Tacaná, to Velasco, 18 Aug. 1952, and Velasco's reply, 25 Aug. 1952, both in Guat. Doc., reel 51.

40. See the file on the finca San José Real Alotepeque, Concepción las Minas, owned by José Iten, in Private Fincas, Chiquimula, INTA, esp. letter from twenty-six petitioners to the DAN, 28 Feb. 1953.

41. Secretary-general of the unión campesina, Chicazango, to Castillo Flores, 30 Mar. 1953, and Castillo Flores's reply, 30 July 1953, both in Guat. Doc., reel 51.

42. For further examples of such unrest, much of it violent, see telegram from the secretary-general of the unión campesina, Chiquimulilla, to Castillo Flores, 8 Mar. 1954, and Castillo Flores to the Guardia Civil, 9 Mar. 1954, forwarding the complaint, both in Guat. Doc., reel 50; *Tribuna popular*, 7 Jan. 1954, p. 3; *El Imparcial*, 23 Jan. 1953; and a scribbled note from the CAL, Las Brisas, Fraijanes, n.d., in Guat. Doc., reel 3.

43. Wasserstrom, "Revolution in Guatemala."

44. *Censo agropecuario, 1950*, 3:117–26, 1:19–26.

45. Reina, "Chinautla," 575–87.

46. Adams, "Magdalena Milpas Altas, 1944–1951," in "Political Change in Guatemalan Indian Communities," ed. Adams, 15–17.

47. *El Imparcial*, 12 Apr. 1951; *Censo agropecuario, 1950*, 1:34, 3:141; *Sexto censo de población, 1950*, 104.

48. Otilio Marroquín to secretary of organization of the CNCG, 16 June 1952, Guat. Doc., reel 52.

49. *El Imparcial*, 15 Jan. 1953.

50. See, for example, Alberto Valenzuela to Castillo Flores, 24 Jan. 1954, and Castillo Flores to the president of the CAL, Puerto San José, Escuintla, 8 Feb. 1954,

both in Guat. Doc., reel 51; and governor of Jalapa to Castillo Flores, 26 Jan. 1954, Guat. Doc., box 10.

51. *Sexto censo de población, 1950*, xxxi–xxxii; *Censo agropecuario, 1950*, 3:117–18.

52. See Adams, *Encuesta sobre la cultura de los ladinos*; Ewald, "San Antonio Sacatepéquez," 192; Tumin, "San Luis Jilotepeque"; and Gillen, *The Culture of Security*.

53. Silvert, *A Study in Government*, 71.

54. *Censo agropecuario, 1950*, 3:141; Gillen, *San Luis Jilotepeque*, 51.

55. Gillen, *San Luis Jilotepeque*, 205–6. See also Gillen's discussion in "Political Change in Guatemalan Indian Communities," ed. Adams, 26; secretary-general of the unión campesina, San Luis, to Castillo Flores, 30 Mar. 1952, and Castillo Flores's reply, 8 Apr. 1952, both in Guat. Doc., reel 52; *Octubre*, 19 Feb. 1953.

56. Forester, " 'No Somos Mozos — We're Nobody's Boys.' "

Chapter 6

1. Beals, "Acculturation," esp. 466; Wasserstrom, "Revolution in Guatemala"; C. Smith, "Local History in Global Context." For further discussion of these arguments, see Handy, "National Policy, Agrarian Reform, and the Corporate Community."

2. See Síntesis socio-económico de una comunidad indígena, AMC, esp. the reports on San Raymundo, 1949; Tecpán, 1948; Zacualpa, 1954; and San Ildefonso Ixtahuacán, 1956. The clearest expression of this pattern can be found in the report on San Juan Sacatepéquez, 1947.

3. See Nash, *Machine Age Maya*, 87–96, 130–35, and McDowell, "Political and Religious Change," 280–81, for a discussion of this process in Cantel. See also Síntesis socio-económico de una comunidad indígena, Patzité, El Quiché, 1948, AMC.

4. See Reina, "Chinautla"; Lincoln, "An Ethnological Study of the Ixil Indians"; and Síntesis socio-económico de una comunidad indígena, Santo Domingo Xenacoj, Sacatepéquez, 1947, p. 28, AMC.

5. For a discussion of the amount of time spent on these community posts, see Tax, *Penny Capitalism*, 10. For refusals to continue to do this work, see McDowell, "Political and Religious Change," 115, 278; Hinshaw, *Panajachel*, 44; secretary-general of the Regional Democratic Workers' Front (Frente Regional Democratico de Trabajadores), zona fria, San Marcos, to Amor Velasco, secretary of organization of the CNCG, 2 July 1952, Guat. Doc., reel 50; secretary-general of the unión campesina, Choanla, San José Ojetenán, San Marcos, to Castillo Flores, secretary-general of the CNCG, 7 Oct. 1951, Guat. Doc., reel 50; and *Tribuna popular*, 19 Feb. 1954, p. 3, 20 Feb. 1954, p. 2.

6. Holleran, *Church and State in Guatemala*; Nash, *Machine Age Maya*, 78, 85; Mendelson, "Religion and World View in Santiago Atitlán," 111–23; Ewald, "San Antonio Sacatepéquez," 189–90. See also *Sexto censo de población, 1950*, liii.

7. Rossell cited in Warren, *Symbolism of Subordination*, 89.

8. Mendelson, *Los Escándolos de Maximón*, 65–79, and "Religion and World View in Santiago Atitlán," 340–42.

9. Ebel, "Political Change," 91–104; McDowell, "Political and Religious Change," 290–93; report of Manuel Monroy Flores, secretary-general of the federación campesina, Sacatepéquez, to Castillo Flores, 12 Apr. 1954, Guat. Doc., box 54; *El Imparcial*, 10 Apr. 1952.

10. *Octubre*, 17 July 1952; *El Imparcial*, 10 Apr. 1952.

11. Tax, "World View and Social Relations," 27.

12. Cited in Hawkins, *Inverse Images*, 74–77.

13. Lovell, "Landholding in Spanish Central America," 225–26.

14. The official results of the election were Arévalo, 257,416; Recinos, 20,403; Colonel Guillermo Flores, 10,902; Teodoro Díaz Medrano, 8,222; and others, 347. *El Imparcial*, 3 Feb. 1945. See CIA report, 27 July 1950, pp. 9–13, CIA-RR, and *El Imparcial*, 6 Feb. 1945, for assessments of the fairness of the elections. See also Handy, "Guatemalan Revolution and Civil Rights."

15. Diós Rosales, "Notes on Santiago Chimaltenango." I would also like to thank John Watanabe for information on Santiago Chimaltenango.

16. *Tribuna popular*, 11 Sept. 1953, p. 2. See also the file on the finca in Private Fincas, Sacatepéquez, INTA.

17. Private Fincas, Sacatepéquez, INTA; quote is from denunciation, 30 Aug. 1952.

18. Private Fincas, Alta Verapaz, INTA, esp. unión campesina to the president of the CAD, 18 Mar. 1953.

19. *Mensaje quincenal de estadística*, Dec. 1951, Feb. 1952. Note that the 1950 agricultural census, from which these numbers are supposedly drawn, gives a substantially smaller number of comuneros — 20,547. *Censo agropecuario, 1950*, 3:147. See also Síntesis socio-económico de una comunidad indígena, esp. Chinique, El Quiché, 1948, AMC, which reported no communal land; Santa Bárbara, Huehuetenango, 1955, which reported nineteen caballerías of land used for wood at no cost; San Juan Sacatepéquez, Guatemala, 1947, which reported forty-two manzanas of land where a few people grazed cattle for the relatively high charge of Q1 per year per head; and San Bartolomé Milpas Atlas, Sacatepéquez, 1946, which reported two caballerías of land rented for corn cultivation at 50 centavos per cuerda.

20. Report of the agrarian inspector, 28 Dec. 1952, Municipal Lands, Huehuetenango, INTA.

21. *Censo agropecuario, 1950*, 3:137; *Sexto censo de población, 1950*, 100, 111. See also *El Imparcial*, 26 Aug. 1947.

22. Statutes of the comunidad campesina of San Agustín Acasaguastlán, 28 Dec. 1946, Municipal Lands, El Progreso, INTA.

23. Report of Rubén Gustavo España, the agrarian inspector of the DGAA, 5 Jan. 1957, and declaration of Regino Umul Much to the DGAA, 15 Feb. 1956, Municipal Lands, Suchitepéquez, INTA.

24. *Ley de reforma agraria, decreto 900*, art. 33. The total was arrived at by summarizing the Carátulas para expedientes, Municipal Lands, INTA. It should be noted

that José Luis Paredes Moreira, working with the same documents in the 1960s, argued that 443,393 manzanas were taken. See his *Reforma agraria*, 113. In a previous article, I reported that 520,971 manzanas were taken under the agrarian reform. This was an error in calculation that escaped my attention in the final editing process. See Handy, "National Policy, Agrarian Reform, and the Corporate Community," esp. 715.

25. For the number of prisoners in San Martín, see Factor Salán C., secretary of organization of the executive committee of the CNCG, Chimaltenango, to Castillo Flores, 23 Apr. 1954, Guat. Doc., reel 51. For further discussion of the enforcement of the forestry law, see "Informe de la secretaria de asuntos agrarios, CNCG," n.d., Guat. Doc., box 10, and Castillo Flores to minister of agriculture, 8 Apr. 1954, Guat. Doc., reel 50.

26. *Ley de reforma agraria, decreto 900*, art. 10, par. 11. See also the file on Patzicía, Municipal Lands, Chimaltenango, INTA, esp. letter from vecinos to the CAD, 12 Nov. 1952.

27. Municipal Lands, INTA. The quote is from a letter from vecinos to the chief of the DAN, 5 Aug. 1953. See Private Fincas, Sacatepéquez, finca La Candelaria, INTA, for expropriations of private fincas by the unión campesina, and Moore, "Social and Ritual Change," esp. 329–50, for further background on Paxel.

28. See letter from ninety-five people to the alcalde of Mazatenango, 30 Sept. 1952, and report of J. Armando Fonseca, agricultural expert, to the DGAA, 15 Dec. 1954, Municipal Lands, Mazatenango, INTA.

29. *Censo agropecuario, 1950*, 1:20–26. See, for example, denunciations of municipal land from San Miguel Ixtahuacán and from Esquipulas Palo Gordo, both by uniones campesinas from four different aldeas, 3 Sept. 1953, Municipal Lands, San Marcos, INTA.

30. Finca El Pilar, Private Fincas, Baja Verapaz, INTA.

31. See denunciation by the unión campesina, 12 Oct. 1952, and report of the CAL, 26 Jan. 1953, both in Municipal Lands, Jalapa, INTA.

32. Resolutions of the meeting of the alcaldía of Santiago Atitlán, 17 Sept. 1953, Municipal Lands, Sololá, INTA.

33. Municipal Lands, Baja Verapaz, INTA; quotes are from denunciation of the unión campesina, 28 Aug. 1952, and testimony before the CAD, 9 June 1952.

34. Municipal Lands, Jutiapa, INTA; quote is from denunciation presented to the CAL, 26 Aug. 1952.

35. Municipal Lands, Sololá, INTA; quote is from report of the CAD, 1 June 1953. See also Síntesis socio-económico de una comunidad indígena, San Lucas Tolimán, 1947, AMC, in which a decision was made by the principales to rent five cuerdas of municipal land to vecinos but was apparently not enforced.

36. Municipal Lands, Baja Verapaz, INTA.

37. Private Fincas, San Pedro Pinula, INTA; quote is from the protest by the comunidad indígena, 13 Feb. 1953.

38. Municipal Lands, Huehuetenango, INTA; quote is from report of the CAD, 7

Sept. 1953. See also the testimony of Diego Ortiz M. to the DGAA, 20 June 1956, ibid., and *Tribuna popular*, 6 Sept. 1954, pp. 2, 4.

39. Municipal Lands, Totonicapán, INTA, esp. denunciation, 27 Jan. 1954.

40. See Simón Morales, secretary-general of the unión campesina, to Castillo Flores, 12 Apr. 1953, Guat. Doc., reel 52.

41. See unión campesina, Senahú, to Castillo Flores, n.d., Guat. Doc., box 10; report from Aldolfo Noguerra, CGTG representative on the CAD, Zacapa, to Víctor Manuel Gutiérrez, 14 May 1954, Guat. Doc., reel 16; and statement from the CAD, Izabal, to Arbenz, 7 June 1954, Guat. Doc., reel 20.

42. On Chuarrancho, see *Octubre*, 3 Apr. 1952, and *Sexto censo de población, 1950*, 105, 94.

43. Municipal Lands, Huehuetenango, INTA, esp. denunciation of the various uniones, 24 Oct. 1953, and report of the municipality to the DGAA, 19 July 1956.

44. Municipal Lands, Chimaltenango, INTA, esp. records of the unión campesina, aldea of El Camán, n.d., and reply of the alcalde, 6 Oct. 1952. See also report of the CNCG to the governor of Chimaltenango, 5 Jan. 1951, Guat. Doc., reel 52, and Síntesis socio-económico de una comunidad indígena, Patzicía, 1951, AMC.

45. On San Jerónimo and Santa Cruz Muluá, see Municipal Lands, Baja Verapaz and Retalhuleu, respectively, INTA. See also *Sexto censo de población, 1950*, 99, 102, 110, 112.

46. Municipal Lands, Guatemala, INTA; quote is from report of the CAD, 19 Dec. 1952.

47. *El Imparcial*, 17 Aug. 1944, 5 Apr. 1948; *Diario de Centroamérica*, 5, 7 Apr. 1948.

48. See telegram from Gustavo Adolfo Solares, governor of Chimaltenango, to secretary-general of the CGTG, 26 May 1954, Guat. Doc., reel 16; Max Salazar, regional representative of the CTCG, to governor of Chimaltenango, 18 May, 1 June 1954, Guat. Doc., reel 37; *Diario de Centroamérica*, 28 Aug. 1953; Municipal Lands, Chimaltenango (for San Andrés Itzapa), El Quiché (for Uspantán), and Huehuetenango (for Santa Eulalia). See Muncipal Lands, Huehuetenango, INTA, for San Rafael La Independencia, esp. report of the agrarian inspector to the DGAA, 29 June 1956.

49. Municipal Lands, Huehuetenango, INTA, esp. denunciation of Augustín Cardona, 22 Sept. 1952; denunciations by the uniones campesinas of Chanchocal and San Juan Ixcoy, 13 Feb. 1953; report of the department's agrarian commission's interview with Marcos García, in whose name the San Juan Ixcoy denunciation was made, 21 July 1956; and report of the meeting of the alcaldía, 24 July 1956.

50. Municipal Lands, Sololá, INTA, esp. report of the municipality of Santa Clara to the CAD, 9 Oct. 1953; report of the CAD, 4 Nov. 1953; and Bernabe Xacvin Cox, secretary-general of the unión campesina, Santa María, to the CAL, 18 Dec. 1953. See also Síntesis socio-económico de una comunidad indígena, Santa María Visitación, 1949, pp. 30–32, AMC. For a discussion of San Pedro and San Juan, see Diós Rosales, "Notes on San Pedro La Laguna."

51. Municipal Lands, Quezaltenango, INTA; quotes are from vecinos of Salcajá to

Arbenz, 15 Jan. 1953; "vecinos de los cantones Chirijquiac, la Estancía, Xecam, Urbina, y Pachaj" to the alcalde municipal, Cantel, 11 Aug. 1952; and "los agricultores y vecinos del municipio de Salcajá" to the Ministry of Agriculture, 13 Jan. 1955. See also *Sexto censo de población, 1950*, 97–98, and *Censo agropecuario, 1950*, 3:134.

52. Municipal Lands, Huehuetenango, INTA, esp. denunciation by Antonio Gaspar Pablo, 17 Nov. 1952, and ruling by the CAD, 4 Feb. 1953.

53. Municipal Lands, San Marcos, INTA, esp. petition from seventy members of the aldea of Venecia to the municipality, 27 Dec. 1952, and ruling of the CAD, 24 Jan. 1953.

54. Municipal Lands, San Marcos, INTA, esp. records of the unión campesina of the aldea San Luis, 18 Sept. 1952, and report of the CAD, 29 Sept. 1952.

55. Municipal Lands, Chimaltenango, INTA, esp. denunciation by the unión campesina, Parramos, 23 Sept. 1952; renters to the governor of Chimaltenango, 20 Nov. 1952; report from the síndico municipal to the CAD, 2 Nov. 1952; report from Efraín Castillo, chief of the land sections of the DAN, to the CAD, 7 Nov. 1952; and note from renters to the CAD, 6 Nov. 1952. See also Síntesis socio-económico de una comunidad indígena, Parramos, 1947, AMC, in which it was reported that the average size of lot rented from the municipality was seven cuerdas.

56. Municipal Lands, El Quiché, INTA, esp. comuneros of the comunidad indígena, Santa María Joyabaj, to the CAD, 16 Jan. 1955.

Chapter 7

1. Reprinted in *Tribuna popular*, 20 June 1954.

2. Clark to Wells, 23 Apr. 1951, USNA-DS, dec. ser. 714.

3. Resolution 18 from the CTG national congress, 24–27 Oct. 1946, included in Norman Stines, secretary of the U.S. embassy, to Department of State, USNA-DS, dec. ser. 814. See also Bauer Paiz, *La Frutera ante la ley*.

4. On the UFCo, see *El Imparcial*, 17 Sept. 1951, and *Octubre*, 30 Aug., 13 Sept. 1951. On the IRCA, see *Diario de Centroamérica*, 26 June 1951, and *El Imparcial*, 23 Apr., 13 June 1951. For the protest over coffee prices, see *Octubre*, 14 Feb. 1951.

5. Schoenfeld to Department of State, 14 Aug. 1953, USNA-DS, dec. ser. 714; Cleveland McKnight, economic attaché, to Department of State, 5 Nov. 1953, USNA-DS, dec. ser. 814. The incomplete records of the expropriation of UFCo land are located in INTA. See also the DAN figures published in *Tribuna popular*, 22 Nov. 1953, p. 5.

6. *Diario de Centroamérica*, 16 Nov. 1953. See also INTA.

7. State Department memorandum, 28 Apr. 1953, USNA-DS, dec. ser. 814; *Diario de Centroamérica*, 21, 22 Sept. 1953; State Department memorandum, 24 May 1954, Guat. Doc., box 1.

8. Wells to Department of State, 17 May 1950, USNA-DS, dec. ser. 714.

9. Included in Schoenfeld to Department of State, 26 June 1953, USNA-DS, dec. ser. 714.

10. Mosely, *Dulles*, esp. 92; Schlesinger and Kinzer, *Bitter Fruit*. See also letters from Congressmen Walter S. Baring, 14 Apr. 1952, Hubert Humphrey, 15 Apr. 1952, and James Byrnes, 5 May 1952, all to J. K. McFall, assistant secretary of state for congressional relations, USNA-DS, dec. ser. 714.

11. *Octubre*, 9 Apr. 1952; Krieg to Department of State, 30, 31 Mar. 1953, and Schoenfeld to Department of State, 12 Apr. 1953, all in USNA-DS, dec. ser. 714; *El Imparcial*, 6, 8, 19, 20 Feb. 1952.

12. Cook, *The Declassified Eisenhower*, 61, 112–13; Clark to Department of State, 4 Dec. 1952, and Krieg to Clark, 22 Nov. 1952, both in USNA-DS, dec. ser. 714.

13. Silvert, *A Study in Government*, 55; William Krieg, interview with author, Antigua, Feb. 1983. For a further discussion, see Handy, "Guatemalan Revolution and Civil Rights."

14. *La Hora dominical*, 21 Oct. 1951. For the coverage in *El Imparcial*, see "Amenaza Roja," 1–5 Jan. 1951. In 1952 it gave front-page coverage to a purported communist plot discovered in El Salvador (ibid., 30 Sept. 1952). It also carried a series of letters from Colonel Roberto Barrios Peña on the communist menace, with detailed descriptions of the abuse of liberties in the Soviet Union (ibid., 7 July 1951). For formation of the anticommunist leagues, see ibid., 4, 5 July, 11 Oct. 1951.

15. *Acción social cristiana*, 19 July 1945, p. 16, 19 Aug. 1945; pastoral letter, 25 May 1950, reprinted in *El Imparcial*, 26 May 1950; pastoral letter, 14 Apr. 1954, included in Krieg to Department of State, 14 Apr. 1954, USNA-DS, dec. ser. 714.

16. See, for example, PAR secretary-general in the department of Suchitepéquez to the editor of *El Imparcial*, 29 Jan. 1952, Guat. Doc., box 1, and memorandum of conversation with Toriello and John Moors Cabot, 6 Mar. 1953, USNA-DS, dec. ser. 714.

17. See, for example, minutes of the round table discussion of the PAR national executive, 28 Aug. 1948, Guat. Doc., box 6, and José Manuel Fortuny, *Informe sobre la actividad del Comité Central de PCG* (Guatemala City, 1953).

18. CIA report, 27 July 1950, p. 16, CIA-RR; Miller to Barret, 16 Aug. 1951, USNA-DS, dec. ser. 714; William Krieg, interview with author, Antigua, Feb. 1983; "National Intelligence Estimate: Probable Developments in Guatemala, May 19, 1953," pp. 1–6, CIA-RR.

19. Eisenhower, *White House Years*, 421–22. See also Schoenfeld to Department of State, 22 July 1952, USNA-DS, dec. ser. 714, discussing the new PAR executive. For reports on the peace campaign, see *Diario de Centroamérica*, 2 Apr. 1951; *Octubre*, 11 July, 13 Sept. 1951, 9 Mar. 1953; "Chronology of Events," Schoenfeld to Department of State, 13 Mar. 1952, USNA-DS, dec. ser. 714; and PGT bulletin, "Por la paz," 13 Jan. 1954, Guat. Doc., box 1.

20. Memorandum of conversation, 13 May 1952, USNA-DS, dec. ser. 714.

21. On the Organization of Central American States, see Raul Osequeda, Guatemalan foreign minister, to the United Nations, 1 Apr. 1953, reprinted in *Octubre*, 9 Apr. 1953. Schlesinger and Kinzer suggest that the *Alfhem* was able to elude the U.S. blockade. Schlesinger and Kinzer, *Bitter Fruit*, 149–50. Krieg argued that it was the

ship's arrival that finally precipitated action; the State Department was prepared to wait to see if the army would allow a communist to win the next presidential election, but with the arrival of the arms, it feared that the military would no longer be able to control the situation. William Krieg, interview with author, Antigua, Feb. 1983. This idea is seconded by E. Howard Hunt, one of the CIA operatives in the intervention. However, Hunt also says that Arbenz's close personal friend, Colonel Anselmo Getellá, had been providing the CIA with information on the government's search for arms, and it knew when the ship was to arrive and presumably could have stopped it. Hunt, *Undercover*, 99–100. This information is supported by the comments in John Peurifoy, U.S. ambassador, to Department of State, 5 Jan. 1954, USNA-DS, dec. ser. 714. B. W. Cook has used this information to suggest that the United States wished to use the delivery of the arms as a pretext for intervention. Cook, *The Declassified Eisenhower*, 266. The best discussion of Caracas is in Toriello, *Tras la cortina*, 107–70.

22. The Canadian representative to the United Nations in 1954 provides a particularly clear and interesting account of the various debates in the UN over the issue of whether it or the Organization of American States should deal with the intervention as well as an account of the U.S. bullying of the Security Council. The final vote on the question of control was 4 in favor of UN deliberation and 5 opposed. Voting with the United States in opposing UN deliberation were China, Turkey, Brazil, and Colombia. Voting against the United States were the Soviet Union, New Zealand, Denmark, and Lebanon. The French and United Kingdom representatives abstained. The UN General Assembly debates over the issue were rambunctious affairs with large crowds of Guatemalan supporters as spectators, a number of whom were thrown out of the gallery. Report of the Permanent Representative to the Secretary of State, 21, 25 June 1954, in "Guatemala: Political and Economic Conditions," vol. 1, RG 20, PAC.

23. Memorandum of conversation with the Canadian ambassador to the United States, 25 June 1954, in "Guatemala: Political and Economic Conditions," vol. 1, RG 20, PAC.

24. Colonel Carlos Enrique Díaz, "Diario de sesiones," Guat. Doc., box 3. See also speech by Colonel Enrique Parinello broadcast over the government radio station, 26 May 1954, in *Tribuna popular*, 27 May 1954. For independent assessments of the army's loyalty, see memorandum of conversation between Costa Rican ambassador and Robert Wilson, 4 Sept. 1952, USNA-DS, dec. ser. 714, and memorandum of conversation between Leo Suslow and Wilson, 2 Sept. 1952, and CIA report, 1953, pp. 1–2, both in CIA-RR.

25. For an interesting comment on this aspect of the military, see an editorial in the *El Imparcial*, 8 Jan. 1945.

26. *Constitución, 1945*, art. 151; *La Prensa* (Mexico City), 20 Apr. 1948, reprinted in *Diario de Centroamérica*, 11 May 1948.

27. *Constitución, 1945*, art. 156. See also the discussion of the workings of the council in Paz Tejada, "Un Militar honesto," 41.

28. CIA report, 27 July 1950, p. 39, CIA-RR.

29. Sierra Roldán, *Diálogos con el coronel Monzón*, 23–24.

30. Schneider, *Communism in Guatemala*, 24.

31. CIA report, 27 July 1950, p. 39, CIA-RR. For Arbenz's record, see Escuela Politécnica, *Anales*, vol. 4 (1947); Samayoa Coronado, *La Escuela Politécnica*, 2:113–16; "Curriculum del Coronel Jacobo Arbenz Guzmán," n.d., Guat. Doc., box 6.

32. Memorandum of conversation between Britnell and Assistant Secretary of State Miller, 28 Aug. 1950, USNA-DS, dec. ser. 714; CIA report, 27 July 1950, pp. 45–46, CIA-RR.

33. Sierra Roldán, *Diálogos con el coronel Monzón*, 25; Paz Tejada, "Un Militar honesto," 43–45; Cehelsky, "Habla Arbenz," 120–21. The killing of Arana remains one of the most controversial acts of the Arévalo administration. Arévalo never admitted the government's part in the killing, instead arguing publicly that he was killed by rebels in the revolt that occurred at the time of his death in 1949. Thus for a few years after the revolt, Arana was honored as one of the martyrs of the revolution. Arbenz indicated that Arana was killed resisting arrest and that his death was one of the events he regreted most. Opposition forces soon argued that Arana was killed in a deliberate ambush set by Arbenz and Arévalo. See *Informe del ciudadano presidente de la república, doctor Juan José Arévalo* (1950), 30–32, and Monteforte Toledo, *Una Democracia a prueba del fuego.*

34. Wells to Department of State, 1 Aug. 1949, USNA-DS, dec. ser. 714.

35. Schoenfeld to Department of State, 14 Aug., 11, 25 Sept. 1953, USNA-DS, dec. ser. 714; *El Imparcial*, 6 July 1951, 15 Mar. 1952; *Octubre*, 22 Aug. 1951. For Castillo Armas's claims, see "Coronel Castillo Armas," 19 Jan. 1950, CIA-RR.

36. For the various promociones, see Escuela Politécnica, *Anales*, 4:177–204 (1947). For elections to the Superior Council of National Defense and chief of the armed forces in 1951, see *El Imparcial*, 6 Mar., 11 July 1951. For a further discussion of the various divisions in the military, see Schneider, *Communism in Guatemala*, 31; Monteforte Toledo, *Guatemala*, 364–74; Baker, *Study in Military Status*, 41; Adams, *Crucifixion by Power*, 257; and Cehelsky, "Habla Arbenz," 121.

37. For a fuller discussion, see Handy, " 'Anxiety and Dread.' "

38. Quote is from an address by Vicente Nájera, 1 May 1951, Guat. Doc., reel 2; Carmack, *Historia social de los Quichés*, 271–300.

39. *Informe del ciudadano presidente de la república, doctor Juan José Arévalo* (1950), 19.

40. Cehelsky, "Habla Arbenz," 119. The number given in Cehelsky's article is 70,000, which is either a typographical error or an exaggeration on Arbenz's part.

41. *Tribuna popular*, 3 Oct. 1953. Arbenz claimed that he met with the top military commanders to explain the law before it was passed by congress and that they reacted favorably to it. Cehelsky, "Habla Arbenz," 121. For a discussion of soldiers acquiring land under the law, see Castillo Flores to Díaz, 4 June 1952, Guat. Doc., box 10; *Tribuna popular*, 15 Aug. 1953; and Sierra Roldán, *Diálogos con el coronel Monzón*, 27. For a description of Major Arreaga's role on the CAN, see Torres Moss to Arreaga, 15 Apr. 1953, Guat. Doc., reel 50.

42. *Octubre*, 7 Feb., 6 Mar. 1952; *Tribuna popular*, 26 Aug. 1953, p. 2; *Diario de Centroamérica*, 26 Feb. 1954; Castillo Flores to governor of Chimaltenango, 11 Sept. 1952, and telegram from secretary-general of the unión campesina, Casillas, Nuevo Santa Rosa, to the CNCG, n.d., both in Guat. Doc., reel 52.

43. Schoenfeld to Department of State, 12, 14 Aug. 1953, USNA-DS, dec. ser. 714. For examples of CNCG influence over the guard, see guard commander, San Marcos, to Castillo Flores, 18 May 1953, Guat. Doc., reel 51; guard commander, Jalapa, to Castillo Flores, 5 June 1953, Guat. Doc., box 2; and Castillo Flores to Cruz Wer, 18 Jan. 1953, 30 Jan., 4 Feb., 13 May 1954, Guat. Doc., box 10.

44. For complaints against commissioners, see secretary of records of the sindicato, finca Camonathulul, Santa Lucia Cotzumalguapa, Escuintla, to the CGTG, 6 June 1952, Guat. Doc., reel 2; the CAL, San Antonio Aguas Calientes, to Castillo Flores, 16 Jan. 1954, Guat. Doc., reel 52; *Octubre*, 20 Dec. 1951; Gutiérrez to governor of Guatemala, 31 July 1952, Guat. Doc., reel 2; and secretary-general of the unión campesina, Santa Julien, San Rafael Pie de la Cuesta, to the CNCG, 27 Jan. 1954, Guat. Doc., box 1. For requests for transfers that were not successful, see two letters from the secretary of armed forces to Castillo Flores, 1 Apr. 1952, Guat. Doc., box 1. For successful requests, see Díaz to Castillo Flores, 25 Jan. 1951, Guat. Doc., reel 50. See also Castillo Flores to Díaz, 13 June 1952, Guat. Doc., box 1, asking for the removal of thirty-six military commissioners.

45. See Otilio Marroquín R. to all uniones campesinas, department of Guatemala, 16 June 1954, Guat. Doc., reel 50; Castillo Flores to Simón Morales, 10 Jan. 1954, Guat. Doc., box 1; *El Imparcial*, 24 Jan. 1953; and the plan presented by the Superior Council of National Defense, 19 May 1954, Guat. Doc., box 1.

46. Arévalo Bermejo, *Guatemala, la democracia y el imperio*, 37–40; Cehelsky, "Habla Arbenz," 123; Philip Williams, chargé in Guatemala, to Department of State, 25 Oct. 1950, Miller to Elliot, 27 Dec. 1949, and Clark to Murray Wise, 18 Oct. 1949, all in USNA-DS, dec. ser. 714. For an analysis of the air force, see CIA report, 27 July 1950, pp. 39–40, CIA-RR.

47. Cehelsky, "Habla Arbenz," 123. For background on distributing arms to civilians, see Gutiérrez and Pinto Usaga, both of the CTG, to minister of national defense, 16 Aug. 1949, Guat. Doc., box 1; *El Imparcial*, 23 June 1950; "Current Intelligence Digest," 3 June 1954, and "Current Intelligence Bulletin," 22 June 1954, both in CIA-RR; Peurifoy to Department of State, 21 June 1954, USNA-DS, dec. ser. 714; and *Tribuna popular*, 2 June 1954.

48. See Wasserstrom, "Revolution in Guatemala," 474–75, for the argument that peasants refused to defend the revolution. For offers of support and instructions from national offices, see telegram from the unión campesina, Arizona, Puerto San José, to Castillo Flores, 17 June 1954, Castillo Flores to the CAL, San Antonio Aguas Calientes, 2 June 1954, telegram from secretary-general of the peasant federation, San Marcos, zona calida, to Castillo Flores, 29 May 1954, and Castillo Flores to director-general of the Guardia Civil, Chiquimula, 10 Feb. 1954, all in Guat. Doc., reel 51; telegram to secretary-general of the PAR from president of the league of renters, 14

June 1954, telegram from governor of Chiquimula to Arbenz, 8 June 1954, telegram from alcalde municipal, San Vicente Pacaya, to minister of gobernación, 20 June 1954, all in Guat. Doc., box 6; *Tribuna popular*, 18 June 1954; Castillo Flores to all uniones campesinas, department of Guatemala, 21 June 1954, and Castillo Flores to departmental federations, 17 June 1954, both in Guat. Doc., reel 50; and Humberto González, secretary of organization of the PAR, to all members, 19, 21 June 1954, Guat. Doc., box 6.

Piero Gleijesis has argued that revolutionary stalwarts in the capital were disappointed by the fact that only a few people responded to their calls to come forward to defend the revolution. Gleijesis, *Shattered Hope*, 342–43. However, this stands in sharp contrast to the response of peasants throughout the country who rallied to the defense of the revolution whenever possible.

49. See, for example, "Effect upon Guatemala of Arms Procurement by El Salvador, Honduras, and Nicaragua, 12 June 1953," in W. Park Armstrong to Cabot, 16 June 1953, cited in Cook, *The Declassified Eisenhower*, 240–41, and Schoenfeld to Department of State, 24 June 1952, USNA-DS, dec. ser. 714.

50. Memorandum of conversation between Schoenfeld and Peralta, 21 Aug. 1953, USNA-DS, dec. ser. 714.

51. "Current Intelligence Digest," 15, 17 June 1954, CIA-RR; *Tribuna popular*, 16 June 1954; Cehelsky, "Habla Arbenz," 122–23; *Impacto*, 30 June, 25 July 1954.

52. "Current Intelligence Digest," 25 June 1954, CIA-RR; Peurifoy to Department of State, 28 June 1954, USNA-DS, dec. ser. 714.

53. Cehelsky, "Habla Arbenz," 123; Peurifoy to Department of State, 28 June 1954, USNA-DS, dec. ser. 714.

Military officers themselves, in discussing their failure to confront the Liberation forces, have stressed their fear of the power of the United States, which supported the Liberation, and the demoralizing effect of the rebel aircraft. Gleijesis, *Shattered Hope*, 338–42. I believe both of these arguments to be self-serving attempts by these officers to escape the blame for refusing to defend the constitutionally elected president.

Chapter 8

1. *Parisien libére*, cited in Dillen, U.S. embassy in Paris, to Department of State, 1 July 1954, USNA-DS, dec. ser. 714.

2. Peurifoy to Department of State, 6 July 1954, USNA-DS, dec. ser. 714; "Current Intelligence Digest," 29 June 1954, CIA-RR.

3. The transition through the various juntas is described in Peurifoy's dispatches to Department of State, 28 June 1954, at noon, 5, 8, and 9 o'clock, and 29 June 1954, USNA-DS, dec. ser. 714.

4. Peurifoy to Department of State, 7 July 1954, USNA-DS, dec. ser. 714. For a discussion of U.S. relations with Castillo Armas at this point and the role of Córdova Cerna, see Brockett, "Building a Showcase for Democracy."

5. Peurifoy to Department of State, 6, 8 July 1954, and Krieg to Department of State,

9, 11 Aug. 1954, all in USNA-DS, dec. ser. 714. On people seeking asylum, see Krieg to Department of State, 6, 16, 17 Aug. 1954, USNA-DS, dec. ser. 714.

6. See Krieg to Department of State, 17, 18 Aug. 1954, USNA-DS, dec. ser. 714, and *Discursos del vocal de la junta de coronel Elfego H. Monzón en la celebración del día de "La Unidad Nacional del Ejército"* (Guatemala City: Tipografía Nacional, 1954).

7. Brockett, "Building a Showcase for Democracy," 6–7.

8. Castillo Armas's position is reported in U.S. embassy to Department of State, 17 Dec. 1954, USNA-DS, dec. ser. 714, cited in Brockett, "Building a Showcase for Democracy," 5.

9. Brockett, "Building a Showcase for Democracy," 9–11.

10. Falla, *Masacres de la Selva*, viii; Jane Lyons, interview with author, Antigua, Mar. 1993.

11. Peurifoy to Department of State, 28 June 1954, Krieg to Department of State, 16, 17 Aug. 1954, and memorandum of conversation with W. F. Woodward, all in USNA-DS, dec. ser. 814; Brockett, "Building a Showcase for Democracy," 11. See also *New York Times*, 29 June 1956, p. 5.

12. Secretaría de Propaganda, *Estatuto agrario: decreto número 31*, esp. 3, 5–7, 12–13, 16.

13. Secretaría de Propaganda, *Estatuto agrario: decreto número 559*, esp. 3–4, 9–10, 19–21, 27–29, 41.

14. Secretaría de Propaganda, *Estatuto agrario: decreto número 31*, art. 3, p. 4.

15. Secretaría de Propaganda, *Estatuto agrario: decreto número 559*, arts. 21, 22, 29, and 35–38.

16. These totals come from the records of the DGAA in INTA.

17. See, for example, Jonas Bodenheimer, *Guatemala*, 239, and Comisión Interamericano de Desarrollo Agrícola, *Tenencia de la tierra*. It appears that these figures are taken primarily from a DGAA statement in 1956 that only about .4 percent of the beneficiaries of decree 900 were still on their land. This, of course, is not the same thing as saying that all but .4 percent of the land had been returned, and DGAA inspectors had important reasons for underestimating the number of beneficiaries still on the land.

18. See, for example, report of M. Antonio Montenegro M., agrarian inspector, to the DGAA, 29 Aug. 1955, Private Fincas, Baja Verapaz, INTA, concerning the finca Rabinala, owned by the García Rosales brothers, in Baja Verapaz.

19. Secretaría de Propaganda, *Estatuto agrario: decreto número 31*, art. 254. See, for example, the report of the president of the department's agrarian commission, El Quiché, to the DGAA, 9 Aug. 1956, concerning the fincas Buena Vista, Faldas de Coyoya, and Río Grande, owned by Cruz Velásquez, Private Fincas, El Quiché, INTA. The decisions concerning Gutiérrez's property are in the same record group.

20. Report of the department's agrarian commission to the DGAA, 16 Feb. 1955, Private Fincas, Escuintla, INTA, concerning the property of Manuel de Jesús Arana in Escuintla.

21. Report of Manuel de Jesús Paiz to the DGAA, 3 Sept. 1956, Private Fincas, San

Marcos, INTA; Arenas to the DGAA, 21 Sept. 1954, Private Fincas, Chimaltenango, INTA.

22. See the file in Private Fincas, Baja Verapaz, INTA, and report from agrarian inspector to the DGAA, 3 June 1956, Private Fincas, Escuintla, INTA.

23. Parcelarios to the DGAA, 1 Oct. 1955, Private Fincas, Sacatepéquez, INTA.

24. Private Fincas, Escuintla, INTA.

25. Reports on the finca Louisiana, Private Fincas, San Marcos, INTA. See especially Joaquin Velasco, alcalde of Malacatán, to the DGAA, 26 Mar. 1956, Private Fincas, San Marcos, INTA, and reports on the finca Cerro Azul, owned by the Brol brothers, Private Fincas, El Quiché, INTA. It should be noted that the latter case was complicated by the hesitant attitude of the DGAA toward the Brol family. It was not sure if the whole family should suffer because of Nicolás's association with Arbenz.

26. Finca Torolita, Private Fincas, Escuintla, INTA, esp. the letter from sixty-one parcelarios to the DGAA, 19 Aug. 1991.

27. Finca La Florida, Private Fincas, Huehuetenango, INTA, esp. Manuel de Léon Granada to the attorney general, 7 Sept. 1956.

28. Resolution 739 of the DGAA, 27 Apr. 1957, in finca Las Trojes, Private Fincas, Guatemala, INTA; finca Santo Domingo Los Ocotes, Private Fincas, El Progreso, INTA; finca La Trinidad, Private Fincas, Huehuetenango, INTA.

29. Petition to the DGAA, 3 June 1955, in finca Monte María, Private Fincas, Sacatepéquez, INTA.

30. Eduardo Galeano, "Language, Lies, and Latin Democracy," *Harper's Magazine*, Feb. 1990, p. 19.

31. Finca Palmilla or Vega Grande, Private Fincas, Izabal, INTA.

32. *Prensa libre*, 23 Aug. 1989, p. 3, 27 Aug. 1989, p. 12.

GLOSSARY

alcalde mayor and chief justice of a municipio
alcaldía local (municipio) government
aldea outlying hamlet, part of a municipio
cabacera capital of a municipio
caballería approximately 110 acres (64 manzanas)
cantones districts of a municipio
cofradía brotherhood honoring a specific saint
comunidades campesinas local organizations of rural cultivators, given legal status in 1946
comunidades indígenas local organizations of Maya, given legal status in 1946
cuerda approximately .3 acres, although throughout rural Guatemala the size varied to some extent
finca de mozos farm, usually in the highlands, in which land is rented out to workers in return for work contracts
habilitador (enganchador) labor contractor
manzana 1.7 acres
mozos colonos resident workers, given land on a finca in return for working on that finca
principales town or municipio "elders"
quintal 100 pounds
reducciones (congregaciones) policy of settling Maya in "official" towns begun in the sixteenth century
regidores "councilmen" in the alcaldía
sindicatos local, rural affiliates of the CTG or the CGTG
terratenientes large landowners
uniones campesinas "peasant" organizations, locals of the CNCG

BIBLIOGRAPHY

Archival Sources

Among the number of archival sources consulted for this study, by far the most important were the records of the Departamento Agrario Nacional. These records contain the investigations and deliberations concerning every denunciation of land (private finca, national finca, or municipal land) received by agrarian officials during the revolution, whether the denunciation was successful or not. The files also contain information concerning the return of the land under the auspices of the Dirección General de Asuntos Agrarios following the overthrow of the Arbenz administration. The lengthy file on each property includes the denunciation itself as well as the reports of the various levels of agrarian officials, evidence brought forward in the appeals, and often extensive reports from the agrarian commissions. These files are located in the Archivos Generales of the Instituto Nacional de Transformación Agraria in Guatemala City. I wish to thank the director of the institute for granting me access to these files.

Other valuable archival sources were the Guatemalan Documents or Guatemalan Transcripts, located in the Manuscript Division of the Library of Congress, Washington, D.C. The partial records of the political parties, revolutionary organizations, and unions active during the revolution, these documents were found and copied following the overthrow of the Arbenz administration and used extensively first by Ronald Schneider at the University of Pittsburgh. They were given to the Library of Congress in 1958. Although they are incomplete and concentrate on the Arbenz administration, they do provide valuable insights into the operation of various organizations. Of the 58 reels of microfilm, a portion has been reproduced into 94 boxes of documents. A guide to the material is available from the Library of Congress.

Also helpful were the files of the General Records of the Department of State, Record Group 59, relating to Guatemala, located at the U.S. National Archives, Washington, D.C. Most useful for the purposes of this study were the decimal series 714 and 814 and the joint weeka series. These records not only provide an essential guide to U.S. views and actions toward the two administrations of the revolution but also document embassy and consular officials' views on internal politics. The yearly political and economic summaries are particularly informative. Other works that concentrate more fully on U.S. involvement in the revolution discuss these sources in more detail; see particularly Piero Gleijesis, *Shattered Hope: The Guatemalan Revolution and the United States, 1944–1954* (1991).

Also of use for more specific purposes were the reports of the Canadian trade commissioner to Guatemala for the years 1950 to 1954. These are collectively entitled Political and Economic Conditions in Guatemala, Record Group 20, in the Public

Archives of Canada, Ottawa. Reel 5 of the Research Reports of the Central Intelligence Agency, part of a microfilmed series on Latin America, while limited, was also useful. The surveys of economic, cultural, and political conditions in fifty-six Guatemalan communities that were carried out primarily in the 1940s and 1950s under the auspices of the Instituto Indigenista Nacional, collectively titled Síntesis socio-económico de una comunidad indígena and located in the Archivos de Materiales Culturales of the institute in Guatemala City, were also useful in drawing the portrait of Guatemalan communities presented in chapter 2. Although they are not strictly archival materials, the various reports and field notes of a number of anthropologists active in Guatemala in the 1930s and 1940s, collected in the Microfilm Collection of Manuscripts on Middle American Cultural Anthropology, University of Chicago, are also of great interest in understanding the nature of Guatemalan communities, especially before the reforms of the revolution began to have an effect.

Government Publications

Also essential for this study was a wide variety of government publications, organized below according to ministry or department. They are all printed by the Tipografía Nacional in Guatemala City unless otherwise indicated.

CONGRESO DE LA REPÚBLICA

Boletín del congreso de la república. Vols. 1–17. 1944–51.
Código de trabajo. 1947.
Código de trabajo, contenido en los decretos números 330, 526, y 623, del congreso de la república. Editorial del Ministerio de Educación Pública, 1950.
Ley de reforma agraria, decreto 900. 1952.
Ley de renta forzada, decreto 712. 1949.
Ley de renta forzada, decreto 853. 1951.

DEPARTAMENTO AGRARIO NACIONAL

Expediente de expropriación sequido contra la Compañía Agrícola de Guatemala de conformidad con la ley de reforma agraria. 1954.
Reglamento del artículo 28 de la ley de reforma agraria. 1952.
Reglamento de cooperativas agrícolas organizadas de acuerdo con el decreto 900. 1952.

DIRECCIÓN GENERAL DE ESTADÍSTICA

Departamentos, municipios, ciudades, villas, pueblos, aldeas, y caserios de la república de Guatemala. 1953.
Censo agropecuario, 1950. 3 vols. 1954.
Censo de la república de Guatemala, 1921. 1924.
Censo general de la república de Guatemala levantado el 26 de febrero de 1893. 1894.

Censo general de población levantado el 1 abril de 1940. 1942.

Mensaje quincenal de estadística. 1950–54.

Sexto censo de población, 1950. 1957.

MINISTERIO DE ECONOMÍA Y TRABAJO

Bauer Paiz, Alfonso. *La Frutera ante la ley: los conflictos laborales de Izabal y Tiquisate.* Publicación 1. 1949.

———. *La Frutera y la discriminación: réplica al senador Lodge y CIA.* Publicación 3. 1949.

———. *La Organización obrera: cómo debe enfocarse en Guatemala.* 1947.

La Empresa Eléctrica de Guatemala, S.A., un problema nacional. Publicación 5. Consejo de Economía, 1950.

Los Ferrocarriles en Guatemala. Compiled by César G. Solis. 1952.

SECRETARIA DE PROPAGANDA Y DIVULGACIÓN DE LA
PRESIDENCIA DE LA REPÚBLICA

A los dos años de la revolución: discursos oficiales. 1946.

Crítica al proyecto de ley agraria de la Asociación General de Agricultores (AGA). 1952.

Dentro del círculo vicioso: "El Ataque al comunismo es un ataque a la patria." Bajo este sofisma tenebroso la prensa independiente de Guatemala vivía años de terror durante el régimen de los comunistas. Imprenta Iberia, 1954.

Discursos del doctor Juan José Arévalo y del teniente coronel Jacobo Arbenz Guzmán en el acto de transmisión de la presidencia de la república, 15 de marzo de 1951. 1951.

Discursos del presidente de la república, ciudadano Jacobo Arbenz Guzmán, en el mitin del 1 de mayo, 1954. 1954.

Discursos pronunciados en las fiestas de 20 de Octubre de 1950. 1951.

Exposición del presidente de la república ciudadano Jacobo Arbenz Guzmán ante la opinión pública nacional y el Consejo Nacional de Economía sobre su programa de gobierno. 1951.

Historia de un golpe rojo. El Gobierno de la república informó acerca del origin y desarrollo de los acontacimientos políticos de junio de este año. Imprenta Iberia, 1954.

Indice de los principales obras materiales realizados en cuatro años del gobierno del doctor Arévalo. 1949.

Informe del ciudadano presidente de la república, coronel Jacobo Arbenz Guzmán, al congreso nacional en su primer período de sesiones ordinarias del año de: 1952, 1953, 1954. 1952–54.

Informe del ciudadano presidente de la república, doctor Juan José Arévalo, al congreso nacional en su primer período de sesiones ordinarias del año de: 1946, 1947, 1948, 1949, 1951. 1946–49, 1951.

Informe del ciudadano presidente de la república, doctor Juan José Arévalo, al con-

greso nacional en su primer período de sesiones ordinarias del año de 1950: sín-
tesis de la labor de cada uno de los ministerios durante el quinto año de gobierno:
1949. 1950.
Informe presidential sobre la situación política del país. 1947.
Primer colonia agrícola de Poptún. 1950.
Reyes Cardona, Julio Antonio. *Sobre la legalidad de la inexistencia del amparo en*
juicios administrativos agrarios y constitucionalidad del acto del congreso al des-
truir a la Corte Suprema de Justicia Guatemala. 1953.

MISCELLANEOUS DEPARTMENTS

Asamblea Constituyente. *Comisión de los quince encargada de elaborar el proyecto*
de constitución. 1953.
——. *Diario de sesiones: Asamblea Constituyente de 1945. 1951.*
Escuela Politécnica. *Anales de la Escuela Politécnica.* 5 vols. Editorial del Ejército,
1940–41, 1942–43, 1944–45, 1947, and 1949–50.
Ministerio de Educación Pública. *El Maestro rural, guía metodológica para la en-*
senanza del idioma nacional a los niños analfabetos. 1945.
Ministerio de Gobernación. *Leyes de gobernación, administración de los departa-*
mentos, de municipalidades, su contabilidad, categorias, arbitrios, generales, va-
gancia, y contratos de trabajo agrícola. Compiled by Rosendo P. Méndez. 1946.
Secretaría de Propaganda y Divulgación de la Junta de Gobierno. *Estatuto agrario:*
decreto número 31. 1954.
——. *Estatuto agrario: decreto número 559. 1956.*
Secretaría de Relaciones Exteriores. *Guatemala ante América: la verdad sobre la*
cuarta reunión de consulta de cancilleres americanos. 1951.

U.S. GOVERNMENT PUBLICATIONS

U.S. Congress. House Select Committee on Communist Aggression. *Communist Ag-*
gression in Latin America. Washington, D.C.: Government Printing Office, 1954.
U.S. Department of State. *Foreign Relations of the United States.* Washington, D.C.:
Government Printing Office, yearly.
——. *Intervention of International Communism in Guatemala.* Publication 5556,
Inter-American Series 48. Washington, D.C.: Government Printing Office, 1954.
——. *Penetration of the Political Institutions of Guatemala by the International*
Communist Movement. Washington, D.C.: Government Printing Office, 1954.

Newspapers and Periodicals

The following is a listing of newspapers and periodicals consulted and the relevant
run of dates. All are published in Guatemala City unless otherwise indicated.
Acción social cristiana (1945–54).
Alerta! Organo de publicidad de la Guardia Civil de Guatemala (Nov. 1944–June
1946).

El Campesino. Dirección General de Agricultura (1945–49).
Correo de Occidente. Quezaltenango (1950–53).
Diario de Centroamérica (1944–54).
La Hora (Jan. 1950–Aug. 1954).
Impacto (June–July 1954).
El Imparcial (1944–54).
Informaciones nacionales (published irregularly, Apr. 1941–49).
El Mes económico y financiero (1947–54).
Nuestro diario (1946–50).
Octubre (June 1950–Aug. 1953).
Revista cafetalera de Guatemala (1948–53).
Revista de economía (bimonthly, 1946–54).
Revista de la Guardia Civil (June 1946–June 1954).
Revista de maestro (bimonthly, 1946–54).
Revista militar (1945–53).
Tribuna popular (Aug. 1953–June 1954).
Universidad de San Carlos (1945–54).
Verbum (May 1954).

Books, Articles, and Other Sources

Acosta L., Augustín, and Ignacio Acosta L. "La Reforma agraria en Guatemala." *Revista de economía*, Dec. 1952, 374–79.
Adams, Richard. *Crucifixion by Power: Essays on Guatemalan National Social Structure, 1944–1966*. Austin: University of Texas Press, 1970.
———. "The Development of the Guatemalan Military." *Studies in Comparative International Development* 4 (1968): 91–110.
———. *Encuesta sobre la cultura de los ladinos en Guatemala*. Seminario de Integración Social, no. 2. Guatemala City: Editorial del Ministerio de Educación Pública, 1964.
———. "Ethnic Images and Strategies in 1944." In *Guatemalan Indians and the State, 1540–1988*, edited by Carol Smith, 141–62. Austin: University of Texas Press, 1990.
———. "The Patzicía Massacre of 1944: A Reinterpretation." Paper presented at the Sixteenth Latin American Studies Association International Congress, Washington, D.C., April 1991.
——— [Newbold Stokes, pseud.]. "Receptivity to Communist Fomented Agitation in Rural Guatemala." *Economic Development and Cultural Change* 5 (July 1957): 338–61.
———, ed. "Political Change in Guatemalan Indian Communities: A Symposium." In *Community Culture and National Change*, 1–54. Middle American Research Institute, no. 4. New Orleans: Tulane University, 1972.
Alcántara Pons, Edwin. "Hacía una programación de desarrollo económico de Guatemala." Thesis, Universidad de San Carlos, 1954.

Amin, Samir, and Kostas Vergopoulos. *La Cuestión campesina y el capitalismo*. 3d ed. Mexico City: Editorial Nuestro Tiempo, 1980.

Amurrio González, J. J. *El Positivismo en Guatemala*. Guatemala City: Editorial Universitaria, 1970.

Anderson, Thomas. *Matanza: El Salvador's Communist Revolt of 1932*. Lincoln: University of Nebraska Press, 1971.

Appelbaum, Richard. *San Ildefonso Ixtahuacán*. Guatemala City: Editorial del Ministerio de Educación Pública, 1968.

Aquirre Beltrán, Gonzalo. *Regiones de refugío*. Mexico City: Instituto Indigenista Interamericano, 1967.

Arévalo Bermejo, Juan José. *La Adolescencia como evasión y retorno*. 2d ed. Guatemala City: Tipografía Nacional, 1945.

——. *Anti-Kommunism in Latin America*. New York: Lyle and Stuart, 1963.

——. *El Candidato blanco y el huracán, 1944–1945*. Guatemala City: Editorial Académica Centroamericana, 1984.

——. *Discursos en la presidencia, 1945–1948*. Guatemala City: Tipografía Nacional, 1948.

——. *Escritos políticos*. 2d ed. Guatemela City: Tipografía Nacional, 1946.

——. *Guatemala, la democracia y el imperio*. Mexico City: Editorial América Nueva, 1954.

——. *Lo que no dije en memorias de aldea*. Guatemala City: Editorial "José de Piñeda Ibarra," 1973.

——. *Memorias de aldea*. 2d ed. Guatemala City: Edita, 1980.

——. *The Shark and the Sardines*. New York: Lyle and Stuart, 1961.

Arriola, Jorge Luis, ed. *Integración social en Guatemala*. Vol. 1. Seminario de Integración Social, no. 3. Guatemala City: Editorial del Ministerio de Educación Pública, 1964.

Asturias, Miguel Angel. *Hombres de maíz*. Buenos Aires: Editorial Losada, 1949.

——. *The President*. Translated by Francis Partridge. London: Victor Gollanz, 1967.

——. *El Problema social del indio y otros textos*. Paris: Centre de Recherches de l'Institut d'Études Hispaniques, 1971.

Aybar de Soto, José. *Dependency and Intervention: The Case of Guatemala in 1954*. Boulder, Colo.: Westview Replica, 1978.

Baker, R. K. *A Study in Military Status and Status Deprivation in Three Latin American Armies*. Washington D.C.: American University Center for Research in Social Systems, 1967.

Banaji, Jarius. "Modes of Production in a Materialist Conception of History." *Capital and Class* 3 (1970): 1–44.

Barahona, Oscar, and J. Walter Dittel. *Bases de la seguridad social en Guatemala*. Guatemala City, 1947.

Bartra, Roger. *Campesinado y poder político en México*. Mexico City: Ediciones Era, 1982.

————. *Estructura agraria y clases sociales en México*. Mexico City: Serie Popular Era, 1974.

Bauer Paiz, Alfonso. *Cómo opera el capital yanqui en Centroamérica: el caso de Guatemala*. Mexico City: Editorial Ibero-Mexicana, 1956.

Beals, Ralph. "Acculturation." In *Social Anthropology*, edited by Manning Nash, 449–68. Vol. 6 of *Handbook of Middle American Indians*, edited by Robert Wauchope. Austin: University of Texas Press, 1967.

Benites, Tulio. *Meditaciones de un católico ante la reforma agraria*. Guatemala City: Ministerio de Educación Pública, 1952.

Bennholdt-Thomsen, Veronika. "Los Campesinos en las relaciones de producción del capitalismo periférico." *Historia y sociedad* 10 (1976): 29–38.

————. "Subsistence Production and Extended Reproduction: A Contribution to the Discussion about Modes of Production." *Journal of Peasant Studies* 9 (July 1982): 241–53.

Bishop, Edwin Warren. "The Guatemalan Labor Movement, 1944–1949." Ph.D. diss., University of Wisconsin, 1959.

Brintnall, Douglas. *Revolt against the Dead*. New York: Alfred A. Knopf, 1976.

Britnell, George E. "Factors in the Economic Development of Guatemala." *American Economic Review* 53 (May 1953): 104–14.

————. "Problems of Economic and Social Change in Guatemala." *Canadian Journal of Economic and Political Science* 17 (1951): 468–81.

Brockett, Charles. "Building a Showcase for Democracy: The U.S. in Guatemala, 1954–1960." Paper presented at the Sixteenth Latin American Studies Association International Congress, Washington, D.C., April 1991.

Bryant, M. A. "Agricultural Interest Groups in Guatemala." Master's thesis, University of Texas at Austin, 1967.

Bulmer-Thomas, Víctor. "Central America in the Inter-War Years." In *Latin America in the 1930s: The Periphery in World Crisis*, edited by R. Thorp, 279–314. London: Macmillan, 1984.

————. "Economic Development over the Long-Run: Central America since 1920." *Journal of Latin American Studies* 15 (Nov. 1983): 269–94.

————. *The Political Economy of Central America since 1920*. Cambridge: Cambridge University Press, 1987.

Bunzel, Ruth. *Chichicastenango: A Guatemalan Village*. American Ethnological Publication no. 22. Locust Valley, N.Y.: J. J. Augustin, 1952.

Bush, Archer. "Organized Labor in Guatemala, 1944–1949." Ph.D. diss., Colgate University, 1950.

Cáceres, Carlos. *Aproximación a Guatemala*. Culiacán, Mex.: Universidad Autónoma de Sinaloa, 1980.

Cardoza y Aragón, Luis. "Guatemala y el imperio bananero." *Cuadernos americanos* 64 (Mar. 1954): 19–45.

Carmack, Robert. "Estratificación y cambio social en las tierras altas occidentales de Guatemala: el caso de Tecpanoco." *América Indígena* 36 (1976): 253–301.

———. *Historia social de los Quichés*. Seminario de Integración Social, no. 38. Guatemala City: Editorial "José de Piñeda Ibarra," 1979.

———. *The Quiché-Maya of Utatlán: The Evolution of a Highland Guatemala Kingdom*. Norman: University of Oklahoma Press, 1981.

———. "Spanish-Indian Relations in Highland Guatemala, 1800–1944." In *Spaniards and Indians in Southeastern Mesoamerica*, edited by Murdo MacLeod and Robert Wasserstrom, 215–53. Lincoln: University of Nebraska Press, 1983.

Carmack, Robert, John Early, and Christopher Lutz, eds. *The Historical Demography of Highland Guatemala*. Institute for Mesoamerican Studies, no. 6. Albany: State University of New York, 1982.

Casey, Dennis R. "Indigenismo: The Guatemalan Experience." Ph.D. diss., University of Kansas, 1979.

Castellano Cambranes, Julio. *Aspectos del desarrollo económico y social de Guatemala a la luz de fuentes históricas alemanas, 1868–1885*. Guatemala City: Publication of the Instituto de Investigaciones Económicas y Sociales, Universidad de San Carlos, 1975.

———. *Coffee and Peasants in Guatemala*. Stockholm: Swedish Agency for Research and Cooperation with Developing Countries and the Plumsock Foundation, 1985.

Castelló, Julio. *Así cayó la democracia en Guatemala: la guerra de la United Fruit*. Havana: Ediciones Faro, 1961.

Caute, David. *The Great Fear: The Anti-Communist Purge under Truman and Eisenhower*. New York: Touchstone, 1978.

Cehelsky, Marta. "Guatemala's Frustrated Revolution: The Liberation of '54." Master's thesis, Columbia University, 1967.

———. "Habla Arbenz, su juicio histórico retrospectivo." *Alero* 3 (Sept.–Oct. 1975): 118–25.

Chardkoff, Richard B. "Communist Toehold in the Americas: A History of Official United States Involvement in the Guatemalan Crisis, 1954." Ph.D. diss., Florida State University, 1967.

Colby, Benjamin, and Pierre L. Van Den Berghe. *Ixiles y ladinos*. Seminario de Integración Social, no. 37. Guatemala City, 1977.

Collart Valle, Angel Antonio. "Problemas económico-sociales de Guatemala." Thesis, Universidad Nacional Autónoma de México, 1950.

Comisión Interamericano de Desarrollo Agrícola. *Tenencia de la tierra y desarrollo socio-económico del sector agrícola*. Washington D.C.: Pan-American Union, 1965.

Cook, Blanche Wiesen. *The Declassified Eisenhower: A Divided Legacy*. Garden City, N.Y.: Doubleday, 1981.

Coronado P., J. Adrian. *Monografía del departamento de Sacatepéquez*. Guatemala City: Editorial del Ministerio de Educación Pública, 1953.

Correa, Gustavo. *La Novela indigenista de Mario Monteforte Toledo y el problema de una cultura integral en Guatemala*. Mexico City: Studium, 1957.

de Janvry, Alain. *The Agrarian Question and Reformism in Latin America*. Baltimore: Johns Hopkins University Press, 1982.

Dessaint, Alain Y. "Effects of the Hacienda and Plantation Systems on Guatemala's Indians." *América Indígena* 22, no. 4 (1962): 323–54.

Díaz Rozzotto, Jaime. *El Caracter de la revolución guatemalteca: ocaso de la revolución democrática-burguesa corriente*. Mexico City: Ediciones Revista "Horizonte," 1958.

Dion, Marie Berthe. *Las Ideas sociales y políticas de Arévalo*. Santiago, Chile: Prensa Latinoamericana, 1958.

Diós Rosales, Juan de. "Notes on Aguacatán." Microfilm Collection of Manuscripts on Middle American Cultural Anthropology, no. 24. University of Chicago, 1949.

———. "Notes on San Pedro La Laguna." Microfilm Collection of Manuscripts on Middle American Cultural Anthropology, no. 25. University of Chicago, 1949.

———. "Notes on Santiago Chimaltenango." Microfilm Collection of Manuscripts on Middle American Cultural Anthropology, no. 30. University of Chicago, 1950.

Dorner, Peter, ed. *Land Reform in Latin America: Issues and Cases*. Madison, Wis.: Land Tenure Center, 1971.

Dosal, Paul. "The Political Economy of Guatemalan Industrialization, 1871–1948: The Career of Carlos F. Novella." *Hispanic American Historical Review* 68 (May 1988): 321–58.

———. "The Political Economy of Industrialization in Revolutionary Guatemala, 1944–1954." *Canadian Journal of Latin American and Caribbean Studies* 15, no. 29 (1990): 17–36.

Dupré, George, and Pierre-Philippe Rey. "Reflections on the Pertinence of the Theory of Exchange." *Economy and Society* 2 (1973): 131–63.

Early, John. *The Demographic Structure and Evolution of a Peasant System: The Guatemalan Population*. Boca Raton: University Presses of Florida, 1982.

———. "Revision of Ladino and Maya Census Populations of Guatemala, 1950 and 1964." *Demography* 11 (1974): 105–17.

Ebel, R. H. "Political Change in Guatemala Indian Communities." *Journal of Inter-American Studies* 6 (Jan. 1964): 91–104.

Ebel, R. H., and Harry S. McArthur. *Cambio político en tres comunidades indígenas de Guatemala*. Cuadernos del Seminario de Integración Social, no. 21. Guatemala City: Editorial "José de Piñeda Ibarra," 1969.

Egginton, Everett, and Mark Ruhl. "The Influence of Agrarian Reform Participation on Peasant Attitudes: The Case of Colombia." *Inter-American Economic Affairs* 28 (1974): 27–43.

Eisenhower, Dwight D. *The White House Years: Mandate for Change, 1953–1956*. Garden City, N.Y.: Doubleday, 1963.

Ewald, R. H. "San Antonio Sacatepéquez: Culture Change in a Guatemalan Community." Ph.D. diss., University of Michigan, 1955.

Falla, Ricardo. "Actitud de los indígenas de Guatemala en la época de la independencia, 1800–1850: el problema de los limites entre los comunidades indígenas de Santa María Chiquimula y San Antonio Ilotenango." *Estudios centroamericanos* (1971): 702–18.

———. "Evolución política-religiosa del indígena rural en Guatemala." *Estudios sociales centroamericanos* 1 (1970): 22–43.

———. *Masacres de la Selva: Ixcán, Guatemala, 1975–1982.* Guatemala City: Editorial Universitaria, 1992.

———. *Quiché rebelde: estudio de un movimiento de conversión religiosa, rebelde a las creencias tradicionales en San Antonio Ilotenango, Quiché, 1948–1970.* Collección "Realidad Nuestra," no. 7. Guatemala City: Editorial Universitaria, 1978.

Farrell, William T. "Community Development and Individual Modernization in San Lucas Toliman, Guatemala." Ph.D. diss., University of California at Los Angeles, 1977.

Figueroa Ibarra, Carlos. *El Proletariado rural en el agro guatemalteco.* Guatemala City: Editorial Universitaria, 1980.

Fletcher, Lehman, et al. *Guatemala's Economic Development: The Role of Agriculture.* Ames: Iowa University Press, 1970.

Flores Alvarado, Humberto. *Proletarización del campesino de Guatemala: estudio de la estructura agraria y del desarrollo de la economía capitalista en el sector campesino.* Guatemala City: Editorial Escolar "Piedra Santa," 1971.

Forester, Cindy. " 'No Somos Mozos — We're Nobody's Boys': Rural Organizing and National Revolution in San Marcos." Paper presented at the Latin American Studies Association Meeting, Los Angeles, October 1992.

Fortuny, José Manuel. *Por un frente único de masas: para impulsar el movimiento revolucionario y rechazar la intervención extranjera: informe presentado al pleno ampliado del Comité Central del Partido Guatemalteco del Trabajo.* Guatemala City: Ediciones del PGT, 1953.

Foster-Carter, Aiden. "The Mode of Production Controversy." *New Left Review* 107 (1978): 44–77.

Frankel, Anita. "Political Development in Guatemala, 1944–1954: The Impact of Foreign, Military, and Religious Elites." Ph.D. diss., University of Connecticut, 1969.

Galich, Manuel. "The Dangers of Practicing Democracy." *U.N. World* 5 (1951): 43, 59.

———. *Del pánico al ataque.* Guatemala City: Tipografía Nacional, 1949.

———. *Por qué lucha Guatemala.* Buenos Aires: Elmer Editores, 1956.

García Bauer, José. *Nuestra revolución legislativa.* Vol. 1. Guatemala City: Tipografía Nacional, 1948.

———. *Religión y comunismo.* Guatemala City: Editorial del Ministerio de Educación Pública, 1954.

Gerassi, John. *The Great Fear in Latin America.* New York: Collier Books, 1965.

Gillen, John. *The Culture of Security in San Carlos.* Middle American Research Institute, no. 16. New Orleans: Tulane University, 1951.

———. "Race Relations without Conflict: A Guatemalan Town." *American Journal of Sociology* 53 (1948): 337–43.

———. *San Luis Jilotepeque.* Seminario de Integración Social, no. 7. Guatemala City: Editorial del Ministerio de Educación Pública, 1958.

Girón Cerna, Carlos. "La Nueva paz del indio." *Universidad de San Carlos* 4 (July–Sept. 1946): 60–111.

Gleijesis, Piero. "The Agrarian Reform of Arbenz." *Journal of Latin American Studies* 21 (Oct. 1989): 453–80.

———. *Shattered Hope: The Guatemalan Revolution and the United States, 1944–1954*. Princeton, N.J.: Princeton University Press, 1991.

González Casanova, Pablo. "Internal Colonialism and National Development." *Studies in Comparative International Development* 1 (1965): 27–37.

Goubaud Carrera, Antonio. "El Grupo étnico-indígena: criterios para su definición." *Boletín del Instituto Indigenista Nacional* 1 (Mar.–June 1946): 13–30.

———. "Notes on San Juan Chamelco." Microfilm Collection of Manuscripts on Middle American Cultural Anthropology, no. 23. University of Chicago, 1949.

———. "Notes on the Indians of Eastern Guatemala." Microfilm Collection of Manuscripts on Middle American Cultural Anthropology, no. 22. University of Chicago, 1949.

———. "Notes on the Indians of Finca Nueva Granada." Microfilm Collection of Manuscripts on Middle American Cultural Anthropology, no. 21. University of Chicago, 1949.

———. "La Nueva escuela rural." *Boletín del Instituto Indigenista Nacional* 2 (Mar.–June 1946): 53–56.

———. "Organización de municipalidades indígenas." *Boletín del Instituto Indigenista Nacional* 2 (1946): 9–26.

———, ed. *Indigenismo en Guatemala*. Guatemala City: Editorial del Ministerio de Educación Pública, 1964.

Goubaud Carrera, Antonio, Juan de Diós Rosales, and Sol Tax. "Reconnaissance of Northern Guatemala, 1944." Microfilm Collection of Manuscripts on Middle American Cultural Anthropology, no. 17. University of Chicago, 1947.

Gramsci, Antonio. *Selections from the Prison Notebooks*. New York: International Publishers, 1971.

Grieb, Kenneth. *Guatemalan Caudillo: The Regime of Jorge Ubico, Guatemala, 1931–1944*. Athens: Ohio University Press, 1979.

———. "The Guatemalan Military and the Revolution of 1944." *Americas* 32 (Apr. 1976): 524–43.

Guzmán-Bockler, Carlos, and Jean Loup Herbert. *Guatemala: una interpretación histórico-social*. Mexico City: Siglo Veintiuno Editores, 1970.

Handy, Jim. " 'Anxiety and Dread': State and Community in Modern Guatemala." *Canadian Journal of History* 26 (Apr. 1991): 43–66.

———. "The Corporate Community, Campesino Organizations, and Agrarian Reform, 1950–1954." In *Guatemalan Indians and the State, 1540–1988*, edited by Carol Smith, 163–82. Austin: University of Texas Press, 1990.

———. *Gift of the Devil: A History of Guatemala*. Toronto: Between the Lines, 1984.

———. "The Guatemalan Revolution and Civil Rights: Presidential Elections and Judicial Process under Juan José Arévalo and Jacobo Arbenz Guzmán." *Canadian Journal of Latin American and Caribbean Studies* 10, no. 19 (1985): 3–21.

———. " 'The Most Precious Fruit of the Revolution': The Guatemalan Agrarian Reform, 1952–1954." *Hispanic American Historical Review* 68 (Nov. 1988): 675–705.

———. "National Policy, Agrarian Reform, and the Corporate Community during the
Guatemalan Revolution, 1944–1954." *Comparative Studies in Society and History*
30 (Oct. 1988): 698–724.

———. "Reforma y contrareforma: la política agraria en Guatemala, 1952–1957." In
*500 años de lucha por la tierra: estudios sobre propiedad rural y reforma agraria
en Guatemala*, vol. 1, edited by Julio Castellano Cambranes, 379–400. Guatemala
City: FLACSO, 1992.

———. "Revolution and Reaction: National Policy and Rural Politics in Guatemala,
1944–1954." Ph.D. diss., University of Toronto, 1985.

———. " 'A Sea of Indians': Ethnic Conflict and the Guatemalan Revolution, 1944–
1952." *The Americas: A Quarterly Review of Inter-American History* 46 (Oct.
1989): 189–204.

Hawkins, John. *Inverse Images: The Meaning of Culture, Ethnicity, and Family in
Post-Colonial Guatemala*. Albuquerque: University of New Mexico Press, 1984.

Hernández Sifontes, Julio. *Realidad jurídica del indígena guatemalteco*. Guatemala
City: Editorial "José de Piñeda Ibarra," 1965.

Herrera, Francisco. *Agrarismo guatemalteco: sinopsis histórica*. Guatemala City: Editorial Landivar, 1966.

Herrick, Thomas. *Desarrollo económico y político de Guatemala durante el período
de Justo Rufino Barrios*. Guatemala City: Editorial Universitaria, 1974.

Higbee, E. "The Agricultural Regions of Guatemala." *Geographical Review* 37, no. 2
(1947): 177–201.

Hinshaw, Robert. *Panajachel: A Guatemalan Town in Thirty Year Perspective*. Pittsburgh: University of Pittsburgh Press, 1975.

———, ed. *Currents in Anthropology: Essays in Honor of Sol Tax*. New York: Mouton
Publishers, 1979.

Holleran, Mary. *Church and State in Guatemala*. New York: Columbia University
Press, 1949.

Hoyt, Elizabeth. "El Trabajador indígena en las fincas cafetaleras de Guatemala."
Ciencias sociales: unión panamericana 6 (1955): 258–68.

Huizer, Gerrit. "Community Development, Land Reform, and Political Participation:
Preliminary Observations on Some Cases in Latin America." *American Journal of
Economics and Sociology* 28 (1969): 159–78.

———. "Community Development and Conflicting Rural Interests." *América Indígena* 28 (1968): 619–29.

Hunt, E. Howard. *Undercover: Memoirs of an American Secret Agent*. Berkeley:
Berkeley Publishing Company, 1974.

Immerman, Richard. *The CIA in Guatemala: The Foreign Policy of Intervention*.
Austin: University of Texas Press, 1982.

———. "Eisenhower and Dulles: Who Made the Decisions?" *Political Psychology* 1
(Autumn 1979): 21–38.

Inman, Samuel Guy. *A New Day in Guatemala: A Study of the Present Social Revolution.* Wilton, Conn.: Worldover Press, 1951.

International Bank for Reconstruction and Development. *The Economic Development of Guatemala.* Washington, D.C., 1951.

Jamail, Milton. "Guatemala, 1944–1972: The Politics of Aborted Revolution." Ph.D. diss., University of Arizona, 1972.

James, Daniel. *Red Design for the Americas: Guatemalan Prelude.* New York: John Day Company, 1954.

Jiménez G., Ernesto. *La Educación rural en Guatemala.* Guatemala City: Editorial "José de Piñeda Ibarra," 1967.

Jonas, Susanne. *The Battle for Guatemala: Rebels, Death Squads, and U.S. Power.* Boulder, Colo.: Westview Press, 1991.

Jonas Bodenheimer, Susanne. *Guatemala: plan piloto para el continente.* San José, Costa Rica: Editorial Universitaria, 1981.

Jones, Chester Lloyd. *Guatemala, Past and Present.* Minneapolis: University of Minnesota Press, 1940.

———. "Indian Labor in Guatemala." In *Hispanic American Essays*, edited by A. C. Wilgus, 299–323. Chapel Hill: University of North Carolina Press, 1942.

Kendall, Carl, John Hawkins, and Laurell Bossen, eds. *Heritage of Conquest: Thirty Years Later.* Albuquerque: University of New Mexico Press, 1976.

Kepner, Charles David. *Social Aspects of the Banana Industry.* New York: Columbia University Press, 1936.

Kepner, Charles David, and Jay Soothill. *The Banana Empire: A Case Study of Economic Imperialism.* New York: Vanguard Press, 1938.

King, Arden. *Cobán and the Verapaz.* Middle American Research Institute, no. 37. New Orleans: Tulane University, 1974.

Kirk, William. "Social Change among the Highland Indians of Guatemala." *Sociology and Social Research* 23 (1939): 321–33.

Kitchen, James. "Municipal Government in Guatemala." Ph.D. diss., University of California at Los Angeles, 1955.

Krehm, William. *Democracia y tiranías en el Caribe.* Mexico City: Unión Democrática Centroamérica, 1949.

LaBarge, Richard Allen. *Impact of the United Fruit Company on the Economic Development of Guatemala, 1946–1954.* Middle American Research Institute, no. 29. New Orleans: Tulane University, 1974.

LaCharité, Norman, et al. *Case Study in Insurgency and Revolutionary Warfare: Guatemala, 1944–1954.* Washington, D.C.: American University, 1964.

LaFarge, Oliver. "Maya Ethnology: The Sequence of Cultures." In *The Maya and the Neighbors*, 281–89. New York; D. Appleton-Century Company, 1940.

———. *Santa Eulalia: The Religion of a Cuchumatán Indian Town.* Chicago: University of Chicago Press, 1947.

LaGuardia, García. *El Pensamiento liberal de Guatemala.* San José, Costa Rica: Editorial Universitaria, 1977.

Leonard, Thomas M. *The United States and Central America, 1944–1949: Perceptions of Political Dynamics.* University: University of Alabama Press, 1984.

Leon-Porras, Fernando de. "Educación y militarismo." *Universidad de San Carlos* 9 (1948): 27–38.

Lincoln, Jackson Steward. "An Ethnological Study of the Ixil Indians of the Guatemalan Highlands." Microfilm Collection of Manuscripts on Middle American Cultural Anthropology, no. 1. University of Chicago, 1945.

Lommel, Anne Warrick. "United States Efforts to Foster Peace and Stability in Central America, 1923–1954." Ph.D. diss., University of Minnesota, 1967.

López Villatora, Mario. *Por los fueros de la verdad histórica, una voz de la patria escarnida, Guatemala, ante la diatriba de uno de sus hijos renegados.* Guatemala City, 1956.

Lovell, George. "Landholding in Spanish Central America: Patterns of Ownership and Activity in the Cuchumatán Highlands of Guatemala, 1563–1821." *Transactions of the Institute of British Geographers* 8, no. 3 (1983): 214–30.

———. "Surviving Conquest: The Maya of Guatemala in Historical Perspective." *Latin American Research Review* 23, no. 2 (1988): 25–57.

Luxemburg, Rosa. *The Accumulation of Capital — An Anti-Critique.* Edited by Kenneth Tarbuck. New York: Monthly Review Press, 1972.

McBryde, Felix. *Geografía cultural e histórica del suroeste de Guatemala.* 2 vols. Seminario de Integración Social, nos. 25 and 26. Guatemala City: Editorial "José de Piñeda Ibarra," 1969.

McCreery, David. "Coffee and Class: The Structure of Development in Liberal Guatemala." *Hispanic American Historical Review* 56, no. 3 (1976): 438–60.

———. "Debt Servitude in Rural Guatemala, 1876–1936." *Hispanic American Historical Review* 63, no. 4 (1983): 735–59.

———. " 'An Odious Feudalism': Mandamiento and Commercial Agriculture in Guatemala, 1858–1920." *Latin American Perspectives* 13 (Winter 1986): 99–118.

———. "State Power, Indigenous Communities, and Land in Nineteenth Century Guatemala, 1820–1920." In *Guatemalan Indians and the State, 1540–1988,* edited by Carol Smith, 96–115. Austin: University of Texas Press, 1990.

McDowell, Paul. "Political and Religious Change in a Guatemalan Community." Ph.D. diss., University of British Columbia, 1974.

MacLeod, Murdo. *Spanish Central America: A Socio-economic History, 1520–1720.* Berkeley: University of California Press, 1973.

MacLeod, Murdo, and Robert Wasserstrom, eds. *Spaniards and Indians in Southeastern Mesoamerica.* Lincoln: University of Nebraska Press, 1983.

Madigan, Douglas. "Santiago Atitlán, Guatemala: A Socioeconomic and Demographic History." Ph.D. diss., University of Pittsburgh, 1976.

Marroquín, Alejandro. "Panorama de indigenismo en Guatemala." *América Indígena* 32 (1972): 291–317.

Marroquín Rojas, Clemente. *Crónicas de la constituyente del 45.* Guatemala City: Imprenta La Hora Dominical, 1945.

Meillassoux, Claude. "From Reproduction to Production." *Economy and History* 1 (1972): 93–105.

Mejía, Medardo. *Juan José Arévalo: o el humanismo en la presidencia.* Guatemala City: Tipografía Nacional, 1951.

——. *El Movimiento obrero en la revolución de Octubre.* Guatemala City: Tipografía Nacional, 1949.

Melville, Thomas, and Marjorie Melville, M. *Guatemala: The Politics of Land Ownership.* New York: Free Press, 1971.

Mendelson, E. Michael. *Los Escándolos de Maximón.* Seminario de Integración Social, no. 19. Guatemala City, 1965.

——. "Religion and World View in Santiago Atitlán." Microfilm Collection of Manuscripts on Middle American Cultural Anthropology, no. 52. University of Chicago, 1956.

Méndez Domínguez, Alfredo. *Zaragoza: la estratificación social de una comunidad ladina guatemalteca.* Seminario de Integración Social, no. 21. Guatemala City: Editorial "José de Piñeda Ibarra," 1967.

Méndez Montenegro, Julio César. "444 años de legislación agraria." *Revista de la Facultad de Ciencias Jurídicas y Sociales de Guatemala* 6 (Jan. 1960).

Monteforte Toledo, Mario. *Una Democracia a prueba del fuego.* Guatemala City: Tipografía Nacional, 1949.

——. *Guatemala: monografía sociológica.* 2d ed. Mexico City: Universidad Nacional Autónoma de México, 1965.

——. "La Reforma agraria en Guatemala." *El Trimestre económico* 19 (1952): 422–51.

——. *La Revolución de Guatemala, 1944–1954.* Guatemala City: Editorial Universitaria, 1975.

Moore, Granville Alexander, Jr. "The Guatemalan Plantation System in Historial Perspective." Master's thesis, Columbia University, 1963.

——. "Social and Ritual Change in a Guatemalan Town." Ph.D. diss., Columbia University, 1966.

Mosely, Leonard. *Dulles: A Biography of Eleanor, Allen, and John Foster Dulles and Their Family Network.* New York: Dell, 1978.

Mosk, Sanford. "The Coffee Economy of Guatemala, 1850–1918." *Inter-American Economic Affairs* 9 (Winter 1955): 6–55.

Mulet de Cerezo, María Luisa. "Bibliografía analítica de la revolución del 20 de Octubre de 1944." Thesis, Universidad de San Carlos, 1967.

Murphy, Brian. "The Stunted Growth of Guatemalan Peasant Movements." In *Crucifixion by Power: Essays on Guatemalan National Social Structure, 1944–1966,* edited by Richard Adams, 438–78. Austin: University of Texas Press, 1970.

Nájera Farfán, Mario Efraín. *Los Estafadores de la democracia: hombres y hechos en Guatemala.* Buenos Aires: Editorial Glem, 1956.

Náñez Falcón, Guillermo. "Erwin Paul Dieseldorf, German Entrepreneur in the Alta Verapaz of Guatemala, 1889–1937." Ph.D. diss., Tulane University, 1970.

Nash, Manning. "The Impact of Mid-Nineteenth Century Economic Change upon the Indians of Middle America." In *Race and Class in Latin America*, edited by Magnus Morner, 170–83. New York: Columbia University Press, 1970.

———. *Machine Age Maya: The Industrialization of a Guatemalan Community*. Chicago: University of Chicago Press, 1967.

Noriega Morales, Manuel. "El Indio como factor económico de Guatemala." *Anales de la Sociedad de Geografía e Historia* 18 (1942): 99–106.

Oakes, Maud. *Beyond the Windy Place: Life in the Guatemalan Highlands*. New York: Farrar, Straus and Young, 1951.

———. *The Two Crosses of Todos Santos: Survivals of Mayan Religious Ritual*. Princeton, N.J.: Princeton University Press, 1951.

Ordóñez Arguello, Alberto, ed. *Transformación económica de Guatemala: hacia una reforma agraria*. Guatemala City: Ediciones de "Estrella Centro Americana," 1951.

Paredes Moreira, José Luis. *Aplicación del decreto 900*. Guatemala City: Publication of the Instituto de Investigaciones Económicas y Sociales, Universidad de San Carlos, 1964.

———. "Aspectos y resultados económicos de la reforma agraria en Guatemala." *Economía* 12 (Dec. 1966): 26–61.

———. *Reforma agraria: una experiencia guatemalteca*. Guatemala City: Imprenta Universitaria, 1963.

Partido Guatemalteco de Trabajadores. *La Intervención norteamericana y el derrocamiento del régimen democrático*. Guatemala City, 1955.

Partido Nacional de Trabajadores al pueblo de Guatemala. Guatemala City: Tipografía Sánchez y de Guise, 1946.

Partido Revolucionario Obrero de Guatemala. *Recopiliación de leyes agrarias de Guatemala anteriores a la revolución de Octubre*. Guatemala City, 1951.

Paz Tejada, Carlos. "Un Militar honesto." In *Aproximación a Guatemala*, by Carlos Cáceres, 36–51. Culiacán, Mex.: Universidad Autónoma de Sinaloa, 1980.

Pearson, Neale J. "The Confederación Nacional Campesina de Guatemala and Peasant Unionism in Guatemala, 1944–1954." Master's thesis, Georgetown University, 1964.

Pellecer Duran, Carlos Manuel. *Renuncia al comunismo*. 3d ed. Mexico City: Costa-Amic, 1964.

Peterson, John. "The Political Role of University Students in Guatemala, 1944–1968." Ph.D. diss., University of Pittsburgh, 1969.

Pitti, Joseph. "General Jorge Ubico and Guatemalan Politics in the 1920s." Ph.D. diss., University of New Mexico, 1975.

"Principios de la acción económica del estado." *Revista de economía* 2 (1950): 7–10.

Raby, David L. *Educación y revolución social en México, 1921–1940*. Mexico City: Sep Setantas, 1974.

Raúl González, Otto. "Bases para una reforma agraria en Guatemala." Thesis, Universidad Nacional Autónoma de México, 1951.

Recinos, Adrian. *Monografía del departamento del Huehuetenango.* 2d ed. Guatemala City: Editorial del Ministerio de Educación Pública, 1954.

Redfield, Robert. "Culture Contact without Conflict." *American Anthropologist* 41 (1939): 514–17.

——. *The Little Community: Viewpoints for the Study of the Human Whole.* Uppsala, Sweden: University of Uppsala Press, 1955.

——. *Peasant Society and Culture.* Chicago: University of Chicago Press, 1956.

——. "The Relations between Indians and Ladinos in Agua Escondido, Guatemala." *América Indígena* 16 (1956): 253–76.

Reina, Rubén. "Chinautla, a Guatemalan Indian Community: A Field Study in the Relationship of Community Culture and National Change." Ph.D. diss., University of North Carolina, 1957.

——. *La Ley de los santos.* Seminario de Integración Social, no. 32. Guatemala City: Editorial "José de Piñeda Ibarra," 1973.

Rene Cruz, Oscar. "La Reforma agraria de Guatemala." *Revista de economía* (1958): 326–28.

Rey, J. A. "Revolution and Liberation: A Review of Recent Literature on the Guatemalan Situation." *Hispanic American Historical Review* 38 (1958): 239–55.

Rey, Pierre-Phillipe. *Les Alliances des classes.* Paris: Maspero, 1976.

Ricketson, Oliver. "Municipal Organization of an Indian Township in Guatemala." *Geographical Review* 29 (1939): 634–47.

Ríos, Efraín de los. *Ombres contra hombres.* Guatemala City: Tipografía Nacional, 1948.

Roberts, Robert. "A Comparison of Ethnic Relations in Two Guatemalan Communities." *Acta americana* 6 (1948): 135–51.

Rojas Lima, Flavio, ed. *Los Pueblos del lago de Atitlán.* Seminario de Integración Social, no. 23. Guatemala City: Editorial "José de Piñeda Ibarra," 1968.

Roosevelt, Kermit. *Counter-Coup: The Struggle for Control of Iran.* New York: McGraw-Hill, 1979.

Ruiz Franco, Arcadio. *Hambre y miseria: fermentas de lucha.* Guatemala City: Tipografía Nacional, 1950.

Samayoa Chinchilla, Carlos. *El Quetzal no es rojo.* Guatemala City: Arana Hermanos, 1956.

Samayoa Coronado, Francisco Armando. *La Escuela Politécnica á través de su historia.* 2 vols. Guatemala City: Tipografía Nacional, 1964.

Schlesinger, Jorge. *Revolución comunista: Guatemala en peligro.* Guatemala City: Editorial Unión Tipografía, 1946.

Schlesinger, Stephen, and Stephen Kinzer. *Bitter Fruit: The Untold Story of the American Coup in Guatemala.* Garden City, N.Y.: Doubleday, 1982.

Schmidt, Lester. "Migrant Labor on the Pacific Coast of Guatemala." Ph.D. diss., University of Wisconsin, 1966.

Schneider, Ronald. *Communism in Guatemala, 1944–1954.* New York: Frederick A. Praeger, 1958.

Scott, James. *The Moral Economy of the Peasant: Rebellion and Subsistence in Southeast Asia.* New Haven: Yale University Press, 1976.

Seligson, Mitchell. *Agrarian Capitalism and the Transformation of Peasant Society: Coffee in Costa Rica.* State University of New York Council on International Studies, Special Studies no. 69. Albany: State University of New York Press, 1975.

Selsor, Gregorio. *El Guatemalazo: la primera guerra sucia.* Buenos Aires: Edición Iguazá, 1961.

Siegel, B. J., and Ralph Beals. "Pervasive Factionalism." *American Anthropologist* 62 (1960): 394–417.

Sierra Roldán, Tomás. *Diálogos con el coronel Monzón: historia viva de la revolución guatemalteca.* Guatemala City: Editorial "San Antonio," 1958.

Silvert, Kalman. *The Conflict Society: Reaction and Revolution in Latin America.* New York: American University, 1960.

———. *A Study in Government: Guatemala.* Middle American Research Institute, no. 21. New Orleans: Tulane University, 1954.

Skinner-Klée, Jorge. *Legislación indigenista de Guatemala.* Mexico City: Instituto Indigenista Interamericano, 1954.

Sloan, John. "The Electoral Game in Guatemala." Ph.D. diss., University of Texas at Austin, 1969.

Smith, Carol. "Beyond Dependency Theory: National and Regional Patterns of Underdevelopment in Guatemala." *American Ethnologist* 5 (Aug. 1978): 574–617.

———. "Does a Commodity Economy Enrich the Few while Ruining the Masses?: Differentiation among Petty Commodity Producers in Guatemala." *Journal of Peasant Studies* 11, no. 3 (1984): 60–95.

———. "Exchange Systems and the Spatial Distribution of Elites: The Organization of Stratification in Agrarian Societies." In *Regional Analysis*, edited by Carol Smith, 2:309–74. New York: Academic Press, 1976.

———. "Local History in Global Context: Social and Economic Transitions in Western Guatemala." *Comparative Studies in Society and History* 26, no. 2 (1984): 193–228.

———. "Origins of the National Question in Guatemala: A Hypothesis." In *Guatemalan Indians and the State, 1540–1988*, edited by Carol Smith, 72–95. Austin: University of Texas Press, 1990.

———, ed. *Guatemalan Indians and the State, 1540–1988.* Austin: University of Texas Press, 1990.

———, ed. *Regional Analysis.* 2 vols. New York: Academic Press, 1976.

Smith, Wlademar. *The Fiesta System and Economic Change.* New York: Columbia University Press, 1977.

Solórzano F., Valentín. *Evolución económica de Guatemala.* Seminario de Integración Social, no. 28. Guatemala City: Editorial "José de Piñeda Ibarra," 1977.

Speilberg, Joseph. "San Miguel Milpas Altas: An Ethnological Analysis of Interpersonal Relations in a Peasant Ladino Community of Guatemala." Ph.D. diss., Michigan State University, 1965.

Stavenhagen, Rudolfo. *Clases, colonialismo, y aculturación: ensayo sobre un sistema de relaciones interétnicas en Mesoamérica*. Cuadernos del Seminario de Integración Social, no. 19. Guatemala City: Editorial "José de Piñeda Ibarra," 1977.

———. *Social Classes in Agrarian Societies*. New York: Anchor Books, 1975.

Suslow, Leo. "Social Security in Guatemala: A Case Study in Bureaucracy and Social Welfare Planning." Ph.D. diss., University of Connecticut, 1954.

Tax, Sol. "La Economía regional de los indígenas de Guatemala." *Boletín del Instituto Indigenista Nacional* 2 (1948): 170–79.

———. "Ethnic Relations in Guatemala." *América Indígena* 2 (1942): 43–48.

———. "Notes on Santo Tomás Chichicastenango." Microfilm Collection of Manuscripts on Middle American Cultural Anthropology, no. 16. University of Chicago, 1947.

———. "Panajachel: Field Notes." Microfilm Collection of Manuscripts on Middle American Cultural Anthropology, no. 29. University of Chicago, 1950.

———. *Penny Capitalism: A Guatemalan Indian Economy*. Washington, D.C.: Smithsonian Institute, 1953.

———. "World View and Social Relations in Guatemala." *American Anthropologist* 43 (Jan.–Mar. 1941): 27–42.

———, ed. *Acculturation in the Americas*. Proceedings of the Twenty-ninth International Conference of Americanists. Chicago, 1949.

———, ed. *Heritage of Conquest: The Ethnology of Middle America*. Glencoe, Ill.: Free Press, 1952.

Taylor, John. *From Modernization to Modes of Production: A Critique of the Sociologies of Development and Underdevelopment*. London: Macmillan, 1979.

Tilly, Charles. "Do Communities Act?" *Sociological Inquiry* 43 (1973): 221–29.

Toriello, Guillermo. *La Batalla de Guatemala*. Mexico City: Cuadernos Americanos, 1955.

———. *Tras la cortina de banano*. Mexico City: Fonda de Cultura Económica, 1976.

Torres-Rivas, Edelberto. *Crisis del poder en Centro-américa*. San José, Costa Rica: Editorial Universitaria, 1981.

———. "Crisis y conjuntura crítica: la caída de Arbenz y los contratiempos de la revolución burguesa." *Revista mexicana de sociología* 41 (1979): 297–323.

El Triángulo de Escuintla: conclusiones del primer congreso regional de economía celebrado en Escuintla del 27 de mayo al 3 de junio de 1945. Guatemala City: Tipografía Nacional, 1946.

Tumin, Melvin. *Caste in a Peasant Society*. Princeton, N.J.: Princeton University Press, 1952.

———. "San Luis Jilotepeque: A Guatemalan Pueblo." Microfilm Collection of Manuscripts on Middle American Cultural Anthropology, no. 2. University of Chicago, 1945.

Valle Matheu, Jorge del. *La Verdad sobre el "caso de Guatemala."* Guatemala City, 1956.

Vergopoulos, Kostas. "El Capitalismo disforme." In *La Cuestión campesina y el capitalismo*. 3d ed. Mexico City: Editorial Nuestro Tiempo, 1980.

Wagley, Charles. *Economics of a Guatemalan Village*. Memoirs of the American Anthropological Association, no. 58. Menasha, Wis.: American Anthropological Association, 1941.

———. *Santiago Chimaltenango*. Seminario de Integración Social, no. 4. Guatemala City: Editorial del Ministerio de Educación Pública, 1957.

Warren, Kay. *The Symbolism of Subordination: Indian Identity in a Guatemalan Town*. Austin: University of Texas Press, 1978.

Wasserstrom, Robert. "Revolution in Guatemala: Peasants and Politics under the Arbenz Government." *Comparative Studies in Society and History* 17 (Oct. 1975): 443–78.

———. "Spaniards and Indians in Colonial Chiapas, 1528–1790." In *Spaniards and Indians in Southeastern Mesoamerica*, edited by Murdo MacLeod and Robert Wasserstrom, 92–126. Lincoln: University of Nebraska Press, 1983.

Watanabe, John. "Cambios económicos en Santiago Chimaltenango." *Mesoamérica* 1, no. 2 (1981): 20–41.

———. " 'We Who Are Here': The Cultural Conventions of Ethnic Identity in a Guatemalan Indian Village, 1937–1980." Ph.D. diss., Harvard University, 1984.

Whetten, Nathaniel. *Guatemala: The Land and the People*. New Haven: Yale University Press, 1961.

Wilgus, A. C., ed. *Hispanic American Essays*. Chapel Hill: University of North Carolina Press, 1942.

Wise, David, and Thomas Ross. *The Invisible Government: The CIA and U.S. Intelligence*. New York: Vintage Books, 1974.

Wolf, Eric. "Closed Corporate Peasant Communities in Mesoamerica and Central Java." *Southwestern Journal of Anthropology* 13 (1957): 1–18.

———. "Materialists vs. Mentalists." *Comparative Studies in Society and History* 24 (1982): 148–52.

———. "Types of Latin American Peasantry." In *Tribal and Primitive Economies: Readings in Economic Anthropology*, edited by George Dalton, 501–23. Austin: University of Texas Press, 1967.

———. "The Vicissitudes of the Closed Corporate Community." *American Ethnologist* 13, no. 2 (1986): 325–29.

Woodward, Ralph Lee, Jr. *Central America: A Nation Divided*. New York: Oxford University Press, 1976.

———. "The Economic Development of Guatemala in the Nineteenth Century." Paper presented at the Social Science History Association Annual Meeting, Toronto, 28 October 1984.

———. "*Octubre*: Communist Appeal to the Urban Labor Force of Guatemala, 1950–1953." *Journal of Inter-American Studies* 4 (1962): 363–74.

———. "Population and Development in Guatemala, 1840–1870." *SECOLAS Annual* 14 (1983).

Wortman, Miles. *Government and Society in Central America, 1680–1840*. New York: Columbia University Press, 1982.

Ydígoras Fuentes, Miguel (with Mario Rosenthal). *My War with Communism*. Englewood Cliffs, N.J.: Prentice-Hall, 1963.

Zamora Castellanos, Pedro. *Vida militar de Centro América*. 2 vols. Guatemala City: Editorial del Ejército, 1966.

INDEX

DEMCO